∽ IRISH AT LAW ∽

John Philpot Curran (1750–1817)

James Comyn

1883 51

IRISH AT LAW

A Selection of Famous and Unusual Cases

Secker & Warburg
London

BY THE SAME AUTHOR

Their Friends at Court
Wills and Intestacies *(with Robert Johnson)*
Contract *(with Robert Johnson)*

First published in England 1981 by
Martin Secker & Warburg Limited
54 Poland Street, London W1V 3DF

Copyright © James Comyn 1981

British Library Cataloguing in Publication Data
Comyn, James
  Irish at Law
  1. Law – Ireland – Cases
  I. Title
  344.1507 '0264   KDK102

ISBN 0-436-10580-2

Printed in Great Britain by
Redwood Burn Limited
Trowbridge & Esher

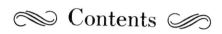

Contents

Acknowledgments	vii
Foreword	viii
Colonel Thomas Blood (1671)	1
Oliver Plunket (1681)	4
Patrick Hurly (1701)	12
The Lamberts (1767)	17
Introducing John Philpot Curran (1750–1817)	22
Lord Doneraile (1780)	24
Counsel and a Judge (c. 1780)	27
The Lord Mayoralty of Dublin (1790)	29
The King v. Peter Finnerty (1797)	31
Wolfe Tone (1798)	35
Lady Pamela Fitzgerald (1799)	43
R. v. Sir Henry Hayes (1799)	49
Major Sirr (1802)	56
Robert Emmet (1803)	61
The Rev. Massy v. The Marquess of Headfort (1804)	66
The King v. Mr Justice Johnson (1805)	73
Adieu to Curran (1817)	78
Lord Powerscourt (1824)	79

Byrne v. Frere (1828)   82

The Anonymous Attorney (1828)   85

James Joseph Hardy (1842)   89

Daniel O'Connell (1844)   93

John Mitchel (1848)   105

Re Peter Mulligan (*c.* 1860)   111

Travers v. Wilde (1864)   114

Peter O'Brien and Mr Justice Keogh (1877)   122

The Twoheys (1883)   125

Charles Stewart Parnell (1889/90)   128

Oscar Wilde (1895)   135

McCartney v. Londonderry and Lough Swilly
    Railway (1904)   144

Patrick Pearse (1906)   149

Big Jim Larkin (1907 and 1914)   155

Irish Workmen's Compensation (1908 and 1914)   161

Cooke v. Midland Great Western Railway (1909)   167

Roger Casement (1916)   171

Tim Healy (1855–1931)   189

John Boyd Dunlop (1920)   194

Erskine Childers (1922)   199

Hayes v. Duggan (1929)   212

Re O'Connor (1930)   216

Miss M'Greene (1931)   219

General O'Duffy (1933/34)   222

Sinclair v. Gogarty (1937)   227

Bernard Kirwan (1943)   234

Dr Paul Singer (1961/62)   241

Noel and Marie Murray (1976)   256

❧ Acknowledgments ❧

I HAVE BEEN fortunate to have considerable family records, my father and uncle (James and Michael Comyn) having left a good deal of material spanning their period of over fifty years at the Irish Bar.

I have consulted all the leading Irish and English Reports, including that bloodthirsty series known as the State Trials.

I have referred to the files over a great many years of the main Irish and English newspapers, notably the *Freeman's Journal*, its successor the *Irish Independent*, the *Irish Times* and the *Morning Post* (now incorporated in the *Daily Telegraph*).

My indebtedness to individual authors is in some cases shown in the text.

In respect of the case concerning Oscar Wilde's father I am grateful to Mr Terence de Vere White, the distinguished Irish author and Literary Editor of the *Irish Times*, who has written the leading book on Oscar Wilde's parents.

Mr Ulick O'Connor, famous Irish writer and biographer of Oliver St John Gogarty, has kindly allowed me to draw on that book.

Three Irish friends have been of great assistance – Mr Justice D'Arcy of the Irish High Court, Owen Keane, Barrister-at-Law, and Brian Michael Curtin, Barrister-at-Law.

I, however, remain solely responsible.

∽ Foreword ∽

IN THIS BOOK I have sought to be an objective observer and
commentator, not a partisan. Since it deals with Irish legal
matters, I cannot be the man on the Clapham omnibus, but
can at least be the man on the old Donnybrook tram, which
moved slowly and cynically through the heart of Dublin
observing all, and being missed by many.

I confess to strong bias in favour of one man mentioned in
these pages: the immortal advocate and wit John Philpot
Curran. If he were alive now and were given a six-month
refresher pupillage with a member of the Irish Bar, or the
English Bar, so as to bring him up to date and adapt his
language a little, I know that he would set both the Liffey and
the Thames on fire. He would have taken in Strasbourg for a
certainty, but I doubt if he would have done any EEC work.

My choice of people and of cases has been capricious, save
to the extent that it has been designed to give a miniature
history of Ireland and the Irish. There are many other cases
and as an Irish counsel once said in a rather irritated way to
the Court of Appeal in Dublin, "If you want them you shall
have them." I do hope your response will not be quite what
theirs was.

The date given beside each chapter heading is the date of
the main or last case concerning the person involved; if dealing
with the person, his years of birth and death are given.

I have researched widely and the main sources and acknow-
ledgments are set out separately.

For the rest, all I can do is to mention a story which has
always delighted me. Two barristers returning home from the

Colonel Thomas Blood
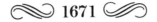 1671

THE IRISH CROWN JEWELS were stolen from what might be called a weak strongroom in Dublin Castle in July 1907, just before a Royal visit. Despite intense police activity in Ireland, Britain and internationally, no trace of them has ever been found. A formal Commission, which was set up to enquire into the matter, was critical of the custodians (a somewhat obvious point) but produced no culprits and no clues.

For centuries Dublin Castle had been to Irishmen the seat of British power: a large, impressive, impregnable fortress. But it would never, of course, measure up in anybody's mind to the great Tower of London, where the *real* Crown Jewels are kept.

Colonel Thomas Blood, commonly and most aptly described as "an Irish adventurer", connected himself in his lively career with Dublin Castle and the Tower of London.

His rank was, one would guess, of his own giving and the wonder is that he promoted himself no higher.

He was an anti-Royalist at the time when it most paid and he received estates in Ireland, but these were forfeited at the time of the Restoration. In 1663, when he was about forty-five, he organised and headed an attempt to take Dublin Castle from the Royalists. In Irish history many attempts were made to achieve that feat, which one can quite understand from ground level as looking distinctly possible. The Castle is not on a great height, the approaches seem many and easy and a successful attack looks to be a worthwhile chance – from outside. But for one reason or another all attacks have failed, and so did Colonel Blood's.

The lives of those who failed in an attack on Dublin Castle were uninsurable and usually brief. Colonel Blood, however, got away without being captured. It is perhaps interesting,

1

even appropriate, to note that Dublin Castle is now, amongst other things, the seat of the Irish Revenue Commissioners.

The Colonel fled to Holland. Eventually he came to England and engaged in various activities on the fringe of the ever-changing politics of the time.

In 1671 he decided to steal the Crown Jewels from the Tower. He struck up a friendship with the elderly Deputy Keeper, a man named Edwards.

With accomplices he arrived at the Tower, where he was by now well known, at 7 o'clock in the morning of 9 May 1671. He suggested a look at the Crown Jewels and when in the chamber his gang knocked down and stabbed the keeper. Thereupon Colonel Blood took the crown, one of the accomplices took the orb and they were about to cut the sceptre in half when they were disturbed.

They got away from the Tower with crown and orb, but only a few hundred yards. Blood was then arrested and found on him was one of the most priceless objects ever known – the crown of England; squashed under his cloak.

He was on arrest lodged – suitably – in the Tower. One would think that in the circumstances he was most unlikely to leave it alive. For far less many had died there. That fascinatingly forbidding fort had a long history of punishment behind it, and even if antecedents were taken into account Colonel Blood had an unsatisfactory record royally.

But the man was a charmer and a trimmer. He actually gained audience of Charles II and, having done so, won the King's favour. It was a remarkable achievement. Not only did he save his head but he got back his forfeited Irish estates.

It grieves me to say it, but he needed no barrister, no King's Counsel. Indeed, sad though it is to say, counsel would surely have failed. Frankly, I have never come across – or heard of – a more splendid litigant in person.

Honourable retirement for the Colonel was disturbed towards the end of his life by his being committed by the Court of King's Bench in England for slander of his erstwhile friend, Buckingham. But his luck held; he was released on bail, and no more was heard of the matter.

He had a son, Holcroft Blood, who lived a more conventional life and became a real General.

Four Courts in Dublin were walking up Kildare Street past the National Library. They saw a colleague, renowned for his lack of grey matter, going into the Library. "What on earth is he doing?" said one. "I think he's bringing out a book," said the other. "No, that can't be right," replied the first, "they keep too close a watch on them." This is the book I have brought out.

James Comyn
London WC1 and
Tara, Co. Meath, Ireland

The harp that once through Tara's halls
    The soul of music shed,
Now hangs as mute on Tara's walls
    As if that soul were fled.
So sleeps the pride of former days,
    So glory's thrill is o'er,
And hearts that once beat high with praise
    Now feel that pulse no more.

No more to chiefs and ladies bright
    The harp of Tara swells,
The chord alone that breaks at night
    Its tale of ruin tells.
Thus Freedom now so seldom wakes,
    The only throb she gives
Is when some heart indignant breaks,
    To show that still she lives.

Thomas Moore

Pride of county exists very much in Britain, and the several alterations of boundary and of name recently made are more unpopular than perhaps the authorities really realise. Such a thing could never be done in Ireland, where counties have always counted for a lot and alteration would not be accepted. Even when settling down in a city the Irishman does not leave his county loyalty behind. And it is fostered by two things: the fact that so much is done at county level, with the county town being a very real centre; and, two, because so much in sport is organised as between counties.

In general history and legal history the counties have long played an important part in Ireland. Each county is said to have, and has, its own characteristics, its own characters, its own accent and its own humour.

There is, however, another geographical feature in Ireland, which is missing in Britain: the Provinces. In Britain when one speaks of "the provinces" it is of the country at large outside London and the Home Counties. Thus, plays do "a provincial tour" of "provincial towns" before opening in London.

The position is entirely and importantly different in Ireland. There are four historic Provinces – Ulster, Leinster, Munster and Connaught (or Connacht) – each comprising a number of counties. They have all had separately identifiable parts in Irish history, and unfortunately there is to be seen in part of one of the Provinces, the part of Ulster which is in Northern Ireland, unhappy relics of that history. But, nevertheless, the happier side also exists in the Provinces, where again both in local government and in sport one sees a continued and healthy inter-Provincial administration and friendly rivalry.

In things Irish, then, there are not only the counties to remember but also the four Provinces.

Oliver Plunket

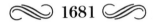 1681

SIR THOMAS MORE, that most English of Englishmen, was beheaded in 1535 for refusing to recognise King Henry VIII's religious supremacy. He was canonised as a Saint some twenty-five years ago.

His counterpart in Ireland nearly a hundred and fifty years later was Oliver Plunket, Catholic Archbishop of Armagh and Primate of All Ireland. Born in 1629 he died at Tyburn in London in 1681. It was there, just beside where Marble Arch now stands, that many of those condemned for high treason and other offences were executed. The name was taken from a stream which flowed down to the Thames. It is now covered in and the name has disappeared from geography but not from history.

The Plunkets were a well-known and highly respected family. Amongst its branches were at the time, and still remain, the Earldom of Fingall and the Barony of Dunsany; later the Barony of Plunket itself, whose fourth holder was Protestant Archbishop of Dublin from 1884 until 1897.

Early destined for the Church, Oliver Plunket went to Rome when he was sixteen and studied there at the Irish College. He was an outstanding student and in 1657 was appointed to the chair of theology at the Propaganda College, a position he held for twelve years until in 1669 he was nominated to the See of Armagh.

Armagh is the See of St Patrick and its Archbishopric carries with it – both for the Church of Ireland and the Catholic Church – the Primacy of All Ireland. The second See in each case is that of Dublin. Armagh and Dublin thus correspond to Canterbury and York.

4

Oliver Plunket was a cultivated man, dedicated to his faith but anxious to live on peaceful terms with the authorities in Dublin so long as he did not compromise his religion and position. This was no easy task in those dark days of the Penal Laws, but the authorities recognised his character and saw him in a not unfriendly light. They were prepared to tolerate him.

Feeling in England, however, eventually led to their having to arrest him and charge him with high treason. This consisted of allegedly seeking the King's death, allegedly encouraging France to create strife within the realm and (this was the vital one) seeking "to alter Ireland to the superstitions of the Romish Church and against the Established Church".

There could only be a Protestant jury to try him but Plunket knew and respected his Protestant fellow-countrymen and felt some hope, indeed some confidence, at their hands.

But when the time came for his trial in Ireland no witnesses against him were forthcoming. It would appear that no verdict was obtained, but even if there had been a formal acquittal there would have been little difficulty in reviving the charge, if only by alleging a renewed and continuing treason to the same effect.

What happened was that the idea of a trial in Ireland was abandoned and Oliver Plunket was removed to London for trial there. He had already been eighteen months in custody when, on 3 May 1681, he was arraigned before the Court of King's Bench at Westminster on the same charge of high treason with substantially the same particulars.

On arraignment Plunket took two preliminary points before pleading to the charge. First, he raised the point that he had already been brought before the Court in Ireland on this charge but it could not be pursued for lack of evidence. Second, he questioned the jurisdiction of this Court in England to try him in respect of matters alleged to have arisen solely in Ireland. On this latter point he said that he had been advised by counsel that the English Court did not have any jurisdiction.

The Lord Chief Justice, Sir Francis Pemberton, rejected both objections and it is clear that he was right in law.

Oliver Plunket was then called upon to plead and pleaded Not Guilty. He applied for an adjournment of the trial to enable him to get witnesses, documents and records from

Ireland. The importance of documents and records was that part of the case against him was that he had made levies on the Catholic clergy and laity for the purpose of funding acts of treason, including provision for French forces to invade Ireland, and that he had taken various steps to promote recruitment in Ireland for such forces.

Oliver Plunket and the Lord Chief Justice engaged in courteous but outspoken debate on this question of adjournment. The Court was not anxious to grant it but eventually did, putting the case over for five weeks, until 8 June 1681.

The Accused, arraigned as "Doctor Oliver Plunket, Titular Primate of Ireland", still was not ready. In a spirited application to the Court for a further adjournment he stressed that he of course had been continuously in custody and that it was difficult in such circumstances to assemble evidence, but he had done his best. Messengers whom he had sent to Ireland had been held up by bad weather in the Irish Sea, public documents which he wanted would not be released without authority, witnesses would not be granted passes to come and he had run up against innumerable other difficulties.

Lord Chief Justice Pemberton would not hear of any further adjournment. Addressing the Accused throughout as "Mr Plunket" he said that ample indulgence had been given. There had been plenty of time – as much as had been originally agreed – for the evidence to be obtained. "Mr Plunket," he said, "it is vain for you to talk and make this discourse now." He assured him, "You shall have as fair a trial as if you were in Ireland."

The jury of twelve were then sworn. Their names may be of interest – Sir John Roberts, Thomas Harriat, Henry Ashurst, Ralph Bucknall, Richard Gowre, Richard Pagett, Thomas Earsby, John Hayne, Thomas Hodgkins, William Patherich, Samuel Becker and William Hardy.

The evidence called against Oliver Plunket by the Attorney-General and Solicitor-General was – as is now generally acknowledged – very unsatisfactory. It came in large part from clergy or ex-clergy who had been disciplined by Plunket, and for the remainder from witnesses who had an interest in seeing him condemned. Much of the evidence was hearsay and the contents of documents were freely allowed to be given in evidence without proper account of the un-availability of the documents. One witness, Edmund Murfey (no doubt Murphy), called by the prosecution failed to come up to proof and was scornfully described by the Lord Chief Justice as having clearly been "tampered with" by the Catholics. The other witnesses were men called Wyer, O'Neal, Owen Murfey, Macheage, Moyer and Hanlet.

There can be no doubt, however, that in spite of their imperfections the witnesses did establish a *prima facie* case against the Accused on the religious charge, and a less strong but a still case to answer on what I may call the French connection.

In the course of cross-examination of the witnesses Oliver Plunket said that all he personally had ever had was £60 a year at most, a single servant and a small thatched home.

When it came to witnesses on his behalf he said that he had just been given the names of three – the witnesses he wanted not having been able to come. The three names were David Fitzgerald, Eustace Commines and Paul Gorman. For some reason, unexplained, only the latter was called and he simply said, "I never heard of any misdemeanour of his," and, "I thought you did more good to Ireland than bad."

In his final speech Plunket reverted to his inability to produce evidence for want of time and criticised the prosecution evidence as proving nothing.

In his brief summing-up to the jury, which began, "Look you", the Lord Chief Justice treated the case as virtually undefended. "I leave it to you it is a pretty strong evidence; he does not say anything to it."

After considering the matter for only a quarter of an hour the jury brought in a unanimous verdict of Guilty of High Treason. The prisoner was remanded in the custody of the Keeper to come up for sentence on 15 June.

On that day there was a fairly long debate between Oliver Plunket and Lord Chief Justice Pemberton, principally on two subjects: one, that of the denial of an adjournment (he now had witnesses, he said, arrived as far as Coventry); and two, the Lord Chief Justice's exhortation that he should repent his religion and no longer offend God and the King. He should seek without delay a minister of religion, a Protestant minister.

The Lord Chief Justice was resentful of any suggestion that

7

"Mr" Plunket had been denied justice. He had had as fair a trial as any man had ever had. Had we been bent on injustice, he said, "we could have hurried you out of the world by a sudden trial."

Sentence was then pronounced. It was the common one of being hung, drawn and quartered. "You must go from here to the place from whence you came, that is to Newgate [the prison sited where the Old Bailey now stands], and from thence you shall be drawn through the City of London to Tyburn, there you shall be hanged by the neck but cut down before you are dead, your bowels shall be taken out and burnt before your face, your head shall be cut off and your body be divided into four quarters to be disposed of as His Majesty pleases. And I pray God to have mercy upon your soul."

To those who know London the road from the present Old Bailey (Newgate as was) to Tyburn ran in a westerly direction dead straight past Holborn and up Oxford Street to what is now Marble Arch, a distance of about four miles.

"Drawing" through the City of London to Tyburn meant being pulled on a hurdle along that route, usually to the accompaniment of jeers and catcalls from spectators in the houses or in the street. Many did not know the identity or the crime of the man being drawn past them. It was the spectacle that attracted them – just as happened in Ireland and in England until not much more that a hundred years ago when public executions were abolished.

On 1 July 1681 the sentence pronounced upon Oliver Plunket a fortnight before was carried into effect in every particular.

That he was "guilty" of promoting the Catholic religion as against the Established Church there can be no doubt. You could hardly avoid doing so if you were Catholic Archbishop of Armagh and Primate of All Ireland. He certainly levied money on clergy and laity by way of church collections and some he undoubtedly sent on to Rome. He also issued Church Orders. All he did on this front was entirely consistent with his duties as a "Popish" Church leader. But everything to do with Popery was then illegal and his conduct High Treason. It would not have been necessary to allege anything more to convict him of a capital offence.

8

That he encouraged or promoted the King's death there was no evidence at all.

With regard to the French connection Oliver Plunket doubtless did have sympathy and contact with the French but he would have been the first to realise that at the time they would have had no hope of a successful invasion of Ireland and that an attempted invasion would only bring more misery on his country. The evidence at his trial that he had money and men for the French and had been seen inspecting harbours and possible landing-places for them rested on the unsatisfactory evidence of a few unsatisfactory men with motives for perjuring him. Where it connected him with religious matters it was strong and credible, because it was basically true. When it sought to connect him with a French invasion it lapsed into the preposterous (a list of 70,000 available men and money collected for the support of French forces). It was a mixture of hearsay, confusion and invention. But it did amount to some evidence.

A prisoner in those days was not allowed a counsel to defend him, nor was he able to give evidence on his own behalf. The King's father, Charles I, denied a King's Counsel, overcame these difficulties brilliantly by speaking – with great effect – for himself. He showed at the time, and to history, what a farce his so-called trial was. Acting perforce for himself, Oliver Plunket was indirectly enabled to give evidence for himself by contradicting the witnesses and engaging in exchanges with the Court. But his lack of an advocate is all too painfully clear from the inadequacy of his cross-examination and his failure to drive home his best points. The result would have been no different, but there would have been a considerable difference about the trial.

It seems incredible to us who are lucky enough to live today and under a benign system of law that there should have been a time when a man on trial was refused counsel and prohibited from giving evidence. The first is perhaps just understandable – that a man on trial should have no help but must speak for himself – it happens still in other places. The prohibition from giving evidence himself is far more difficult to understand. It was strangely enough said to be for the prisoner's own protection, that he might not be left open to questioning. But one would think he might have been given the option. Such is the legal position now; an Accused need not give evidence but may. The old rule is all the stranger when, as we have observed, a prisoner acting for himself necessarily spoke much on his own behalf in addressing the Court and cross-examining witnesses. Charles I was devastating in his few comments when called on to plead. He was equally devastating in his relatively few subsequent observations.

One of the best points that Oliver Plunket made at his trial was that none would speak against him in his native land, where as we know the authorities were well prepared to tolerate him and where the witness Gorman reckoned he "did more good to Ireland than bad". Another telling point was his assertion that he had been offered his life in return for turning informer. This latter, which he stated during the trial and just before and again after judgment, was undoubtedly true. He rejected the offers, but the making of them put his trial into perspective – that he naturally knew a lot but was himself guilty of nothing more than being an active Catholic Archbishop of Armagh.

The English authorities in Ireland knew Plunket, his people and his influence. Their attitude of toleration towards him was a wise one and spared them much trouble. The insistence of their superiors in England to try him and execute him was a grave mistake. He instantly became in Irish eyes a martyr and his memory was revered down the years. To execute an Archbishop of Armagh, Primate of All Ireland, was as bad to Irishmen as beheading the King was to ordinary Englishmen thirty-two years before. Oliver Plunket was canonised a few years ago.

Local Rules are well known in many activities. For example in golf ("A ball lying on the electric railway running beside the 6th fairway may be lifted and dropped without penalty"). Or the odd admonition in a County Court: "Refrain from Spitting".

Ireland always had certain laws and rules of law solely applicable to her. One, which received recognition by the House of Lords in 1715 in the case of Basil v. Atcheson, was that when there was a period of general and national calamity and accordingly nothing was made out of land which was due to pay mortgage interest, then interest did not run during the period in question. There were over the years many troubles, risings and rebellions which brought this rule into play.

The lands in question in Basil v. Atcheson were plantation lands, that is to say lands taken over and planted with new owners who supplanted the previous owners. They were consequently especially liable to attract trouble.

There was a rebellion in 1641 and the lands lay waste and untenanted for more than fifteen years. For many years after that it was only possible to let them at a very low rent.

In 1681 legal proceedings were started but, as so often happened then, they dragged on for ages, being allowed to lie dormant for years and then being revived by later generations. Thus, it was thirty-four years before this action came on for hearing, and it covered a period stretching back over seventy-four years. The defendant, Basil, resisted part of the substantial claim for arrears of mortgage interest on the "local rule" mentioned above. He won his right to freedom of liability for the calamity years, and a Master in Chancery was given the monumental task of taking an account of what was due.

Patrick Hurly

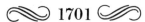 1701

On 31 May 1701 Patrick Hurly, Gentleman, of Moughna in the Barony of Corcomroe in the County of Clare, was tried at the King's Bench in Ireland for (1) Perjury and (2) conspiring with Daniel Hicky and others to cheat the Popish Inhabitants of the County of Clare. The precise nature of the charges was that he pretended to have been robbed and made a claim under oath under a recent Act which allowed compensation for unsolved crimes to be levied on the County and more particularly on the class of inhabitants believed to be involved. There are roughly similar provisions – though not religiously orientated – in Ireland and England today, for Malicious Damage and Criminal Injuries respectively. In Ireland the levy is on the County, in England it comes from public funds.

Patrick Hurly claimed to be affluent, but a number of witnesses spoke to his being a perpetual refugee from his creditors, having twenty-four-hour sentries to warn him of any unwelcome callers, having pistols to frighten them off, building a special wall to keep them at bay and being himself ready at a moment's notice to disappear or to send off such assets as he had. One witness – very oddly his own solicitor – told of Hurly having before the robbery gleefully produced the recent Act and saying that it was the prettiest way of making money that ever he heard of. The solicitor, Captain Charles MacDonagh, said that Hurly offered him two hundred guineas if he would help to get money from the County. He, of course, refused, and told Hurly that it would mean perjury and that he would probably lose his ears for it.

The Crown attached importance to the case and were

represented by both the Attorney-General and the Solicitor-General. The practice of denying a prisoner counsel except to argue points of law was now in process of being relaxed, and Hurly had counsel who were permitted to take part in the actual trial, albeit to a somewhat limited extent. Counsel were by now allowed in Treason cases, but, strictly speaking, were not allowed as participants in cases of felony for over another hundred years. But Perjury, oddly enough, was a misdemeanour. The strangest thing of all, however, was that Hurly could not give evidence in his own defence, which was particularly strange where the charge was Perjury – having given false evidence. The rule that a prisoner could not give evidence (alleged to be a rule for his own protection) remained for nearly two hundred years, until 1898. It seems incredible to modern lawyers, but it was an absolute rule, never relaxed, until abolished just before the turn of this century.

Hurly's case is a good example of the then judges' determination to deal with a criminal case in a single day, however long. His must have lasted a full twelve hours or more. A similar case some twenty years later lasted for over twenty-two hours. The Judge said, "I am, I confess, much fatigued"; then, turning to the jury as if by way of afterthought, he added, "And, to be sure, some of you may feel likewise."

A feature of the Hurly case was that there was a splendid disregard for the rules of evidence and procedure which we have come to venerate. As we have seen, the prisoner's own solicitor gave evidence against him. Hearsay evidence was freely admitted and expressions of opinion were encouraged; thus, more than one witness said that he or she first believed the robbery to be a genuine one but no longer so believed because of what they had been told. Procedurally a rather effective, but to us unthinkable, course was adopted of calling immediately after a witness one who dealt with the same incidents but gave a different version.

The Perjury alleged was in a Sworn Information made by Hurly to support his claim. It was made on 6 March 1699 alleging the robbery on 3 March. It was sworn before a Justice of the Peace, who rejoiced in the name of Dean Neptune Blood, Dean of Kilfenora. It alleged a raid by masked men who tied up Hurly and a friend and who were armed with swords and pistols. They then took 374 golden guineas, 345 pistoles of gold, a gold cross set with diamonds, a number of diamonds and a quantity of Holland sheets and Holland shirts.

A colourful passage in Patrick Hurly's Sworn Information was that during the robbery the raiders upbraided him calling him "rogue, rascal, son of a whore, treacherous villain to his country and words to that effect".

Accomplices gave evidence of Hurly planning a fake robbery, leaving out swords and pistols for their use. The defence attributed to them the motive of literally seeking to save their own necks, for if they were true robbers they would hang.

Calaghan Carty, one of Hurly's servants, was probably the best of these witnesses. In addition to motive, there was put to him an alleged signed recantation of what he now said. He denied that it was genuine and said that he must have been impersonated. Allegations certainly flew around the Court that day.

Walter Neylan, who shared a cell with Hurly in Ennis Gaol, said that the prisoner had confessed to him. The prisoner personally challenged that evidence and said, "He hath a pique to me and I to him."

There was then a perfect field-day of hearsay evidence (but, as one counsel once said, "Yes, but it was strong hearsay"). A surgeon named Charles Cassidy told how the family doctor, Dr Brady, offered him twenty guineas to help arrange a fake robbery for Hurly, later telling him that Hurly would go up to forty guineas. Montague MacCarty said that Mrs Hicky (the wife of the main alleged conspirator) offered him two gold pieces for a cow, but he noticed that they were not coins at all but golden-coloured counters. She admitted that they were from the Hurly robbery and gave them to him in return for three-pence half-penny and some tobacco, wishing to be rid of them, and of the others too.

High Constable Huonin proved discovery of 121 golden-coloured counters under a dung-heap near Hurly's house. He produced them.

Evidence was also given of Patrick Hurly seeking to buy masks in Dublin shortly before the alleged robbery.

The defence called several witnesses as to Patrick Hurly's

affluence, and the fact was that on what they saw and believed the robbery was genuine. The Solicitor-General, who appears to have been in good form, dismissed a number of them by saying, "They are such men as have naught between them and the gallows but this shifting."

A neighbour named Mrs Kemp spoke convincingly of the robbery and said that afterwards one Murough O'Brien tried to bribe her for £10 to put counters in Hurly's house or Hicky's. Promptly, effectively but out of any order that we know Murough O'Brien was called to deny this allegation. "I would not tamper with Hurly's whore," he said. "My Lord, if I would have come on such a business would anyone believe that I should employ this woman that has had a bastard or two by Hurly?"

A young man named Donogh O'Brien Andrews gave evidence of threats to make him say that the robbery was contrived, but that he would not. In another example of prompt confrontation his father was called and said that the young man had admitted to him that it was faked.

It was clear from earlier evidence that Patrick Hurly had been harsh in pursuit of his own brother, John, for debt, but John came as a witness for him. He was permitted to say amongst other (to us inadmissible) things that Patrick's wife had told him before the robbery that Patrick was all right financially and that she had seen him with a bag of gold.

The Solicitor-General and the Attorney-General made very brief speeches because "it is now growing late". Mr Justice Cooke summed-up to the jury, summarising the evidence without very much comment. After an absence of half an hour the jury came back with a verdict of Guilty on both counts. Again surprising to our ears, one of the counsel for the Crown made a suggestion as to penalty. "I hope, my Lord, if it is only a fine it cannot be less than the sum he designed to get from the County by Perjury." The actual result was surprisingly lenient.

Hurly was fined for the Perjury £100 and imprisoned until payment. Judgment on cheating was stood over.

In times past it seems that a jury not only assessed damages but also assessed a sum for costs, which in many ways seems sensible enough. Trouble, however, arose on the occasions when they were perverse, as they were entitled to be and still can be. In one case, Maguire v. Maddin in 1726, there seemed to be no good reason for their perversity because the plaintiff proved to everybody's satisfaction but theirs that he had suffered at least £400 damage because of the malpractices of the defendant's son, whom the defendant had guaranteed for the position of Factor on the plaintiff's merchant ship bound from Dublin for the Madeiras and back. The jury awarded only sixpence damages and sixpence costs. Happily, however, the defendant, who had tried to block the plaintiff at every turn, and in particular tried to deny him his judgment by proceedings in Chancery, ended up by order of the House of Lords having to pay the full costs of everything.

The Lamberts
 1767

W<small>IVES DID NOT</small> do well under the law until the present century, and even now they have complaints and grounds of complaint. One wife who had a particularly hard time was Mrs Catherine Lambert, who, in the end, even had to fight a claim that she was not a wife at all.

She was first married to a Mr Arthur Humphrey, who had a very valuable long lease of some 300 acres of land in County Galway held from a Mr French. Mr Humphrey died in 1740, leaving his widow and several children and the property in Galway. There were, unfortunately, arrears of rent of nearly £120 due to Mr French and he was threatening proceedings for possession, which, if successful, would have left the widow and children very badly off.

Mr Lambert, a widower, was reputed to be a very wealthy man and Mrs Humphrey approached him with a suggestion that if he paid off the arrears she would let him 130 acres of the land at a nominal rent (6s 4d an acre) and assign him the original lease as security. He accepted the proposal and the deal was done.

In 1741 Mr Lambert came to the lady's house and, in the rather charming phrase used in the case, "solicited her in marriage". To encourage her he said that he would surrender her mortgage of the lands to her, and he put this in writing. For two years, however, nothing happened, and then in September 1743 marriage was agreed and "Articles of Marriage" were drawn up. They provided for £20 a year for the wife-to-be and release of the lands and any liability for the arrears of rent. This was to be "in satisfaction of all dower, thirds or jointure".

Married or not, it could not be disputed that the lady moved into his house and lived with him, being treated by him, their respective children and the world at large as his wife.

They lived happily together for twenty years or more, until a clique (including some of his family) began a campaign to persuade him, who had now become infirm, that she was cheating and robbing him and doing so for the benefit of her own children. It was obviously feared that when he died he would make unduly generous provision for her.

There was one person able and willing to poison the old man's mind and that was his resident Overseer or Steward, a man named Edward Cloran. He was assisted by one Lynch, a thatcher by trade. Cloran succeeded fully and quickly. Things came to a head when Cloran struck her son and she complained to Mr Lambert. He flew into a rage with her, made all the accusations with which he had been fed, banished her from bed and board and struck her to the ground with a bill-hook.

He wanted her away from the house, but she would not go and there were some bizarre occurrences. She was allotted a small, cold room, which Lynch closed up at night with an iron chain and padlock. She was fed on what Cloran and Lynch chose to feed her. In addition, Mr Lambert threatened that he would shut up and completely vacate the house, leaving her entirely alone, and he actually put this into effect.

Eventually, she was driven into signing an agreement to separate and to accept £20 a year, £10 in May and £10 in November. If he should die before her she was to have what the articles of marriage provided and no more. The document was dated 29 November 1762.

Mrs Lambert still refused to go and eventually was physically dragged and thrown out by Cloran. It was then that the first denial of the marriage was made. Her cup of sorrow was overflowing because, as a result of Mr Lambert's conduct, she had been refused renewal of the land lease by Mr French. In addition to which, Mr Lambert had kept all her rent for himself.

In December 1763 Mrs Lambert issued proceedings in the Irish Chancery Court for setting aside the separation agreement and the provision of proper maintenance. She sued Mr Lambert, all his children, and Cloran.

The first matter of defence put forward was that no marriage had taken place. It had been intended, hence the articles of marriage, but soon afterwards Mr Lambert found out her true character, came to his senses and declined marriage. Later, believing her with all her faults to be at least a good house-keeper, he had allowed her into his house. He agreed that he had let her be known by his name and had held her out as being his wife. This he had done because of her importunity and to save her embarrassment.

The defence went on to deny the cruelties alleged against Mr Lambert, his family and Cloran, and to allege that Mrs Lambert was the cause of all the trouble, being thoroughly unpleasant and dishonest, regularly stealing from Mr Lambert. It had been necessary to impose moderate restraint on her at night lest she roam the house taking valuables. She had smuggled out a good many. The case, he finally contended, was one for the Matrimonial Court, the Ecclesiastical Court, and not for Chancery.

Marriage did not have the same formal requirements, or the same certificate or registration in those days as now. It could be difficult to prove that a marriage had actually taken place, especially if it were in private with only a few people present. The mere bestowing of a name, the mere living together could be regarded as equivocal.

Mrs Lambert had a strong case on "holding out" and on being treated as a wife, but she had difficulty about actual proof of marriage. The nearest she got to strict proof was by calling as a witness the Reverend Dean Crowe, who testified that he had been sent for to perform the marriage "but that the day being exceedingly wet he had been prevailed upon by the then Bishop of Clonfert not to venture his life on such a day". He went next day, but Mr Lambert said that since he had not come he had the ceremony performed by another, and intro-duced the lady to the Dean as his wife.

A witness named Samuel Simpson said that, knowing about the proposed marriage, he asked Mr Lambert one day if he had cause to wish him joy. Mr Lambert said yes – the marriage had taken place, but he was annoyed with Dean Crowe for not turning up to marry them; he was not prepared to wait and had got another clergyman.

19

The case against the marriage was formidable. Mr Lambert denied it on oath. No date, month or place had been given for the marriage, nobody was identified as having performed the ceremony and nothing was said as to who was present.

The Lord Chancellor of Ireland heard the case for four days in November 1766 and found for Mrs Lambert. The question of maintenance was referred to a Master for enquiry and report. On the day after the decision Mrs Lambert returned to the Court requesting an immediate financial provision for maintenance and in order to enable her to carry on the suit before the Master, which she had no doubt her husband would do everything possible to delay. The Court awarded her £200 and indicated that it would, if necessary, make a further order.

Mr Lambert brought an appeal to the House of Lords against both decisions. The points he ran most strongly were failure to prove the marriage, but that if there were a valid marriage the proper Court to deal with its problems was the Ecclesiastical Court.

Mrs Lambert's counsel raised their previous arguments and also added this neat one – that a strong point in favour of marriage was that the husband had required a Deed of Separation, something which would only be appropriate between man and wife. The counsel claimed that the Orders of the Lower Court were so plainly equitable and just the appeal should be dismissed with "most exemplary costs", a splendid expression.

The House duly dismissed the appeal and ordered Mr Lambert to pay £200 as costs. Exemplary? Perhaps, in view of the date.

Poor Mrs Lambert certainly got herself into a lot of trouble because of those arrears of rent which her first husband left.

Harry Grady was a great eighteenth-century jury advocate at the Irish Bar. He had a most effective mannerism of being able to make his right eye express to a jury varying reactions. Actual winking was only one of the functions of what he proudly called his "jury eye".

One morning he came into counsel's robing room in Cork looking sad and depressed. "What's the matter, Harry?" enquired a friend.

"I'm ruined," he said, "absolutely ruined."

"But Good Heavens, why?"

"I don't know what it is," he replied, "but my jury eye is out of order."

Introducing John Philpot Curran
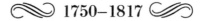 1750–1817

A NUMBER OF the cases which follow will feature John Philpot Curran, who was probably the greatest orator and readiest wit the Irish Bar has ever known. His genius lay in advocacy. A Protestant, he was anti-Unionist and was fearless in appearing for anti-Establishment clients and in what he said on their behalf. He had a cultured and silver-quick mind; he was well educated in the Classics and a master of the English language.

He made his way at the Irish Bar from nothing, was for a time a Member of the short-lived Irish Parliament, making speeches there of the same high quality as in the Courts, and seemed destined for very high office. This, however, eluded him and the appointment he received was of less importance then than later, namely Master of the Rolls in Ireland. He did not gain the greatness as a judge that he enjoyed as a barrister.

He made an early marriage and had a number of children but the marriage turned out unsuccessfully. Then, as a rather lone figure (though loving company), he became more and more a prey to the melancholia or recurrent depression which had dogged his life.

One of his children, Sarah, is forever remembered in Ireland for her tragic love affair with the Irish hero Robert Emmet (q.v.). He was the one rebel whom Curran actually refused to defend, but who going on to defend himself made a speech more remembered than Curran ever made.

John Philpot Curran was born in a small village called Newcastle in County Cork. His parents were poor. He said of his early life there, "I was then a little ragged apprentice to every kind of idleness and mischief, all day studying whatever was eccentric in those older and half the night practising it for the amusement of those who were younger."

His sheer ability got him to Trinity College, Dublin, and to the Bar, to which he was called at the age of twenty-five in 1775. His start was slow but he gradually built up a large general practice. Other Irish advocates have been compared with him – Kendall Bushe, Daniel O'Connell and Isaac Butt – but, though they were brilliant advocates (O'Connell perhaps a public orator even in Court), none match him, particularly in readiness of retort and aptness of allusion. Almost every good legal story has been fathered on him, in recognition of the many which he fathered himself.

Curran was directly comparable to his great contemporary at the English Bar, Erskine, but like many famous racehorses they apparently never took each other on.

The rounded language, the flowery touch and the imagery of Curran's speeches are so different to the style of the present that they may not always appeal, even with the editing which I have permitted myself. But both in Ireland and England matter-of-fact advocacy is of comparatively recent development, and it can be most refreshing to hear a transgressor.

At any rate, no apology is necessary for the style of Curran's advocacy. A man can but be the advocate of his time to the people of the time. If epigrams in Afrikaans go down well with a jury in Kilrush or in Carlisle, then let those who practise in such Courts learn Afrikaans.

Curran was lengthy in his speeches; that was common at the time, which is a little strange when one notes that civil and criminal cases were usually over in a day, albeit a day of twelve-, fourteen- or sixteen-hour sittings. The explanation seems to be that the evidence went quickly and the centre-piece of a trial came with the speeches of counsel.

In Curran's time the trial of capital charges sometimes went on through the night and the death sentence was usually carried out within a few hours of the end of the trial.

Curran was able to be as tough as his times and his legal opponents but he had a culture and polish, a learning and philosophy, which placed him high above them.

Lord Doneraile
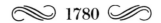 1780

IN OLDEN TIMES it was customary in these islands for barristers to perambulate in their robes in the halls adjoining the Courts where they were prepared to appear. They could not then, any more than now, advertise. They did not have stalls or counters or display even their names. Their appearance in robes showed, as the phrase had it, that they were "on the rank", available for hire. The phrase is in use still and is a homely but graphic illustration of the rule that except for good reason no barrister should decline a case if offered with a proper fee.

This interesting and important custom was practised even more in Ireland than in England, where in London and then progressively elsewhere barristers grouped themselves in professional Chambers.

Young men, freshly called to the Bar, often got their first Briefs in this way. The attorney (or solicitor as he became known) would already have his usual counsel briefed in the bigger matters but for several reasons he might be seeking counsel at the last moment – for a case which had been unexpectedly listed, for a poor client, for an application which had to be made or resisted, for a Brief returned by the counsel he had retained through that counsel being detained in another case, or having failed to arrive, or become ill, etc.

The attorney would know, or know of, most of the barristers on parade, but in the end his choice might well be on intuition or by sheer chance.

In this way the new barrister would get his chance. A few such chances of being seen and heard in Court might lead him on to great things. Given the chance the rest was up to him. Attorneys were, when they could be, generous with chances. Established colleagues were kind with recommendations.

John Philpot Curran was a Protestant of comparatively humble origins and, like so many of his kind, a great friend of the Catholic population in their days of trial under the Penal Laws.

In 1780 a Catholic priest named Neale, living furtively as a Catholic priest then had to do, was sought out by a nobleman in County Cork, Lord Doneraile, and literally horsewhipped. The reason was that a girl with whom Lord Doneraile had been friendly had complained to him that Father Neale had put her brother under some religious penalty. Lord Doneraile required the priest to lift the interdict, and upon the priest saying that he could not do so without leave of his Bishop he was horsewhipped and withdrew into his hovel hiding-place.

Accompanying Lord Doneraile on the occasion in question was a kinsman of his, Captain St Leger. That was the family name, and one of its members instituted the first of the great English classic races – the St Leger.

Through the years some Irish and English counsel have, alas, often found "excuses" for not appearing on the "wrong" side in unpopular cases. Happy it is to reflect that frequently they would have actually enhanced their reputations by doing so.

Father Neale was brave enough to want to take an action against Lord Doneraile. He found an Attorney brave enough to take it up. Lord Doneraile and his family were influential and liked. There was, however, difficulty in finding a barrister prepared to act.

Curran, we know, walked the halls like other barristers, but we do not know whether it was in this way that he received the Brief in the case of The Reverend Neale v. Lord Doneraile. What is known is that where others had refused the Brief with alacrity he accepted it readily.

The position was, therefore, that a young County Cork barrister accepted the Brief against a leading County Cork peer at Cork Assizes. It could easily be professional suicide. After all, he had not yet begun to establish himself locally, much less in Dublin.

Curran was brilliant in his conduct of the case and did nothing to spare the defendant or his relative, Captain St Leger. The latter he described before the jury as "a renegade soldier, a drummed-out Dragoon".

The jury – and be it remembered that under the existing laws it would not have contained a Catholic – found in favour of the priest: thirty guineas damages for assault and battery, and costs.

Captain St Leger demanded satisfaction by duel. Curran, unnecessarily, accepted. When they met, the Captain enquired, "Who fires first?" Curran replied, "You invited me, you open the ball."

There were exchanges of shots without result.

Captain St Leger died shortly afterwards. "He died," said Curran, "of fright. The report of his own pistol was too much for him."

The whole episode went well to Curran's credit. Many lawyers openly stated how disappointed they were to have been precluded from taking the case.

Counsel and a Judge

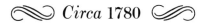 *Circa* 1780

IT APPEARS THAT a certain Judge Robinson was often vitriolic towards parties, witnesses and counsel. He was a small man.

On one occasion he attacked Mr Hoare, a well-known counsel, one of Curran's team in the Reverend Massy's case (see pp. 66–71), and accused him of desiring to bring the King's Commission into contempt. Whereupon Mr Hoare replied as follows: "No, my Lord. I have read in a book that when a peasant during the troubles of Charles the First found the King's crown in a bush he showed to it all marks of reverence; but I will go a step farther, for though I should find the King's Commission even on a bramble, still shall I respect it."

When Curran was a very young man at the Bar, Judge Robinson insulted him. Curran was arguing against legal propositions put forward by the other side and said that he had consulted "all his law books" but could not find a case to support them.

"I expect," said the Judge, "that your law library is rather contracted."

Curran replied, "It is very true, my lord, that I am poor, and the circumstance has certainly rather curtailed my library; my books are not numerous, but they are select and I hope have been perused with proper dispositions; I have prepared myself for this high profession rather by the study of a few good books than by the composition of a great many bad ones. I am not ashamed of my poverty, but I should be of my wealth, could I stoop to acquire it by servility and corruption. If I rise not to rank, I shall at least be honest; and should I ever cease to be so, many an example shows me that an ill-acquired elevation, by making me the more conspicuous, would only make me the more universally and the more notoriously contemptible."

The gown worn by the junior barrister is known as the stuff gown; the gown of the King's or Queen's Counsel is the silk gown – hence "taking silk".

The fact that Curran undertook the defence of several of the prisoners charged with high treason was frowned on by many of the judges, and others. In one of the trials the Judge, Lord Carleton, told him that if he was not careful he would lose his gown as a King's Counsel. "Well, my Lord," replied Curran, "His Majesty may take the silk, but he will leave the stuff behind."

Re the Right of Election of the Lord Mayoralty of Dublin
 1790

A DISPUTE AROSE between on the one hand the Sheriffs and the Common Council of Dublin and on the other the Court of Aldermen as to the right of electing a Lord Mayor for the City. It was heard before the Lord Lieutenant and Privy Council of Ireland and was a dull case, enlivened only by counsel, particularly Curran, who was conscious as he said of "addressing a very large auditory".

It was in the course of his speech on that occasion that he made the famous observation, "The condition upon which God hath given liberty to man is eternal vigilance." Not as well remembered is what followed – "Which condition if he break, servitude is at once the consequence of his crime and the punishment of his guilt."

It was in the same case that he said, "I am aware, my Lords, that truth is to be sought only by slow and painful progress; I know also that error is in its nature flippant and compendious; it hops with airy and fastidious levity over proofs and arguments, and perches upon assertion which it calls conclusion."

Like many lawyers he often had to speak of truth and error. One such was when a country witness complained that his cross-examination was putting her "in a doldrum". "What does she mean by a doldrum?" exclaimed the Judge. "Oh, my Lord," replied Curran, "it's a very common complaint with witnesses of this description – it's merely a confusion of the head arising from a corruption of the heart."

In a criminal trial before a jury, the Judge shook his head at one of Curran's arguments. "I see," said Curran, "the movement of his lordship's head. You might think that it implied a difference of opinion, but you would be mistaken, it is merely accidental. Believe me, gentlemen, if you remain here many days you will perceive that when his lordship shakes his head – there's nothing in it."

When news of the great victory at Algiers arrived, a lady remarked to Curran that, alas, not everything and everybody had been demolished. "My dear madam," he said, "sufficient unto the Dey."

The King v. Peter Finnerty

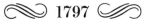

1797

IN THE CASE of Peter Finnerty, Curran made an impressive defence of the liberty of the press. Finnerty published a newspaper called simply the *Press*. It came out three times a week from 28 September 1797 until its sixty-ninth and last copy was seized in March 1798. He was charged with seditious libel against Lord Camden's Administration. He had published a strong and indignant letter in his paper on 26 October 1797 criticising the treatment of a man called Orr, who had been convicted at Carrick Fergus for administering an unlawful oath to a soldier named Wheatley, which was a capital offence.

In that case the jury had been out from 7 p.m. until 6 a.m. They then returned their verdict of Guilty but added to it a recommendation to mercy. Shortly afterwards three of the jury resiled from the verdict, swearing variously that they had been influenced by alcohol, threatened and tricked into agreeing. It has long been a rule, a necessary rule, that a Court will not enquire into the jury-room. There have, over the years, been a number of cases where one juror or more has sought to withdraw his initial consent for one reason or another. But the Courts will not have it. Here it would seem that something unusual had happened because of the long retirement and the strange addition of a recommendation to mercy. At any rate, enough question existed for the Administration to take the unusual course of granting a number of respites in respect of the sentence of death. The general rule in those days was to have the sentence carried out in a matter of hours after the verdict, and in the rare cases of reprieve to have it granted as speedily. After a number of respites in this case, Orr was hanged on 24 October 1797.

The offending letter was published twelve days later. It was signed "Marcus" and was in strong terms. In particular, it accused the Lord Lieutenant of Ireland of lacking mercy and encouraging repression. In the best traditions of journalism, but contrary to the Law, Peter Finnerty refused to disclose the author's name, which was known to him. Had he made the disclosure contemporary opinion was to the effect that he himself would not have been prosecuted.

The author was, in fact, a man called Deane Swift; so far as I can ascertain that was not, as it would seem, a pseudonym, but was the man's true and unaltered name.

In the course of his speech, Curran had much to say about the freedom of the press. Over the years many people have had much to say on that great and precious freedom, but Curran's phraseology and the structure of his speech are, even after nearly two hundred years, of special value and interest.

The main points of the speech were as follows:

"The liberty of the press is inseparably twined with the liberty of the people. The press is the great public monitor; its duty is that of the historian and the witness.

"The learned counsel [for the Crown] has been pleased to say that he comes forward in this prosecution as the real advocate for the liberty of the press, and to protect a mild and merciful government from its licentiousness; and he has been pleased to add, that the constitution can never be lost while its freedom remains, and that its licentiousness alone can destroy that freedom. As to that, gentlemen, he might as well have said that there is only one mortal disease of which a man can die; I can die the death inflicted by tyranny . . . Has he heard of nothing else that has been fatal to the freedom of publication? . . . As to the motives [for prosecution], does history give you a single instance in which the state has been provoked to these conflicts, except by the fear of truth, and by the love of vengeance?

"I see you turn your thoughts to the reign of the second James. I see you turn your eyes to those pages of governmental abandonment, of popular degradation, of expiring liberty, and merciless and sanguinary persecution . . . [Man] sinks but to rise again. It is at that period that the state seeks for shelter in the destruction of the press; it is in a period like that, that the tyrant prepares for an attack upon the people, by destroying the liberty of the press; by taking away that shield of wisdom and of virtue . . . It is at these periods that the honest man dares not speak, because truth is too dreadful to be told. It is then humanity has no ears, because humanity has no tongue . . . the facts are too recent in your mind not to show you that the liberty of the press, and the liberty of the people, sink and rise together . . . the only printer in Ireland, who dares to speak for the people, is now in the dock.

"[Mr Attorney-General] would have the press all fierceness to the people, and all sycophancy to power . . . if you exercise the rigour of a censorship . . . you will reduce the spirit of publication, and with it the press of this country, to what it for a long interval has been, the register of births, and fairs, and funerals, and the general abuse of the people and their friends.

"Upright and honest jurors, find a civil and obliging verdict against the printer! And when you have done so, march through the ranks of your fellow-citizens to your own homes, and bear their looks as they pass along; retire to the bosom of your families; and when you are presiding over the morality of the parental board, tell your children, who are to be the future men of Ireland, the history of this day . . . tell them the story of Orr.

"You are called upon, in defiance of shame, of truth, of honour, to deny the sufferings under which you groan and to flatter the persecution that tramples you under foot."

However, it was all to no avail. Finnerty was convicted and sentenced to two years' imprisonment, a period in the pillory and a £20 fine; in addition, he was required to give sureties for good behaviour.

The prosecution and its result finished Finnerty's paper, but enhanced his popularity and reputation. When going to and in the pillory (for an hour) he was accompanied by a cheering crowd.

Finnerty and Curran deserve to be remembered for their services to the principle of a free press.

A judge was unwise enough to tell Curran that what he was saying "goes in one ear and out the other".

"But of course," replied Curran, "there's nothing to stop it."

Lord Norbury (John Toler) was a contemporary of Curran and, as Attorney-General, prosecuted in many of the famous trials in which Curran defended. He became Chief Justice of the Common Pleas in 1800 and by his partiality and broadness of humour made many enemies. He held the position until 1827 and was then created an Earl. He specialised in *bons mots* on the bench, but many were of the wounding variety.

In one case, a seduction action, he took a dislike to the defendant and also to the pretentiousness, as he saw it, of that unfortunate man's names: Henry William Godfrey Baker Sterne. Summing-up to the jury he rolled the names round his tongue and went on, "So there you have him, Gentlemen of the Jury, from stem to stern. And I am free to observe, gentlemen, that if this Mr Henry William Godfrey Baker Sterne had as many Christian virtues as he has Christian names we would never be here at all dealing with this case."

Wolfe Tone

 1798

THERE ARE TWO things not generally appreciated about Irish independence movements. One, that until 1798 they were not in any way republican in nature. And two, that many of the leaders were Protestant and a number came from the province of Ulster (which contains nine counties, six of which, since 1921, constitute Northern Ireland).

It is also a fact that the Irish risings, rebellions or insurrections, call them what you will, have been short-lived and unsuccessful. The 1798 Rising probably stood the best chance of success, because it was supported by the French, but it was defeated – as so many such enterprises are – by the weather and the sea. The 1798 Rising provided many Irish heroes, including in particular Theobald Wolfe Tone, Lord Edward Fitzgerald (son of the Duke of Leinster) and the Sheares brothers, practising barristers of the Munster Circuit.

Wolfe Tone was born in Dublin in June 1764, the son of a prosperous coachmaker. The family came from farming stock in County Kildare. In February 1781 he entered Trinity College, Dublin. In January 1787 he became a Law student at the Middle Temple in London and was called to the Bar two years later.

He was a founder-member of the Society of United Irishmen, which was formed in Belfast in 1791. In origin its purpose was entirely lawful, having as its purpose the constitutional reform of anti-Catholic oppression. But strongly influenced by the French Revolution and the American War of Independence, in 1794 after full discussion some members withdrew and the remainder changed its character to that of a secret, militant society.

Wolfe Tone, one of the militants, stood in danger when a French emissary with whom he was in contact was caught, but in May 1795 he managed to escape to America. In January 1796 he travelled on to Paris, where he urged the provision of a French force and a supply of arms for Ireland. The French authorities were so impressed by this idea that they fitted out an expedition which sailed from Brest on 16 December 1796. Wolfe Tone, appointed an Adjutant-General in the French forces, was aboard one of the sixty or more craft which carried 15,000 troops and a large supply of arms.

By 27 December the plan was abandoned. Weather scattered the expedition during the voyage, and though part reached Bantry Bay and Wolfe Tone pressed for a landing by the troops available – less than half the original force – further bad weather made this part of the expedition turn for home too.

In the following year, 1797, a similar intervention of prolonged bad weather prevented a Dutch sponsored force even getting under way. A further setback arose when Wolfe Tone found that, despite strong French offers of co-operation, General Bonaparte, who had been given command of "The Army of England", showed no great enthusiasm and indeed in May 1798 sailed off with the fleet – for Egypt.

A few days later the 1798 Irish Rising began without any outside help. When Wolfe Tone heard of it in Paris, he did everything he could to elicit further French assistance. What happened was a case of too little too late. A General Humbert assembled a small force – 1,000 men, 1,000 extra muskets and some artillery – and decided to make a landing in Ireland. A landing was duly effected, but success was short-lived. A force twenty times as strong under the command of General Lake quickly broke the small French army. The Irish members, which included Wolfe Tone's brother, were brought to Dublin in irons, tried and executed.

In September 1798 a larger French force – few ships but 5,000 men – set sail for Ireland with Wolfe Tone on board the Admiral's vessel, the *Hoche*. The expedition took three weeks to reach Lough Swilly. An English squadron was lying in wait there and after a tough battle the French force was defeated. The *Hoche* held out against strong opposition for over six hours, with Wolfe Tone commanding one of the batteries, and it then succumbed.

A number of the French force was taken prisoner, and a few days later Wolfe Tone was identified amongst them and arrested. He was taken to Dublin and put on trial before a court martial.

The ordinary Law Courts were in operation and a court martial clearly had no jurisdiction over him but, defending himself, he took no point about that then.

Indeed, arrayed in French uniform, he offered no defence to the charge of treason. When called upon to plead by the Judge Advocate, he said, "I mean not to give the Court any useless trouble and wish to spare them the idle task of examining witnesses. I admit all the facts alleged and only request leave to read an address which I have prepared for this occasion."

Asked if this meant that he admitted acting traitorously against His Majesty, Wolfe Tone replied, "Stripping the charge of the technicality of its terms, it means, I presume, that I have been found in arms against the soldiers of the King, in my native country. I admit this accusation in its most extended sense, and request again to explain to the Court the reasons and motives of my conduct."

Strictly speaking, I suppose it could be said that Wolfe Tone had not actually entered a plea to the charge, but the court martial took what he said as amounting to a plea of Guilty.

He was then invited to make his address to the Court – provided that he kept it within the bounds of moderation. Lack of moderation soon showed. He spoke of his dedication to the cause of "freeing" Ireland and to having sought the French as allies to that cause.

The President and other members of the tribunal interrupted at that stage and the Judge Advocate observed, perhaps unnecessarily, but certainly truly, that this sort of approach could not be expected to have an extenuating effect on His Excellency the Viceroy.

Wolfe Tone then went on, "I believe there is nothing in what remains for me to say that can give any offence; I wish to express my feelings and gratitude towards the Catholic body, in whose cause I was engaged." He was, like a number of his comrades, a Protestant.

The President interrupted to remark, "That seems to have nothing to say to the charge against you, to which you are only to speak. If you have anything to offer in defence or extenuation of the charge, the Court will hear you, but they beg you will confine yourself to that subject."

In that short passage the President's use of the words "in defence . . . of the charge" are rather interesting because, of course, the matter was proceeding on the basis of a plea of Guilty and no evidence had been given against the prisoner.

At any rate, Wolfe Tone turned to a different subject, his personal connection with the French army. He listed the sacrifices he had made for his native land. He added, "It is no great effort, at this day, to add the sacrifice of my life."

He said that he had indulged in an open fight and that atrocities and horrors could not be charged to him. "In a case like this," he said, "success is everything. Success, in the eyes of the vulgar, fixes its merit."

A little later he said, "I am aware of the fate which awaits me . . . I have spoken and acted with reflection and on principle, and am ready to meet the consequences. Whatever be the sentence of the Court, I am prepared for it. The members will surely discharge their duty – I should take care not to be wanting in mine."

He then asked to be heard as to the mode of punishment and requested that the Court should give him the death of a soldier, by shooting. He prayed in aid that he had long and bona fide been an officer in the French service, and he handed in various papers in proof of what he said. There was a short discussion on the subject and he was then asked if there was anything more he wanted to add. He said there was nothing except that the sooner His Excellency's approbation of the sentence was obtained, the better.

He was sentenced to death and the sentence was confirmed by the Viceroy, who refused the request for a military execution.

A number of dramatic events then followed. On the night of 11/12 November 1798, Wolfe Tone in his cell opened a vein in his neck with a penknife. How he could have been left with such an implement is a mystery. Then on the morning of the 12th, John Philpot Curran applied on his behalf to the Court of King's Bench for Habeas Corpus, to have him transferred to the civil authority.

It is clear that the court martial had no jurisdiction to try Wolfe Tone at all, when the ordinary Courts were fully operating. The point is, however, largely academic because a trial by an ordinary criminal Court would almost certainly have had no other result. The reason that it is not wholly academic is two-fold: that the court martial did not have the jurisdiction which it exercised and, secondly, that because of the jurisdiction point the Chief Justice readily granted the preliminary application for Habeas Corpus.

There then arose a magnificent situation. The Court's Officer went off to execute the order, but was told by the military authorities in charge of Wolfe Tone that they would only obey the orders of their own superiors. On hearing this, the Lord Chief Justice went into action in a big way. He ordered the Sheriff to proceed immediately to take Wolfe Tone into his custody and not only Wolfe Tone, but two named military officers as well. Furthermore, the Sheriff was specifically to show the Court's order to the General in command.

The Sheriff returned to Court to report that Wolfe Tone had wounded himself and could not be moved. Thereupon the Chief Justice ordered that the execution be suspended. The injuries were severe and Wolfe Tone gradually declined. He died a week later, on 19 November, in his cell. He is buried in the churchyard at Bodenstown, County Kildare, and various processions to his grave have taken place over the years and still continue.

There are interesting questions about the trial of Wolfe Tone apart from the question of the jurisdiction of the court martial mentioned above. First, he was arguably of French nationality by adoption and thus in a position to argue the points raised later in the case of Joyce (Lord Haw-Haw) after the 1939–45 War. He hinted at the point, but clearly did not raise it. Secondly, he was, rather than an insurrectionist, clearly and undeniably a bona fide member of an enemy force, namely the French. Again, he made the point, but did not raise it as a defence; only as a plea to mode of punishment.

39

Success on either of the points just mentioned would have meant that Wolfe Tone would have had to have been treated as a prisoner of war and not a traitor – a difference between life and death.

It is difficult but not impossible for a person to prove transfer of allegiance at the relevant time. A classic example in modern terms would be if a subject of country A had, before the events in question, clearly and obviously become a citizen of country B. An artificial or purely strategic change of nationality would be of no avail.

It seems reasonably clear that Wolfe Tone would not have been able to prove the necessary bona fide change of nationality. He remained, however reluctantly, the subject of the King of England – and Ireland; there cannot be a change of allegiance simply by disclaimer. The position was, in the words of the old verse, "Treason doth never prosper, what's the reason? For if it prosper, none dare call it treason."

There is no doubt that in a real and not any artificial sense Wolfe Tone was a member of the French forces, an officer of senior rank in the French army. Should that have availed him at trial before the court martial or a civil court? I believe that the right answer in law is No – because it is treason of itself for a subject to enlist in the forces of an enemy. There is no magic in becoming a military adherent to the enemy instead of a civilian adherent.

The position is that whatever may be said for the wisdom and mercy of treating such as Wolfe Tone as prisoners of war, in strict law they remain subjects and liable to treatment as traitors if they fall into the hands of "their" fellow-subjects. It will always remain a question in each individual case as to whether there has been a due change of nationality before the relevant time.

Irrespective of law, Wolfe Tone remains on one side's view a traitor and on the other side's view a hero, indeed the first of the many.

In the Ireland of 150 and 200 years ago many of the cases were reported in a few lines. They were of the style of "Plaintiff insulted Judge. Plaintiff instantly imprisoned." One which has always intrigued me and I confess rather frightens me is where the Court said, "If this pauper will not submit to arbitration we will de-pauper him." The process has an alarming sound.

On another occasion the Court refused to discharge a pauper from prison unless and until he paid the costs of the proceedings, costs which looked like being on a millionaire scale.

When a poor old pauper won a case he was only given "pauper costs".

A case about turf, the Irish fuel which other people will insist on calling peat, was disposed of in a couple of sentences. A tenant, said the Judge, could cut turf for his own use. He added gratuitously but interestingly that in England a tenant could coal from an existing seam but not open a new seam.

The judges could, however, spread themselves too. Give them some knotty problem of land law (preferably with a forfeiture for high treason thrown in somewhere along the line) and they could go into ecstacies and hundreds of pages. Mortgages, Marriage Settlements, Boundaries, Dower, Wills, these they loved and upon them they waxed eloquent, granting injunctions, dispossessing people and making elaborate orders which often led to further litigation later.

The poor Masters in Chancery were given a terrible time by their judges, being required to take accounts between parties stretching back over the years or to make elaborate investigations and report back to the Court.

There were many different kinds of Court in those days with different, often competing, jurisdictions – Exchequer, Common Pleas, King's Bench – and there was much to-ing and fro-ing between them. But an equal cause of delay and nuisance was the enormously detailed and elaborate written pleadings required to be lodged in Court. They ran to quires of paper and set out all manner of alternative pleas, objections and replies. It was not until just over a hundred years ago that the long necessary streamlining of the whole system took place in Ireland as well as in England.

One would not have dreamt in those days of just alleging, "On the first of September last at a political meeting in Kilkenny the defendant slandered the plaintiff by calling him a thief," or of having a defence which said, "The defendant is a thief. In August last he stole £100 from a widow named Murphy."

Lots of the old words and phrases went with the changes. One which I regret is the pleasant description of an appeal as being laid "In Error".

Lady Pamela Fitzgerald
(And Children)
 1799

WHEN LORD EDWARD FITZGERALD (q.v.) died in prison before trial for treason a Bill was brought into Parliament in Ireland to attaint him after his death. Attainder in respect of a convicted felon meant confiscation of his property to the Crown and forfeiture of all rights. In the case of a living felon where it was pronounced in his lifetime or automatically attached to his sentence no more was necessary. Here, an Act of Parliament would be necessary because the alleged criminal was dead and had never been tried.

Counsel are entitled to be heard in support of or against a Bill and Curran appeared at the Bar of the House of Commons in Ireland for Lord Edward's widow and children against the Bill to have him treated as attainted. He appeared, in fact, for the brother of the deceased; the widow (Lady Pamela); the heir, Edward, aged four; the elder daughter, Pamela, aged two; and the youngest child, Lucy, aged three months.

He said that there were two separate questions: the alleged treason, and the proposal to attaint.

He remarked with astonishment that the Committee of the House had asked him if he had any defence to go into in respect of the treason. "What," he said, "can be more flagrantly unjust than to enquire into a fact the truth or falsehood of which no human being can have knowledge – save the informer who seeks to assert it? I have no defensive evidence! I have no case! It is impossible I should. I have often of late gone to the dungeon of the captive; never have I gone to the grave of the dead to receive instructions for his defence. Nor in truth have I ever been at the trial of a dead man."

43

He protested against the whole enquiry into the alleged treason, not, as he said, in the name of the public but in that of the dead man and his surviving family, to whom it was "a cruelty and an injustice".

The informer in the case was a familiar one, Reynolds. Dealing with him, Curran said that he had admitted to being an informer and a bribed informer and, although he had so sworn on oath, that much of his evidence could be accepted. He had received 500 guineas for this matter. "He is the kind of man to whom the Law resorts with abhorrence and from necessity, in order to set the criminal against the crime. Who is made use of by the Law upon the same reason that the most noxious poisons are resorted to in medicine."

Dealing with Reynolds' evidence, Curran said, "If such the man, look for a moment at his story; he confines himself to mere conversation only – with a dead man, who cannot answer. He ventures not to introduce a third person, living or even dead." Later, "The only assertion to which credit can be given is that he has sworn, and forsworn, that *he* is a traitor, that he has received 500 guineas to be an informer; his general reputation is unworthy of credit."

As to Lord Edward's papers as produced Curran said they proved nothing either way; they were a man's writings and documents, which might be capable of easy explanation. This was a brief and shrewd way of dealing with them, given the absence of a living Accused; because in truth it would have been hard for Lord Edward to explain them away.

On the second part of the case Curran gave a detailed examination of the principles of forfeiture for high treason in many countries and various times. "The laws of the Persians and Macedonians," he said, "extended the punishment of traitor to all his kindred. The law subjected the property and life of every man to the most complicated despotism. The loyalty of every individual of his kindred was as much a matter of wild caprice as the will of the most arbitrary despot could be. But this principle was never adopted in any period as our law. At the earliest times of the Saxons the law of treason acted directly only on the person of the criminal, it took away from him what he actually had to forfeit – his life and property. But as to his children, the law disclaimed to affect them directly;

they suffered, but they suffered by a necessary consequence of their father's punishment, which the law could not prevent and never directly intended. It took away the inheritance because the criminal, at the time of taking it away, had absolute dominion over it and might himself have conveyed it away from his family."

This argument, brilliantly developed, was made as a first forcible submission that it was here too late to forfeit the property as it was already legally vested in the heir.

The next point he made was that historically by our law judgment was only on the traitor "to take effect only upon a condition suggested by the unalterable rules of natural justice, namely a judgment founded upon a conviction, against which he might have made his defence, or upon an outlawry, where he refused to abide his trial."

The great advocate was faced then with the great point – Parliament is omnipotent and can make a special Law. Agreed, he said, "but an argument from existence of a power to the exercise of it in any particular instance is ridiculous and absurd. From such an argument it would follow that it must do whatever it is able to do; that it must be stripped of the best of all power, the power of abstaining from what is wrong."

He said that a retrospective law was wrong; every *ex post facto* law was in itself an exercise of despotical power. The measure proposed here was repugnant to the spirit of the British Constitution.

The statute of Anne and of George II, he declared, provided that after the death of the Pretender and of his sons no such forfeiture should exist.

Bills of Attainder were to be found, he accepted, "in the violent reigns of the Plantagenets and the Tudors, but many of these were revised by the wisdom of cooler and juster times".

He examined various types of Bill of Attainder, such as one establishing the offence and at the same time attainting the criminal for it, or one which did not change the law as to the crime but changed the evidence for proving it. Of these species, he said, "No lawyer has ever spoken with respect. They were the cruel effect of the rancour and injustice of party spirit, nor could anything be said in their excuse except that they were made for the direct punishment of actual criminals – while they were still living."

The only remaining type was the present one. "For this too there was a precedent; but for the honour of humanity let it be remembered that one hundred and forty years have elapsed in which that precedent has not been thought worthy of imitation in Great Britain." He referred, he said, to the attainder of the Regicides upon the Restoration. But then only four of the already dead Regicides were included in the Bill. It came about at all, he declared, only at the behest of hypocrites and turncoats. It was limited as it was by a merciful King and a Ministry of uncommon wisdom.

"This precedent," Curran went on, "has never since been followed in Great Britain although that country has since been agitated by one revolution and vexed by two rebellions."

Referring to Great Britain as "that wise and reflecting country", he said that she had found such measures unjust and ineffectual.

This led him on to a consideration of penal laws in general, and, of course, he obviously had in mind the Penal Laws in Ireland against Catholics and Dissenters. "They have ever been found," he said, "more to exasperate than to restrain . . . The multiplication of penal laws lessens the value of life, and when you lessen the value of life you lessen the fear of death." Posthumous attainders in Ireland, he said, were put through by "the arbitrary Elizabeth" and by William III as means of transferring property to people of their own choice.

Posthumous attainders, he said, were "the result of an unnatural union of the legislative and judicial functions; in which the judicial has no law to restrain it; in which the legislative has no rule to guide it, unless passion and prejudice (which reject all rule and law) can be called rules and laws."

He pointed out that it was for these reasons that such steps had not been taken as a result of the Rebellion of 1715 or that of 1745.

If the principle argued for in this case be right, he declared, must it not be a violation of that principle for anyone to give his clients food and shelter? But nothing could restrain "a rebel tear or a traitorous humanity".

He ended by saying that "punishment can only light upon guilt; it is only vengeance which breaks upon innocence".

Almost inevitably the Bill was passed. Lady Pamela and the children went abroad and she remarried. The Fitzgeralds remained powerful and prosperous in Ireland and much of the effect of the attainder was overcome within a few years. The attainder itself was formally reversed by the British Government in 1819.

A donkey brayed loudly when Curran was addressing a judge who did not like him very much. "One at a time please, Mr Curran," said the Judge, very pleased with his own wit. Shortly afterwards the Judge bent over to pat his large dog. Curran stopped talking. "Go on, Mr Curran, go on."

"I wouldn't like to," said Curran, "while your Lordship is in consultation."

R. v. Sir Henry Hayes

 1799

IN CRIMINAL CASES Curran did not always defend; occasionally, very occasionally, he prosecuted. One such case was the prosecution at Cork Assizes of Sir Henry Hayes for the alleged abduction of Miss Mary Pike, a rich heiress of a well-known local Quaker family. The charge carried the death penalty.

Curran's description of the respective roles of prosecution and defence apply today as much as then and could not be better put:

"My Lord, and Gentlemen of the Jury, it is my duty, as one of the counsel in this prosecution, to state to Your Lordship, and to you, Gentlemen of the Jury, such facts as I am instructed will be established by evidence, in order that you may be informed of the nature of the offence charged by the indictment, and be rendered capable of understanding that evidence, which, without some previous statement, might appear irrelevant or obscure. And I shall make a few such observations in point of law on the evidence we propose to adduce, with respect to the manner in which it will support the charge, if you shall believe it to be true, as may assist in you performing that awful duty which you are now called upon to discharge.

"In doing so I cannot forget upon what very different ground from that of the learned counsel for the prisoner, I find myself placed. It is the privilege, it is the obligation, of those who have to defend a client on a trial for his life, to exert every force, and to call forth every resource, that zeal and genius and sagacity can suggest; it is an indulgence in favour of life; it has the sanctity of usage; it has the permission of humanity; and the man who should linger one single step behind the most advanced limit of that privilege, and should fail to exercise every talent that Heaven has given him in that defence would be guilty of a mean desertion of his duty and an abandonment of his client.

"Far different is the situation of him who is concerned for the Crown. Cautiously should he use his privileges; scrupulously should he keep within the duties of accusation. His task is to lay fairly the nature of the case before the Court and the Jury. Should he endeavour to gain a verdict otherwise than by evidence he was unworthy of speaking in a Court of Justice. If I heard a counsel for the Crown state anything that I did not think founded in law, I should say to myself God grant that the man who has stated this may be an ignorant man, because his ignorance can be his only justification. It shall therefore be my endeavour so to lay the matters of fact and law before you as shall enable you clearly to comprehend them: and, finally, by your verdict to do complete justice between the prisoner and the public."

Later in the course of his opening address he said, "Anything I say, either as to the fact or to the law, ought not to attract anything more than bare attention for a single moment. It should make no impression upon your belief unless confirmed by credible evidence. I am merely stating matters from instruction; I am not a witness. I am also obliged, as I told you, to make observations as to the law, but that is wholly submitted to the Court; to which it is your duty, as well as mine, to bow with all becoming deference and respect."

Towards the end of his opening, which lasted about two hours, Curran counselled the jury against deciding the case on sympathy. He had in mind not only sympathy for the girl, but also possible sympathy for Sir Henry, who was popular locally and had avoided arrest for over two years, living and moving about fairly freely in and around the city of Cork. He had been formally declared an outlaw, which itself meant the death penalty when the outlaw was apprehended. Here, as was usual, the outlawry was revoked after the prisoner was arrested so that he could be tried on his merits for the original offence.

In dealing with the matter of sympathy Curran said, "Justice may weep; but she must strike when she ought not to spare."

Concluding, he said, "Believe nothing upon my statement. Hear and weigh the evidence. If you doubt its truth, acquit without hesitation. By the laws of every country, because of those of eternal Justice, doubt and acquittal are synonymous terms. If, on the other hand, the guilt of the prisoner shall unhappily be clearly proved, remember what you owe to your fame, your conscience and your country. I shall trouble you no further, but shall call evidence in support of the indictments; and I have not a doubt that there will be such a verdict given, whether of conviction or acquittal, as may hereafter be spoken of without kindling any shame in you or your country."

Abduction cases were comparatively rare. They depended for their success on the victim being able and willing to give evidence. Several potential cases foundered for want of a willing prosecutor, and there was much to discourage a prosecutrix; there would be a considerable ordeal in giving evidence and widespread publicity on a lavish scale.

Some twenty years before, there had been a famous abduction case in the area; two Miss Kennedys had been abducted by two young men, forced to go through forms of marriage and detained for many months. When they were freed great pressure was exerted upon them not to give evidence and they had to have a military guard to protect them from intimidation. They gave evidence, the two men were found guilty and were executed.

Miss Mary Pike was a willing witness and the story she told – corroborated in material parts by other witnesses – was a frightening one. She was the only child, and heiress, of a successful Cork businessman who had recently died. Her mother lived in the city and was in poor health. The family were Quakers. Miss Pike lived a little way outside the city with a friend of her father, Mr Cooper Penrose, and his family.

In the summer of 1797 the accused, Sir Henry Hayes, on visiting Mr Penrose's gardens – as many did – met Mr Penrose, greatly admired his grounds, and, having timed things well, got himself invited to remain for dinner.

There he met Mary Pike for the first time. As Curran put it, "His first approach to her was meanly and perfidiously

51

contrived, with the single purpose of identifying her person, in order that he might feloniously steal it, as the title-deed of her estate."

The doctor in charge of old Mrs Pike was a Dr Gibbings. A letter was forged in his name addressed to Mr Cooper Penrose and delivered late at night. It was dated 22 July 1797 and read, "Dear Sir, Our friend Mrs Pike is taken suddenly ill. She wishes to see Miss Pike. We would recommend despatch, as we think she has not many hours to live. Yours Robert Gibbings."

In the early hours of the morning, Miss Pike, accompanied by Mr Penrose's daughter and another lady, set off in his carriage for the city. On the way the carriage was stopped by a group of four or five men on horseback. One was dressed in a greatcoat, had a scarf or handkerchief concealing the lower part of his face, and was armed with pistols.

There was another coach stationed nearby. Miss Pike was forcibly removed from her companions and put in the other chaise. And in it waiting for her was the Accused's sister. She died before the trial.

The traces of Mr Penrose's carriage were cut and the two women and the coachman were left to make their way home as best they might.

Miss Pike was taken to the prisoner's house, Vernon Mount, and when the horses stopped at the foot of the hill leading up the avenue Sir Henry Hayes dismounted from his horse, gave it to one of the others and carried her, struggling strenuously, up to the house. He then carried her upstairs and brought her to a man who was dressed as a priest or clergyman and purported to marry them.

A purported marriage was a regular feature of abduction cases, often believed – stupidly and wrongly – to be recognisable by law and to give the man all the then extensive rights of a husband over a wife's property. An alternative reason, probably the one operating in Sir Henry Hayes' case, was a belief that the ceremony would make the victim compliant and her relatives resigned.

Miss Pike was far from compliant. The rings which had been forced upon her finger she tore off and threw away. Efforts to get her to share a bed with Sir Henry were strongly and successfully resisted. This latter was another familiar ploy in abduction cases; consummation of the "marriage" was regarded, of course wrongly, as something which would go to strengthen its validity or – and this was often right – would deceive or shame the victim and her relations into accepting the situation.

Sir Henry then made Miss Pike write a letter to the Penroses saying that she was married and not to worry about her. She agreed to write the letter but absolutely refused to sign it by her "new" name. She disclaimed being Lady Hayes and signed her true surname.

Just as Mary Pike was not compliant so her relatives and friends were not resigned to her fate. They went in some force to the prisoner's house in order to free her and found it an easier task than expected because the prisoner and his accomplices, including his sister, had fled. Miss Pike was rescued, criminal informations were laid against Sir Henry and rewards to the amount of £1,000 were offered for his apprehension.

Sir Henry did not leave the area but remained in concealment for a time and was then progressively more open in his movements, his two-year freedom constituting, as Curran said, a sad reproach to the city of Cork. Miss Pike, on the other hand, was sent to England for the duration of Sir Henry's freedom. "Sad reverse," said Curran. "It was not for guilt to fly! It was for guilt to stand, and bay at public justice! It was only for innocence to betake itself to flight. It was hers to feel that she could despair even of personal protection in the country which harboured and cherished the delinquent."

Shortly before she was to return to Ireland for the prosecution Miss Pike received a letter from Sir Henry Hayes which was a mixture of entreaties not to give evidence against him and threats as to what would happen if she did.

Nevertheless she came and her evidence was clear, strong and damning.

All this happened a hundred years before it was permissible for an Accused in Ireland or England to give evidence on his own behalf. It is hard to believe that such a precious right is only just over eighty years old. The Accused could, of course, defend himself by cross-examination of the prosecution witnesses and by calling witnesses of his own.

Nothing, however, availed Sir Henry Hayes. There was really no defence he could put forward once Miss Pike gave evidence. He had not attempted to conceal his identity or his residence from her. He had not run away with her abroad or to some hiding-place elsewhere in Ireland. It was of the essence of abduction that the perpetrator should seek to get his hands on his victim's money and property, and for that he had to stay close at hand.

Abduction was indeed a difficult exercise to complete satisfactorily. For entire success it depended on really winning the young woman's consent and affection after the deed or in so frightening her and her friends as to prevent them interfering with the transfer of the property. There was a great risk of failure before one even got to the question of prosecution at all.

Sir Henry Hayes was duly found Guilty and sentenced to death.

The sentence was commuted to transportation for fourteen years. It is not easy to understand the reason for commutation since the case was at least as bad as others where the death penalty was exacted. Sir Henry served his term of transportation and at the end of it returned to Ireland.

It is an interesting contrast between England and Ireland that there are many differences in metaphor between the two countries. In England one speaks of sending somebody to Coventry; in Ireland, after the memory of a local land agent, Captain Boycott, who was shunned, one speaks instead of boycotting. In England a thing is regarded as being as safe as the Bank of England; in Ireland as impregnable as the Rock of Cashel. In Curran's time the art of obtaining money was known in England as "raising the wind", in Ireland as "flying a kite". A friend of his, Plunkett, was asked by the Judge what the latter phrase meant; he had heard of the former, never of the latter. Plunkett replied, "In England, my Lord, the wind raises the kite, but in Ireland the kite raises the wind."

Major Sirr

 1802

ONE OF THE most curious characters to stalk through Irish history was Major Henry Charles Sirr (1764–1841). An ex-Army officer, he became what was known as the Town-Major of Dublin in 1796 and held the office through the Rebellion of 1798 and the insurrectionist movements up to 1803, indeed until 1826.

What was the position of Town-Major? Nominally, until Major Sirr's time, it was a position of emolument rather than activity. A subsequent bearer of the office (Hayes in 1876) established against the Dublin Corporation that it entitled one to be the Registrar of Pawnbrokers (most lucrative) and the Receiver of various obscure Courts (also lucrative), and could not be commuted for a mere salary. For a modern equivalent we must look (with apology and without lucrative analogy) to the office of a Police Chief, and add to it (again with apology) the description non-active. With an advocate's latitude, Curran described it as beginning with "a name scarcely legible in the list of public encumbrances".

Sirr is credited with the arrest of Peter Finnerty (q.v.), of wounding and arresting Lord Edward Fitzgerald (q.v), and of arresting Robert Emmet (q.v.). In fact it is widely suggested that his preference lay in "leading his regiment from behind", and that in each instance he allowed a deputy to perform his duty but assiduously attended upon the deputy.

As is already apparent, he moved from sinecure inactivity to actual activity in the troubled years from 1798 to 1803 inclusive. It is cynical, perhaps unjust, to say that his emoluments were thereby increased. And not legitimately.

In 1802 a brewer named John Heavey sued him for assault and false imprisonment. Curran appeared for the plaintiff and showed yet another side of his genius – the ability to secure a jury by pure compelling narration of events.

In his opening speech he said that he did not call "for a haughty verdict that might humble the insolence of oppression or assert the fancied rights of independence".

He said that he must take the jury back to the melancholy period of 1798. "It was at that sad crisis that the defendant, from an obscure individual, started into notice and consequence. It is in the hot-bed of public calamity, that such portentous and inauspicious products are accelerated without being matured. From being a Town-Major, a name scarcely legible in the list of public encumbrances, he became at once invested with all the real powers of the most absolute authority. The life and the liberty of every man seemed to be given up to his disposal."

Curran then recounted the origins of the trouble. A man named M'Guire was being prosecuted. Mr Heavey was by accident in Court. He heard a prosecution witness, whom he had employed, give evidence. He felt it his duty to tell the defence, subsequently the Court, that the witness was completely unreliable. M'Guire was acquitted.

Sirr met the plaintiff shortly afterwards in the street and upbraided him for giving evidence. He threatened him. "Gentlemen," said Curran to the jury, "there are two classes of prophets: one that derive their prediction from real or fancied inspiration, and who are sometimes mistaken; another who are determined to bring about events themselves. Of this second, and by far the most authentic class, was the Major. Heaven, you see, has no monopoly of prediction."

Next evening, said Curran, Heavey was "dogged in the dark into some lonely alley, where he was seized, he knew not by whom or by what authority". He was imprisoned in a part of Dublin Castle called the Provost – "a mansion of misery" presided over by a Major Sandys.

Curran told how Mr Heavey was held there for seven weeks and was parted from his mare by the duress of Major Sandys. "You are to be sent down tomorrow to Kilkenny to be tried for your life; you will most certainly be hanged; and you can scarcely think that your journey to the other world will be performed on horseback."

At Kilkenny, on invented evidence, Heavey was tried and sentenced to be hanged. Accidentally, said Curran, Lord Cornwallis (the Viceroy) came to know of the proceedings, quashed them and released Mr Heavey.

On return to Dublin, Heavey demanded his mare of Major Sandys, observing that though he might have proceeded to heaven on foot it was more comfortable to perform his earthly journeys on horseback. Curran said that Sandys was "astonished at the impudence and novelty of calling the privileges of official plunder into question". Heavey brought an action for his mare and, by default, got judgment and costs, both of which were satisfied.

Curran described Sandys and Sirr as "You plunderer in the gaol, you tyrant in the street." He challenged both to deny on oath his assertions.

Three years later, said Curran, after a meeting in a coffee-house, Sirr had Heavey arrested and again lodged in Dublin Castle. "The officer of the guard happened to be an Englishman, an Englishman but lately arrived in Ireland; he said to the bailiffs, 'If this was in England I should think this gentleman entitled to bail, but I don't know the laws of this country. However, I think you had better loosen those irons on his wrists or I think they may kill him.'"

In the Hospital of the Provost (six beds, fourteen men, a room about thirteen feet by twelve) Heavey was detained for what Major Sandys frankly described as the crime of insolence to Major Sirr.

Mr Heavey made application for Habeas Corpus but was defeated (so Curran alleged, uncontradicted) by a false return to the Writ which said that he was detained pursuant to a warrant from General Craig on a charge of treason.

Curran went on to say that throughout Sandys set the price of freedom as an abject apology in writing to Major Sirr. After many refusals Heavey signed "a submission dictated by Sandys".

Calling upon the jury to find for the plaintiff, Curran requested this verdict as a message not only to Ireland but to England, and said, "In every point of view, therefore, I recommend to you to find, and to find liberally for the plaintiff."

The plaintiff's case went undisputed and the jury brought in a verdict in his favour for £150 damages and costs.

Major Sirr continued in his office notwithstanding – it was that kind of office. But he evidently adopted what is now known as a lower profile, a lower profile with perhaps even larger profits.

A friend of Curran's went to London to seek fame and fortune. After a short time away he wrote to his mother saying, "Could you at your convenience send me eleven shirts. I find here that every gentleman has a dozen."

Robert Emmet

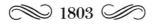 1803

"She is far from the land where her young hero sleeps,
And lovers are round her, sighing:
But coldly she turns from their gaze, and weeps,
For her heart in his grave is lying."

THOMAS MOORE (1779–1852), the great Irish melody-writer, spoke here of his great friend Robert Emmet and Emmet's love affair with Sarah Curran, daughter of the great advocate. It is a romance which has always profoundly stirred Irish people. It, and his speech from the dock when convicted of treason, have ensured him a lasting place in Irish history.

It is ironic that Emmet asked Sarah's father to defend him at his trial and was refused. The reason is not easy to see, but is probably attributable to outside pressure upon Curran, who was usually not susceptible to such interference. He was indeed that ideal advocate, one who would espouse unpopular causes and not count the consequences. Perhaps, however, here he felt a particular embarrassment because of Sarah.

Robert Emmet was born on 4 March 1778, the third son of a well-known Dublin physician. His brother Thomas Addis Emmet, very much older, had been involved in the 1798 Rising. Robert, who was at Trinity College, Dublin, at the time showed his passionate alliance with his brother's views at the college Historical Society, a famous debating club. As a result, he was expelled from the College in February 1798.

The civil authorities in consequence had Robert Emmet on

their list and he departed for the Continent. There he mixed with the large body of Irish refugees, which was augmented in 1802 by the men released after terms of imprisonment for their parts in the 1798 affair. These included his brother.

In the latter part of 1802, buoyed up with promises of French assistance, Robert Emmet returned to Dublin to organise another Rebellion. He moved furtively, using disguise and false names. He spent his time gathering men and weapons.

When war between France and England broke out again in May 1803, Robert Emmet took fresh hope. However, the government were obviously aware of a probable revolt and he was obliged to advance his plans. The 23rd of July 1803 was fixed for the Rising.

Everything possible went wrong for the rebels. The main plan was for an attack on Dublin Castle – the seat of govern-ment – from Thomas Street, about three-quarters of a mile away. To start with the expected numbers did not arrive at their rendezvous and there were in the end only a hundred or less assembled. Next, a mob gathered round, not hostile, but curious and excited, creating a hindrance and ready to grab any personal opportunities which occurred. Worst of all, an incident took place which altered the whole scheme of things and affected both the force and the crowd. A carriage appeared in the street which contained the Chief Justice of the King's Bench (Lord Kilwarden) and his daughter and nephew (the Reverend Mr Wolfe). A man from the crowd suddenly piked and killed the Chief Justice. It was apparently a man whose son had been sentenced to death by the Chief Justice. The nephew was also killed. The daughter was rescued by Robert Emmet personally.

With this incident the Rising – if it could ever have been called such – collapsed completely. The rebels dispersed, and when the government forces came on the scene there was nothing for them to deal with. Emmet and his men had not wanted the murders which occurred and had no part in them, but the mob had taken over.

Robert Emmet, now a particularly marked man, could have escaped abroad had he acted quickly, but he delayed for weeks in order to see Sarah Curran. He was given hiding in several places but eventually, a month after the Rising, he was caught in a house belonging to a Mrs Palmer in Harolds Cross, a suburb of the city.

On 19 September 1803 Robert Emmet was put on trial for high treason at the Courthouse in Green Street, then and now Dublin's main criminal court, the Irish equivalent of the Old Bailey.

He entered no defence and the jury found him guilty without leaving their box. He was then asked why sentence of death should not be passed upon him and he made a long and famous speech frequently interrupted by the presiding Judge, Lord Norbury, for preaching treason.

The main themes of Emmet's speech from the dock were that he passionately wanted freedom for Ireland and that accusations of selling the country to the French were false.

Speaking of his trial and of the attacks on his character he said, "There must be guilt somewhere, whether in the sentence of the court or in the catastrophe. Time must determine."

When interrupted he said, "What I have spoken was not intended for Your Lordship, whose situation I commiserate with rather than envy; my expressions were for my countrymen."

Again in reply to the Judge he said, "By a revolution of power we might change places, but we never could change characters."

Protesting that he had a right to be heard as to the moral and political justification for his actions, he said, "Why insult me, why insult justice in demanding of me why sentence of death should not be pronounced against me? I know, My Lords, that form prescribes you should ask the question. The form also presents the right of answering. This, no doubt, may be dispensed with, and so might the whole ceremony of the trial, since sentence was clearly pronounced at the Castle [Dublin Castle] before the jury were empanelled. Your Lordships are but the priests of the oracle and I insist on the whole of the forms."

With regard to France he said, "Connection with France was, indeed, intended but only as far as mutual interest would sanction or require. Were the French to assume any authority inconsistent with purest independence, it would be the signal for their destruction."

Dealing with a statement by Lord Norbury to the jury that he had been the life and blood of the conspiracy he said, "You do me honour over much; you have given to a subaltern all the credit of a superior."

A little later on, Lord Norbury infuriated Emmet by saying, "Your sentiments and language disgrace your family and your education, more particularly your father, Dr Emmet, who was a man of eminence who would not have countenanced such opinions."

Repudiating this and praising his father's morality and patriotism, Robert Emmet went on to say, "My Lords, you are impatient for the sacrifice . . . Be ye patient! I have but a few more words to say . . . I have but one request to ask at my departure from this world – it is the Charity of its Silence."

Finally came the memorable words, which rank amongst the greatest of history: "Let me rest in obscurity and peace, and my tomb remain uninscribed and my memory in oblivion until other times and other men can do justice to my character. When my country takes her place among the nations of the earth, then and not till then, let my epitaph be written."

At 10 p.m. Emmet was sentenced to death. At midnight he was removed to Kilmainham Jail. At noon the next day, 20 September 1803, he was publicly hanged. His body was then cut down and the neck placed on a block and the head severed. The executioner held up the head, showed it to the crowd – a stunned and horrified crowd – and proclaimed, "This is the head of a traitor."

Walking in St James's Park in London one autumn evening, Curran was with a friend, Charles Philips, when a storm came on and shook the dying leaves of the trees in great quantity. Curran turned to his friend and said, "We are desired by philosophy to take lessons from Nature; yet how foolishly does she seem to act; she flings away her blessings and her decorations; she is busy stripping those defenceless trees at the approach of winter and of cold – at the very season when they most want covering."

The Rev. Charles Massy
v.
The Marquess of Headfort
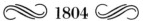 1804

SEDUCTION IS A word and a concept not in much use today. In the period between about 1750 and 1850, it was a quite common source of litigation under the grandiose and pompous legal name of "criminal conversation", known widely as crim. con.

John Philpot Curran, who led for the plaintiff in the Reverend Massy's case, had himself been the successful plaintiff in such a case, against a clergyman (the Reverend Mr Sandys), and had been greatly affected by it, refusing ever after to consider any question of reconciliation.

It seems, however, that Curran – and probably many of his male contemporaries – drew a distinction between a husband's infidelity and a wife's. The year before the Reverend Massy's case, Curran, in a case called Pentland v. Clarke, had – successfully – dealt with allegations of inconstancy against that husband by saying, "The consequence arising from illicit connections is widely different with respect to the husband and the wife; carnal revelry and immorality in the husband is not supposed to count an indelible disgrace upon the wife, and cannot defraud the children of their property, by introducing a spurious offspring, to which the infidelity of the wife may lead. Errors of this kind in the husband may not arise from an actual turpitude of heart; he may have committed errors of this kind, and yet be a good father; he may be a good citizen, he may be a good husband, notwithstanding he may not be entirely without blemish. I am not speaking of a constant scene of riot and debauchery, but of acts which, though they are to be condemned, it is possible to atone for by subsequent good conduct."

The Reverend Massy was a well-to-do young clergyman, the second son of a baronet, who had married in 1796, against his father's wishes, a pretty young lady named Miss Rosslewin who had no money of her own. They had one child, a son. The then Marquess of Headfort, who was himself married, was an extensive landowner in Ireland whose income was an enormous one for those days, at least £30,000 a year. At the time in question he was in the Army with his Meath Militia and stationed in Limerick, near where the Massys lived. He was much older than the Massys, being over fifty. Put in the language of the present day (when in England it is no longer possible to claim damages against a Co-respondent) she went off with him. That happened on a Sunday shortly after Christmas 1803.

The action for criminal conversation was started, claiming damages of £40,000. It was set down for trial at Ennis Assizes, County Clare, and occupied just one day, albeit one of a twelve-hour sitting. The jury brought in their verdict at midnight. The date was 27 July 1804.

Nowadays, most actions in Ireland have at least two counsel a side, but in England even the practice of having a junior counsel when you have a leader is being eroded. On this occasion Curran had nine counsel with him and his opponent Ponsonby had five. The plaintiff's team was Messrs Curran, Hoare, Deane Grady, Carey, Whyte, Hawksworth, O'Regan, Lloyd, McMahon and Bennet; Agent (i.e. Solicitor) Anthony Hogan Esq. The defendant's team was George Ponsonby, Quin, Gould, Francis, Bushe and Richard Pennefather; Agent James Sims Esq.

The trial excited great interest and a lot of publicity. The plaintiff's case was opened by Mr Hoare, and Curran made the closing speech.

Mr Hoare was eloquent. In one passage he described the defendant Marquess as "this hoary veteran in whom, like Etna, the snow above did not quench the flames below". In another he likened him to "The Cornish plunderer, intent on spoil, callous to every touch of humanity, shrouded in darkness [who] holds out false lights to the tempest-tossed vessel and lures her and her pilot to that shore upon which she must be lost for ever, the rock unseen, the ruffian invisible and nothing apparent but the treacherous signal of security and repose."

"The Cornish plunderer" has remained a well-remembered phrase, but for myself I have always wondered about its aptness before a County Clare jury who had no connection whatever with Cornwall. After all, if plundering or piracy were to be introduced, there were nearer felons than Falmouth and nearer pirates than Penzance.

Five witnesses were then called on behalf of the plaintiff, proving the marriage, the happiness of the Massys' household, the elopement and the Marquess' income.

Three witnesses called on behalf of the defendant deposed to the frivolous, flighty nature of the lady. It was what might be described in modern language as the defence line of no resistance, no loss, no damage.

Ponsonby spoke. Then, late in the long day, Curran. Speaking of Ponsonby, he said:

"You have seen even his great talents, perhaps the finest in any country, languishing under a cause too weak to carry him, and too heavy to be carried by him. He was forced to dismiss his natural candour and sincerity, and, having no merits in his case, to take refuge in the dignity of his own manner, the resources of his own ingenuity, from the overwhelming difficulties with which he was surrounded. Wretched client! Unhappy advocate! What a combination do you form! But such is the condition of guilt – its commission mean and tremulous, its defence artificial and insincere, its prosecution candid and simple, its condemnation dignified and austere.

"The learned counsel has told you that this unfortunate woman is not to be estimated at forty thousand pounds – fatal and unquestionable is the truth of this assertion. Alas, gentlemen, she is no longer worth anything; faded, fallen, degraded, and disgraced, she is worth less than nothing! But it is for the honour, the hope, the expectation, the tenderness, and the comforts that have been blasted by the defendant, and have fled for ever, that you are to remunerate the plaintiff by the punishment of the defendant. It is not her present value which you are to weigh, but it is her value at that time when she sat basking in a husband's love, with the blessing of Heaven on her head, and its purity in her heart; when she sat amongst her family, and administered the morality of the parental board. Estimate that past value – compare it with its present deplorable diminution – and it may lead you to form some judgment of the severity of the injury and the extent of the compensation.

"The learned counsel has referred you to other cases, and other countries, for instances of moderate verdicts. I can refer you to some authentic instances of Irish ones. In the next county, £15,000 against a subaltern officer. In Travers and M'Carthy, £5,000 against a servant. In Tighe against Jones, £1,000 against a man not worth a shilling. What then ought to be the rule, where rank, and power, and wealth, and station, have combined to render the example of his crime more dangerous, to make his guilt more odious, to make the injury to the plaintiff more grievous, because more conspicuous?"

He spoke scathingly of the insubstantial material put forward in defence or in mitigation of damage – that the plaintiff was the author of his own wrong, that he connived at what had happened and that he had placed "injudicious confidence" in his wife. It would not be right to say that Curran brushed them aside – he was not at any time a brusher aside – rather he dwelt on them and said that the unjustified making of these charges inflated the damages.

It happened to be on a Sunday that the wife left and Curran prayed that in aid. "In the middle of the day, at the moment of divine worship, when the miserable husband was on his knees, directing the prayers and thanksgivings of his congregation to their God – that moment did the remorseless adulterer choose to carry off the deluded victim from her husband – from her child – from her character – from her happiness, as if not content to leave his crime confined to its inseparable and miserable aggravations unless he also gave it a cast and colour of factitious sacrilege and impiety."

Suggesting to the jury how they personally would have pleaded with the defendant to desist from his purpose, he suggested that they would have said, *inter alia*, "but if you have no pity for the father, have mercy at least upon his innocent and helpless child; do not condemn him to an education scandalous or neglected; do not strike him into that most dreadful of all human conditions, the orphanage that springs not from the grave, that falls not from the hand of Providence, or the stroke of death; but comes before its time, anticipated and inflicted by the remorseless cruelty of parental guilt."

Striking a familiar theme that the jury was Irish and in a position to strike a blow for Ireland, Curran made play with the fact that the defendant had carried off Mrs Massy to England. "He transported his precious cargo," he said, "to a country where her example may be less mischievous than in her own; where – I agree with my learned colleague in heartily wishing – he may remain with her for ever. We are too poor, too simple, too unadvanced a country, for the example of such achievements. When the relaxation of morals is the natural growth and consequence of the great progress of arts and wealth, it is accompanied by a refinement that makes it less gross and shocking; but for such palliations we are at least a century too young. I advise you, therefore, most earnestly to rebuke this budding mischief, by letting the wholesome vigour and chastisement of a liberal verdict speak what you think of its enormity. In every point of view in which I can look at the subject, I see you are called upon to give a verdict of bold, and just, and indignant, and exemplary compensation. The injury of the plaintiff demands it from your justice. The delinquency of the defendant provokes it by its enormity."

On the same subject of damages, and with the same purpose of an appeal to an Irish jury, he said, "I doubt not but that he is at this moment reclined on a silken sofa, anticipating that submissive and modest verdict, by which you will lean gently on his errors; and expecting from your patriotism, no doubt, that you will think again and again, before you condemn any great portion of the immense revenue of a great absentee, to be detained in the country that provided it, instead of being transmitted, as it ought, to be expended in the splendour of another country . . . I am addressing you as fathers, husbands, brothers. I am anxious that a feeling of those

70

high relations should enter into, and give dignity to, your verdict."

There was a splendid passage dealing with the noble Marquess' previous excursions: "But it seems, gentlemen, and indeed you have been told, that long as the course of his gallantries has been – and he has grown grey in the service – it is the first time he has been called upon for damages. To how many might it have been fortunate if he had not that impunity to boast! Your verdict will, I trust, put an end to that encouragement to guilt that is built upon impunity."

The jury brought in a verdict for £10,000 damages, and for that amount and costs judgment was entered in favour of the Reverend Massy.

I have nowhere seen the verdict regarded as otherwise than a great triumph for Curran. The amount in 1804 money was, of course, huge. Myself, I would have expected a verdict of £30,000; not the £40,000 claimed but £30,000, as representing one year's income of the defendant: if not that, then £25,000 or £20,000. But perhaps the fact that the plaintiff himself was well off weighed with the jury.

That Curran could, when required, equally well take the other side in such a matter is shown by his earlier case of Egan v. Kindillan, a father's action for seduction. Mr Kindillan, for whom he appeared, had been prosecuted first for abduction, which carried the death penalty. Curran had appeared for him then and he had been acquitted. In the civil action in the course of his speech to the jury he described the defendant as "more seduced than seducing. It is upon this the father calls to you for damages! For an injury committed – by whom? From what cause? From the indiscreet behaviour, the defective education, and neglected mind of his daughter. He can have no feeling, or he would not have exposed both her and himself; or if he has any feelings, they are such as can be gratified by you, gentlemen of the jury, they are such as can be calmed by money! . . . She goes off unsolicited, she seeks the opportunity, and yet Mr Kindillan is to be the victim!"

Nevertheless the jury awarded £500 damages to the father of the eighteen-year-old Miss Egan.

The origin of the hatred which the Lord Chancellor of Ireland, Lord Clare, exhibited to Curran, to the latter's considerable financial damage at the Bar, goes back perhaps to their days in the Irish Parliament (which sat in College Green and now impressively houses the Bank of Ireland). When the House was discussing a penal and oppressive bill, Curran accused Lord Clare (then Attorney-General Fitzgibbon) of being asleep. He lamented that "the slumber of guilt should so nearly resemble the repose of innocence". A duel followed and Fitzgibbon took a very long and careful aim, but he missed. "It was not your fault, Mr Attorney," exclaimed Curran, "you were deliberate enough."

The King v. Mr Justice Johnson

 1805

HIGH COURT JUDGES in Ireland and England have long enjoyed the status of being removable only on a vote of both
Houses of Parliament. This is a recognition of their need to be
independent and free from any pressure on the part of the
Government or the Executive.

Even High Court judges, however, can disqualify themselves by crime or be forced into the position of having to
resign. An early example of this is to be found in the person
of Mr Justice Robert Johnson, who was called to the Irish
Bar in 1776 and became a Justice of the Common Pleas in
1800. The facts were extraordinary, the procedure adopted
against him was extraordinary and the result was extraordinary.

In November 1803 William Cobbett, the great political
agitator, published in his *Political Register* a letter signed
"Juverna", which was highly derogatory of Lord Hardwicke
(the Lord Lieutenant of Ireland), Lord Redesdale (the Lord
Chancellor of Ireland), Mr Secretary Marsdale and Mr Justice
Osborne (a High Court Judge in Ireland). It spoke of Lord
Hardwicke as being stupid and plausible and as having played
"a vicious role" in Ireland. It called Mr Secretary Marsdale
"a corrupt, unprincipled, rapacious plunderer", and Mr
Justice Osborne "the most corrupt instance of a debased and
degraded government's preferment". It was all good strong
stuff.

When prosecuted, Cobbett, in breach of the journalists'
code, and to obtain leniency, revealed the manuscript

and its probable source. The finger pointed at Mr Justice Johnson.

The government determined to get him to England for trial and used a Fugitive Offenders Act for the purpose. An interesting, not unimportant point is that the Act they used was one passed after the letter in question was written and as Curran (the Judge's counsel) constantly asserted passed specially to deal with his case. The preamble to the Act described it as being in order "to render more easy the apprehending and bringing to trial of offenders escaping from one part of the United Kingdom to the other, and also from one country to another".

Pursuant to the Act a warrant was issued for arrest of the Judge by the Lord Chief Justice of England, Lord Ellenborough, sent to and endorsed by an Irish magistrate.

Mr Justice Johnson was accordingly arrested on 18 January 1805. He immediately proceeded for Habeas Corpus to the Irish Court of Queen's Bench, which at first divided 3–3 (two abstaining), and when re-constituted rejected the application by 2–1.

Curran argued that his client was not a fugitive offender; he had not run away; he was in Ireland, where he always had been; and accordingly he had not fled the scene of the alleged crime. The counter argument was that the crime was publication in England and though Johnson had not left Ireland he was a fugitive from justice for that crime.

There was an application to the Court of Exchequer, which effected a reconciliation between Curran and the presiding Judge, the Irish Lord Chief Justice (Lord Avonmore), formerly Barry Yelverton. Curran said:

"I am not ignorant, My Lords, that this extraordinary construction has received the sanction of another Court, nor of the surprise and dismay with which it smote upon the general heart of the Bar. I am aware that I may have the mortification of being told in another country of that unhappy decision, and I foresee in what confusion I shall hang down my head when I am told of it. But I cherish, too, the consolatory hope that I shall be able to tell them that I had an old and learned friend whom I would put above all the

74

sweepings of their hall, who was of a different opinion, who had derived his idea of Civil Liberty from the purest fountains of Athens and of Rome . . .

"I would add that if he had seemed to hesitate it was but for a moment; that his hesitation was like the passing cloud that floats across the morning sun, and hides it from view and does so hide it by involving the spectator without ever approaching the face of the luminary . . ."

The oration brought tears and reconciliation from Lord Avonmore – but it did not win his verdict. Only one Judge, Baron William Cusack Smith, stood out and denounced the arrest of the Judge as arbitrary and illegal.

The prisoner then finally in Ireland tried his own court, the Common Pleas. It is said that a counsel was added to the team on this occasion in order to fillibuster. He was named Scriven, and having wonderfully fulfilled his function became known as "Leather-lungs Scriven". It is further said in regard to his achievement that having argued for days he was asked by the presiding Judge, Lord Norbury, how long he expected to be and he replied that he had eighteen questions to submit and argue and that he hoped to finish his second point tomorrow night.

All legal remedies in Ireland having been exhausted without success, Mr Justice Johnson was brought to London pursuant to the warrant. Further steps to challenge it there also failed and he was put on trial before the Court of King's Bench at Westminster, before Lord Ellenborough and a jury. William Cobbett gave evidence against him identifying him as the author of the letter in question. The case pursued its full course up to the point when the jury brought in their verdict of Guilty. But before it was registered counsel for the Crown had departed, instructed by the government not to proceed further with the case. Later a formal *nolle prosequi* was entered.

Mr Justice Johnson was allowed to retire on full pension and went to live in Paris, where he continued his agitating.

Serious though the Judge's conduct was, the prosecution and the method of it were surely mistaken. They aroused great professional and popular resentment in Ireland. Various reasons have been put forward for the government's extraordinary and unexpected last-minute withdrawal from the prosecution. It has been put down to various problems and difficulties which they faced, but this seems to me unconvincing. I think the more likely explanation is that establishing guilt sufficed their purpose; sentence would have been only an additional embarrassment.

The great Erskine and the great Curran never appear to have met in Court, but they knew and admired each other.

One of their meetings was as guests of the Prince of Wales at dinner. The Royal host directed the conversation to the profession of his celebrated visitors. Lord Erskine declaimed eloquently on the glories of the Bar. "No man," he said, "need be ashamed to belong to such a profession; for my part, of a noble family myself, I felt no degradation in practising it; it has added not only to my wealth but to my dignity." Curran said nothing at first but when pressed remarked, "Lord Erskine has so eloquently described all the advantages to be derived from the profession that I hardly thought my opinion was worth adding; but perhaps it is, perhaps I am a better practical instance of its advantages even than his Lordship. He was ennobled by birth before he came to it; but it has in my person raised the son of a peasant to the table of a Prince."

Adieu to Curran

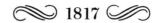 1817

CURRAN HOPED FOR success politically but it never came. The preferment he achieved was to be appointed Master of the Rolls for Ireland in 1806, at the age of fifty-six. He held the position until 1814, when he resigned. It would seem that only one of his judgments was recorded. That was a probate case called Merry v. Power, in which the defendant was referred to in the plaintiff's pleadings as "one Power, a Popish Priest". Curran castigated this description of the Catholic Bishop of Waterford.

Curran always suffered from recurrent fits of severe melancholia. He did not enjoy good health as a judge, and he greatly missed life at the Bar.

After his resignation he made extensive travels to France and England and he finally decided to settle in London. A sufferer from asthma, he found central London in its then condition of smoke and overcrowding too much for him, and he settled in Amelia Place, between Brompton and Chelsea.

He died there on 15 October 1817, aged sixty-seven.

Lord Powerscourt

 1824

THE POWERSCOURT DEMESNE in County Wicklow, under the Sugar Loaf Mountain, is one of the most beautiful in Ireland. It has wonderful gardens and a magnificent waterfall. Every guidebook and every book on stately homes includes it.

The property is now owned by the Slazenger family, who tend it with loving care. Unfortunately a tragic fire destroyed a large part of the great mansion a few years ago.

Powerscourt has always been an honoured name in Ireland. The Viscounts Powerscourt had a very good name with their neighbours and their tenants and work people.

In 1824 a question arose in proceedings which were not in any way contentious but exploratory as to what was to happen about a devise by Richard, Viscount Powerscourt, to Trustees to lay out at their discretion £2,000 per annum until his son came of age "in the service of my Lord and Master and, I hope, Redeemer".

The argument against this very substantial provision was that it was too vague to be defined or enforced. There was no express or implied reference to charity. And the application of the money would not be capable of control or review by the Court.

The contrary argument was fascinating. Counsel cited a case where there was a bequest to God! And the Court held the bequest to be a valid charitable bequest and assigned the money to the parish church where the testator lived when he made the Will. Further citations of valid charitable bequests were "for the diffusion of Christianity amongst infidels", and "to promote and carry on the work of God at Lyndhurst".

The Lord Chancellor of Ireland, Lord Manners, spoke un-characteristically for a judge when he said that he felt great difficulty in deciding the question and had very little con-fidence in the conclusion to which he had come.

He held that pious uses were a branch of charity and that the Viscount's provision obviously was for pious uses. He said that he could refer the matter to the Master to settle a suitable scheme, but on the whole he preferred to leave it to the Executor and Trustees to do so, as the Will intended. But even on this he had serious doubts.

He ended his judgment by hoping that the case might go to the House of Lords! It did not.

In 1821 the famous Dublin silversmiths and jewellers West and Son had to apply to the Court to carry on the business because Mr West, who had died, had left no direction about it in his Will. Lord Chancellor Manners decided that the Executors should carry on the business as they found it but should make no delay in administering the estate. He also held that they would not be liable for any loss incurred in carrying on the business in the way they found it. Later the widow was allowed by his Lordship, on giving security, to carry on the trade until the eldest of the children, who were minors, should come of age, he having been apprenticed to his father.

Byrne v. Frere

 1828

THIS WAS A long, complicated and very dull case about land, but it deserves to be remembered for some observations of the Lord Chancellor of Ireland, Lord Hart, who tried it.

In stating that he would be reserving judgment he said, "I have heard this cause at greater length than any doubt I at any time entertained upon it required for my own satisfaction. I did so for this reason. I wished to hear it so as to satisfy the parties. It is a great point not only to do justice but to leave the parties in the certainty that justice has been done. That is the truest justice that the suitor acknowledges, and therefore the decree which I like best is that with which both parties are content. Perhaps the next best is that with which both parties are dissatisfied."

When giving judgment he began by saying, "There are so many grounds for the dismission of this bill in respect of the principal relief sought that the difficulty is to select amongst them . . . There is a small portion of relief about which there is no dispute, but I shall dismiss the bill generally under the circumstances".

Costs, he said, he had found difficulty about. "It is one of the cases of which the costs give more trouble than [the decision]. Lord Eldon often complained that the costs levied him more anxiety than anything else in the case. They are now often of equal sum in value. Sometimes, I fear, they are far greater. I remember a case in which I was counsel, where two great men, a brewer and a duke, quarrelled about a public house worth £18 a year. There were five hearings and it cost one side £2,500 and the other £3,000 . . . There the parties were men of large fortune and no great harm was done. My client, I remember, was ever quite content because he had the balance in his favour by one triumph over the duke."

In this case he left the parties "to abide their own costs" and thus made no order for costs.

It was a warm, sleepy summer's day in a County Court in Cavan. A youthful counsel of marked efficiency briskly ended the examination of his client by saying in a quiet and even voice, "And I think you have one, but only one, criminal conviction and that was for murder and was a long time ago." As the witness said, "Yes," the aged judge shot up from his near slumber and said, "Good God. Were you hanged?"

The Anonymous Attorney
 1828

THE WORD ATTORNEY as a synonym for solicitor is nowadays resented by that great profession. Perhaps Shakespeare, Dr Johnson and Gilbert bear a good deal of the responsibility. The resentment is not really justified because attorney simply means agent. Thus the Bank of Ireland's employed solicitor has for countless years been known as its Law Agent. And we have, of course, still very much in our law the Power of Attorney, whose attorney is regarded as rather a distinguished and special person.

Until about 150 years ago both in Ireland and England the double description attorney and solicitor for the plaintiff or defendant was common. Then the sole description solicitor took over. Attorney was very much the older word, and indeed until about 1700 the only one used. For a time judges pompously proclaimed that they knew nothing of solicitors but knew and respected the ancient calling of attorney.

In the 1820s in Ireland (probably in England too) there seems to have been a custom of some standing that an attorney should not be imprisoned for debt when about his client's business. It was a doctrine not popular with judges but nevertheless observed by them. Doubtless they thought it open to abuse rather on the basis of the legendary Irish solicitor's bill which contained the item: "To waking up in the night and worrying about your case, 6/8d. per hour for 3½ hours."

In January 1828 an attorney who remained anonymous (because of plurality of creditors, no doubt) presented a petition to the Lord Chancellor of Ireland, Lord Hart, for protection against arrest for a limited period because he had a number of cases on hand and was under "temporary embarrass-ment". He was fearful of arrest from several quarters, and if arrested the interests of his clients would suffer (this was the clever touch) even by his temporary detention until an order for his discharge could be obtained.

Two counsel (unpaid?) supported the petition. They obviously did it beautifully. They said it would be inconvenient to have to have repeated applications for discharge after arrest "which in the circumstances of this gentleman it was probable would occur". Release on application would be automatic, so why not have (though they did not so describe it) an advance amnesty? They said that there were precedents in orders of no less than five previous Lord Chancellors, although admittedly none went as far as they wanted to go, namely for their client to go into the country on client's business.

They said there had been a case before Lord Manners where, with some initial hesitation, he had given six months' protection, but at the end of that time extended the protection "until further order". That was a strong case, they argued, for two reasons: a creditor applied to pierce the protection but was refused; and the attorney had a partner so that absolute necessity for freedom could not have been suggested.

Mr Scott and Mr O'Loghlen, the counsel involved, were neat and disarming in their submission that "The ease and disengagement of the attorney's mind are as important to his client as the freedom of his person."

Lord Hart did not like it. He said that he could not follow the example of his predecessors because he considered that it was contrary to law. He referred to the scandals there were in olden times when men of money or influence, or both, could buy freedom from their creditors.

As to the case decided by Lord Manners, he observed that Lord Manners had said that although he granted the order nobody disobeying it would be guilty of contempt. In grand fashion the Lord Chancellor said he would never make an order simply *in terrorem*, effective only against the ignorant. He would never make any order that did not carry with it the pain of contempt. The order petitioned for was refused.

History is forever not relating what happened to people afterwards. We do not know here, and because of the cloak of anonymity can never know what happened to the several clients. And how did they cope with the constant peril in which their attorney stood and with the unease of his mind?

What we do know is that in July of the same year, 1828, the same Lord Chancellor vented his views of the whole custom in strong language when saying in the case of an attorney named Fitzmaurice, "I also think it is a pernicious privilege; for a man who has been so careless of his own interests will hardly be an efficient agent in attending to the interests of others." Mr Fitzmaurice was arrested on his way to Court for a matter which he engagingly admitted could have been dealt with by his Clerk. While he was inside a number of other creditors applied to keep him inside. The Lord Chancellor condemning the privilege nevertheless regarded this as the classic case of it and freed Mr Fitzmaurice.

In that case reference was made to a decision of Lord Manners, Master of the Rolls, in respect of a Mr Foote, four years earlier. Lord Manners was one of the many impatient of the privilege and rather strangely deprived Mr Foote of it in what one might regard as classic circumstances. Mr Foote was an attorney up from Cork on client's business in Dublin. He had been before a Master in Chancery and was in his lodgings very naturally drafting papers required by the Master when he was arrested for debt. They were, moreover, his registered lodgings because all attorneys had to have a registered place of abode in Dublin, for service of documents and so forth. "Attempts," said the Master of the Rolls ominously, "approaching this [extension of privilege] have frequently been made, which I have always resisted." The application was refused and, ironically, with costs.

A solicitor from the West of Ireland was having a few celebratory drinks with his Dublin agent after an unexpected success in an action at the Four Courts. Questions of pride of ancestry arose, and the country solicitor began to sing the opening words of a well-known Irish song "When Ireland lay broken and bleeding she sent for the Men of the West". The Dublin solicitor interrupted, "She sent for them all right, but they bloody well never came."

An Irish solicitor was finding difficulty in getting payment of his bill from a man whom he had successfully defended for murder. He got over the difficulty and received instant payment by altering the bill to read as follows: "To professional services rendered in connection with your trial for Murder, including divers attendances upon you when you confessed to the said crime."

James Joseph Hardy
 1842

CHIEF BARON PALLES (1831–1920) was one of the great lawyers of the nineteenth and early part of the present century. He was Solicitor-General and Attorney-General of Ireland in turn and then had forty-two years of high judicial office in the course of which he had many famous cases before him.

His early life was blighted, and his whole career might have been ruined, by a most curious episode. His father, Andrew Christopher Palles, was a solicitor in Dublin, and in the seven years of practice before young Christopher was born he had begun to establish himself in his profession. He had a good house in the north side of the city (then professionally fashionable) and had a landed estate in County Cavan.

In 1842, when young Christopher was eleven, his father was peremptorily struck off the Rolls by the then Lord Chancellor of Ireland, Sir Edward Sugden, later Lord St Leonards. The circumstances were extraordinary.

He had a client named Captain Goold who had interests and potential interests in large estates in Cork and Tipperary. There were various legal difficulties and Captain Goold entered into an agreement with his father as to a formal legal re-settlement of certain of the property. Andrew Palles sent the papers to a well-known conveyancing counsel named James Joseph Hardy, who, acting for both Goolds, drew the necessary deed. He appointed himself and Palles as trustees. It so happened, however, that there was a serious error in his draft. This he discovered when later Palles instructed him to draw up a Marriage Settlement for Captain Goold.

Hardy was shocked when he discovered the mistake and

feared that it would affect his reputation. He accordingly decided upon the amazing course of forging a whole set of Deeds, to put the matter right. Andrew Palles knew nothing at all about this.

Captain Goold got into financial difficulties. Palles helped him considerably from his own resources but eventually got committed to the Dublin Debtors' Prison, the Marshalsea, by one of the Goold creditors to whom he had got himself bound.

While Palles was in prison a Chancery suit about the estates came on for trial and the matter of the forged deeds was discovered. Lord Chancellor Sugden straight away struck Andrew Palles off the Rolls, without hearing him, and reported the wretched Hardy to his Benchers at the King's Inns for disciplinary action.

The fate of Hardy, disbarment and oblivion, was of course thoroughly deserved, but it was from one point of view a harsh blow from fate. He was a talented and successful man, he made a mistake, and when he discovered it he sought to put it right but in no way to his own enrichment or benefit. There are, fortunately, very few professional men of the law who have done anything quite like he did.

The striking off the Rolls had a dreadful effect on the Palles family. With the practice gone, Andrew Palles had to move them from their pleasant house in Mountjoy Square to a very much smaller house, and had to scrape around for money to keep them. The future Chief Baron and his elder brother were at the Jesuit school Clongowes Wood College in County Kildare and Mr Palles managed to keep them there, refusing kindly offers from the Jesuit Fathers "to abate the pensions". He himself went to live and work in London for a time.

Andrew Palles would not petition for reinstatement to the Rolls while Sugden was Lord Chancellor. Nearly five years passed before, on the advent of a new Lord Chancellor, he presented his petition on 3 June 1847. The new Lord Chancellor was a man with an unusual first name – Maziere; Maziere Brady. Things moved with a speed that is commendable but rare. The Lord Chancellor referred the matter for investigation to two Masters in Chancery and in just over a month from petition, on 9 July 1847, they reported clearly and definitely that he should be restored to the Rolls. He immediately was.

Andrew Palles presented a copy of the petition to the Clongowes library, and he and his son remained devoted to Clongowes and the Jesuits all their lives.

It was a sad introduction to life and the law for the future Chief Baron, but he got through it, went to Trinity College, Dublin, was called to the Bar in 1853, became a Queen's Counsel in 1865 and went on from there to his Law Officerships and the Bench. Sadness clouded his personal life to the end, for his only child, a boy, was not normal and had to be cared for. He lived on until he was ninety.

The Chief Baron himself lived to the age of eighty-nine and died at his latter-day home Mount Anville, then just outside Dublin. It subsequently became a well-known convent boarding school. His estate, which he left almost entirely for the benefit of his son, amounted to just under £60,000.

Chief Baron Palles was in his long judicial life party to quite a few legal anomalies and oddities.

Taking a highly technical objection in one case which he tried (Pearson v. Dublin Corporation, 1907) he assured it a journey through three further Courts and the attention of no less than fourteen other judges. Four judges in the King's Bench division reversed him, three in the Irish Court of Appeal restored him and then seven in the House of Lords reversed the Court of Appeal and ordered a new trial. I believe the case was then settled.

On another occasion he decided a case but agreed to state a case for the opinion of the Divisional Court. He then sat himself in the Divisional Court with another judge to hear the appeal. This was a curiosity allowed and fairly often exercised until comparatively recent times. In this particular case he agreed with his own decision, but the other judge did not. To establish majority rule he then convened a court of three to hear the matter and duly took his place as one of the three. But – there may be merit in the system – this time he joined in the unanimous verdict that he had been wrong.

He was much interested at various times in his judicial career about bequests for Masses, a subject not even yet exhausted. Masses which were to be celebrated in public he found no difficulty in holding were a charitable bequest. Then in 1906 in O'Hanlon v. Cardinal Logue he took the considerable step forward of holding that whether the Masses were to be celebrated in public or private a bequest for them would be charitable. He was, however, careful in the bequest for Masses which he made in his own Will to stipulate that they should be celebrated in public.

Daniel O'Connell
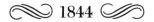 1844

SOME NAMES SEEM to have the shape and sound of fame about them. It would have been difficult to invent a more suitable name than Daniel O'Connell for the man who created such an impact on Ireland, Britain and other countries as well, during the period between about 1810 and 1847 when he died.

He was one of the first Catholics since the Reformation to be able to be called to the Irish Bar; he was the first Catholic since the Reformation to be able to become a Member of the British Parliament. It was eminently suitable, therefore, that he was the person who in 1829 won Catholic Emancipation, freedom at last from most of the remaining Penal Laws against Catholics. It won him the heart of the Irish people and earned him the popular, permanent title of "The Liberator". Some regarded him as "the uncrowned King of Ireland", a title also bestowed later on Parnell.

Daniel O'Connell was a rough, tough, powerfully built man who came from an old County Kerry family. He had a compelling influence over people and the touch of magic in both law and politics which make for greatness. He had a voice which could be quiet and gentle (with an effort) but which was so strong, clear and carrying that it enabled him to be plainly heard without any artificial amplification by a huge crowd; over half a million on one occasion at the Hill of Tara.

He was born in 1775, one of a family of ten children. He spent some years in fosterage with an uncle, Maurice. Fosterage was a very ancient Irish custom, not followed by any means in every case but very frequent. It preserved, indeed extended, the child's rights and these were most

93

elaborately provided for in the old Brehon Laws. The child in effect became a member of what is now known in Child Welfare as "the extended family". The modern laws as to Wardship, Custody, Care and Control and Adoption are less elaborate in their provisions than those of the centuries-long Irish law and tradition of fosterage. The corresponding duty of the young to look after their old remains customary in Ireland still, though (like fosterage) no longer subject to the same elaborate legal provisions.

After home teaching Daniel O'Connell went to university at St Omer and at Douay until the French Revolution disrupted it. He was called to the Irish Bar in 1798, the year of the Rebellion. Although a United Irishman he appears to have regarded that Rebellion, and Robert Emmet's one of five years later, as having been foolish. He could not really appreciate the possible value of a hopeless expedition, and despite his own forcefulness and nature he favoured peaceful pressure rather than warlike force.

His political philosophy as it developed in youth and matured in age was first of all to do everything possible to free his fellow-Catholics from the comprehensive legal restrictions under which they lay; then to break the Union with England not for a republican substitute but to the extent of a true Irish Parliament, which the pre-1800 Irish Parliaments had not been because of religious discrimination. He was always at pains to stress and show his loyalty to the Crown.

His law practice flourished, firmly based, of course, on the Munster Circuit, whose people and problems he knew so well. In Court he could be boorish, bullying – and brilliant. His cross-examinations and his speeches would not have suited the present day quiet, matter-of-fact type of advocacy. When he suspected perjury he went in fighting and was merciless in voice and action when he exposed it. Perhaps the most interesting of all his legal accomplishments was his ability to detect a lie from the particular turn of phrase used by a witness. "There was life in him when the Will was signed," said a Kerry witness in a Will case. "Did somebody put a fly in the dead man's mouth?" enquired O'Connell, and it subsequently transpired that that was what had happened.

In 1813 he defended John Magee, the Editor of the *Dublin*

Evening Post, on a charge of criminal libel. The Court, Lord Chief Justice Downes and other judges, was hostile. The jury was, as often happened, prosecution picked (a "packed jury"). The libel was pretty clear and indefensible even before an impartial Court and jury. The article spoke in the most dreadful terms of the departing Viceroy, the Duke of Richmond, describing the alleged evils of his predecessors and saying that he surpassed them all. O'Connell brilliantly decided that the best course was from start to finish and in every way to mock judges and jury, assuming their impartiality. It did not win the case, nothing could, but it showed up the trial for what it was and won O'Connell an important spur to his legal name. Magee got two years' imprisonment, a fine and the requirement of security for good behaviour for seven years.

There was an interesting sequel to the Magee case. A body in Kilkenny passed a resolution condemning the proceedings. Magee's paper recorded the resolution. And Magee got an extra six months' imprisonment for that!

There were many duel challenges and a few actual duels in O'Connell's life. Some arose from what he said in Court, some from his political utterances. One which particularly added to his fame was when a man named D'Esterre, seeking high office in the Dublin Corporation, bitterly resented some wholesale condemnation of the Corporation as then constituted by Dan O'Connell. He let it be known that he would await O'Connell on any route home from the Courts which he specified, there to horsewhip him. O'Connell specified Grafton Street but took the precaution of a heavy stick and a mass of supporters. D'Esterre withdrew to a shop and O'Connell plus supporters marched triumphantly by. D'Esterre then issued a challenge. Duelling was, of course, long since a crime and if death resulted it was in law murder, though not frequently proceeded against.

The venue was fixed in County Kildare. There were a great many spectators, more than "secret" arrangements would suggest. If the analogy may be forgiven D'Esterre, like a goalkeeper watching a penalty being taken, moved to one side as O'Connell fired – but to no avail. O'Connell not only hit him but shot him dead.

In proceedings at Cork, which became known collectively as the Doneraile Conspiracy, there was a series of cases of conspiracy to murder listed. The first case produced convictions. Those concerned for the men in the second and subsequent cases sent a horseman to ride over a hundred miles to retain O'Connell, who was at his home Derrynane in County Kerry. Daniel O'Connell accepted the retainer immediately, rode to Cork city, threw the reins of his exhausted horse to supporters of his at the entrance to the Courts, stormed into the Court and announced his arrival. He requested the none-too-pleased judges if he might take nourishment while the case progressed and they agreed with ill-grace. Then, in the middle of eating and drinking milk, he barked out interruptions and objections. He immediately became the dominant – and domineering – personality in the whole case. In the end the jury disagreed. In the next cases there were acquittals and the Doneraile Conspiracy proceedings collapsed.

On an occasion in County Kerry Baron McClellan sought to reprove O'Connell by saying, "That was not done when I was at the Bar." The reply was instant, rude in a way that only O'Connell could be rude, "When Your Lordship was at the Bar I did not take you as a model."

In 1828 in a contested election Dan O'Connell was elected to the House of Commons in Westminster as MP for County Clare. The law giving Catholic Emancipation had been passed but was not yet in force when he came to take his seat. There was proffered to him the old Oath condemning Catholicism. He refused to take it and was turned away. He then stood again for County Clare and this time was returned unopposed. The old Oath had gone when he came to take, and took, his seat.

At the time of Emancipation O'Connell was believed to be earning at the Bar about £8,000 a year, a considerable sum when multiplied into today's figures but in many ways a surprisingly low one for a man in his position. He also had an income, perhaps half that amount, from his property in Kerry.

After Emancipation he gave up practice at the Bar and concentrated on politics. A national Tribute was collected for him and amounted to about £50,000. Annual Tributes of about £13,000 were paid to him. This is a most remarkable phenomenon, comparable to the British governmental grants and gifts to Marlborough, Wellington and later war leaders.

The distinction is that the Tributes to O'Connell were from public subscription in Ireland – in times which were far from good. It does not appear that they were solicited by O'Connell – though his style of life and, to be fair, his political activities required them. There is no reason to doubt that they were in origin, and remained, voluntary. But they were not grants from a party in the sense that we know nowadays; they were direct from the public to a particular person. When the famine years came O'Connell refused to take anything.

In the 1830s he spent much of his time campaigning for repeal of the Union and in fighting against such laws as those which provided for the compulsory payment of tithes for the Protestant Church by Catholics, as well, of course, as others.

All his agitations were, it is to be stressed, for peaceful opposition, peaceful progress. He was as it were a fighting man of peace. This attitude and his general personality did not always meet with overall approval and for a time his popularity waned.

His reputation, however, rose to great heights again when in 1841 Dublin got its first Nationalist city council and he was, to the joy of the country, elected Lord Mayor of Dublin. He made the most of it.

1843 was the year of the monster Repeal meetings, including the one at Tara mentioned earlier. A meeting was planned for Clontarf, on the north side of Dublin, and again an historic place in Irish history, being the place where Brian Boru defeated the Danes. The meeting was "proclaimed", the word then and for many years previous used to mean officially banned. It was formally called off but Daniel O'Connell, his son and others concerned with the matter were arrested and charged with a variety, really a permutation, of conspiracies to cause disaffection. As a result, O'Connell was to achieve fame in the law books as well as in the Law.

At the trial in Dublin many points were taken against the charges, some highly technical but one in the plainest of language to the effect that what was being charged was merely lawful political protest. A fundamental objection was made by way of challenge to the whole jury (a challenge to the array) on the ground that some seventy people who should have been on the jury list, which stood at about 700, had been wrongly, indeed fraudulently, excluded. Jury challenges were always an important feature in Ireland, where "packed juries" were a commonplace.

Jury packing seems appalling to us in the present day, although I suppose the recent disclosures about "jury vetting" bear some comparison. In the Ireland of the eighteenth and nineteenth centuries jury packing was a commonplace to secure convictions. Pernicious though the practice was, let this be said – otherwise there would always have been acquittals in cases where religion or politics were concerned.

All objections were over-ruled and all Accused but one were found Guilty on the major counts. Daniel O'Connell was sentenced to twelve months' imprisonment, fined £2,000 and ordered to give surety for good behaviour for a period of seven years. The others were fined and required to give surety of a similar kind.

Daniel O'Connell and the others appealed to the House of Lords, and in the summer of 1844 a famous case ensued. Every possible point, good, bad or indifferent, was taken.

Meanwhile, Daniel O'Connell began his imprisonment, and in prison by being there gained more eminence and reverence than ever, and when visited held court and relayed messages for the outside world.

Five Law Lords presided. They were accompanied by some "lay" peers. And, as was customary then in important cases, they summoned and sought the opinions of the judges, of whom nine attended as representatives. The Law Lords were the Lord Chancellor (Lord Lyndhurst), and Lords Brougham, Denman, Cottenham and Campbell. The judges were Lord Chief Justice Tindal, Mr Justices Patteson, Williams, Coleridge, Coltman and Mark, and Mr Barons Parke, Alderson and Gurney.

There were violent differences of opinion between the consulted judges, but a number of important matters were authoritatively stated. The judges were unanimous in the view that some of the counts were bad in themselves and others rendered bad by bad findings. But they found some counts good and validly supporting conviction. They thought nothing of the technical objections, the challenge to the array or the objection that a general judgment for the Crown and a general sentence could not be supported if some counts were bad. They differed between themselves in individual findings about the counts.

The House of Lords by a majority, 3 to 2, reversed the judgment of the Irish Court and thereby quashed all the convictions and sentences. Some lay Lords expressed a wish to vote, and it was of course remembered that there had been occasions upon which lay Lords had voted in the seventeenth and eighteenth centuries. In this instance they were dissuaded, principally by the two dissenting Law Lords, the Lord Chancellor and Lord Brougham. The latter characteristically used some strong language saying that he urged the lay Lords to abstain though he deeply lamented the decision arrived at: "It will have a tendency to, I was going to say, shake confidence in this House; but without saying that . . . I think it is a decision which will go forth without authority and come back without respect." (Isaac Butt, QC, who succeeded O'Connell in political and legal leadership in Ireland, used the same phrase about authority and respect in a later Irish case.)

It was fortunate for O'Connell that the lay Lords did abstain. None would be likely to have voted for him.

Apart from everything else, therefore, the O'Connell case, taking place in a very political atmosphere, finally confirmed that lay peers (even if themselves lawyers) take no part in deciding appeals to the House.

The strict legal point which decided the case was that "a general judgment for the Crown against an Accused in respect of 'his offences aforesaid', on an indictment containing several counts, one of which is bad, and where the punishment is not fixed by law, cannot be supported".

However, a number of other legal points were decided or clarified, particularly by two of their Lordships that the challenge to the array was valid and vitiated the whole trial. It was in respect of it that Lord Denman made the famous observation: "a delusion, a mockery and a snare". The phrase has been subjected to alterations and permutations, for example it is sometimes cited as "a snare and a delusion". The fuller phrase given above is as Lord Denman spoke it. It is said that later he regretted it as having perhaps been too strong and not sufficiently judicious. The quotation in context is as follows:

"If it is possible that such a practice as that which has taken place in the present instance should be allowed to pass without a remedy (and no other remedy has been suggested), trial by jury itself, instead of being a security to persons who are accused, will be a delusion, a mockery and a snare."

Lord Denman, and others of the Law Lords too, strongly criticised the counts which alleged, in general terms as unlawful, agreements to agitate for constitutional and legal changes in Ireland. Lord Denman said: "Charging as an unlawful act a conspiracy to excite dissatisfaction with the existing tribunals, for the purpose of procuring a better system – I am by no means clear that it may not be an innocent and most meritorious act. I am by no means clear that there is anything illegal involved in exciting disapprobation of the Courts of Law, for the purpose of having other Courts substituted more cheap, efficient and satisfactory."

The House of Lords also pronounced upon the finding of different conspiracies being bad in law when (a) found within a specified conspiracy and (b) being found against different co-accused.

An especially important point was made by the House of Lords – as valid now as it was then – that the prolixity of counts could only lead to trouble. Lord Denman, again, had this to say: "In my opinion there cannot be a much greater grievance or oppression than these endless, voluminous, unintelligible and unwieldy indictments. An indictment which fills fifty-seven closely printed folio pages is an abuse to be put down, not a practice deserving encouragement."

O'Connell was victorious again, and on being freed received a hero's welcome yet again. He was, however, failing in powers and in power. He had but a brief political career left. In the course of it he espoused for a time, and then rejected, the idea of Federalism between Ireland and England. The fact is that he lagged behind the developing idea of Home Rule, as subsequently advanced by Isaac Butt and Parnell.

In May 1847, when on a journey abroad for his health, Daniel O'Connell died at Genoa. On 5 August he was accorded a state funeral in Dublin and buried in Glasnevin Cemetery. There, within a short distance of the cemetery gates, is his vault, above it a large round tower in the ancient Irish model.

The tower looks as modern as it is. People are ambitious in death as in life. There has grown up around his vault a series of vaults and graves of prominent people in what is now known as "the O'Connell circle".

In his masterful stride through life Daniel O'Connell not only won friends and influenced people (the latter was his great power) but he readily made enemies too. The scathing, crushing remark came quickly to his lips and unless he received respect he gave none. On one occasion in Court a solicitor was constantly seeking to interrupt him. Dan finally shouted at him, "Sit down you audacious, snarling pugnacious ram-cat." The unfortunate solicitor was known as ram-cat for the rest of his life.

When a judge in the Four Courts in Dublin announced that he was afraid he might have to send the next case, O'Connell's case, for trial before another judge, Dan managed to be belligerent in saying, "Which one?"

He nearly had a duel with Peel. He had many verbal duels with Disraeli, who probably epitomised all that O'Connell loathed. But in Disraeli he had as good a master of language, and of invective, as himself. He once described Disraeli as "having all the characteristics of the impenitent thief". He could hardly complain (but naturally did) when the latter said of him, "He has committed every crime which did not require courage."

Another opponent, musing on his likely fate, suggested that it would be to be hanged on a scaffold with a statue of himself underneath.

There are statues and streets galore in Ireland named after O'Connell. In Dublin he has a bridge, a street and a statue in the centre of the city. Sackville Street became O'Connell Street and his statue stands at one end of it, the Parnell monument at the other. The intervening Nelson's Pillar, opposite the GPO, has gone.

There are Parnell and Emmet Streets throughout the country, but they do not come within miles of O'Connell's total.

The statue which would probably please him most is in the square in Ennis, the county town of County Clare, the county which first returned him to Parliament and stuck by him to the end. To and from meetings in that square he had his carriage pulled for miles by enthusiastic supporters. In and from that square he had been led by torchlight processions and bands.

De Valera in his time captured and held Clare to the same extraordinary extent that O'Connell did. Indeed, its vote virtually matched the narrow national majority by which de Valera won his second seven-year term as President.

To those who know Irish geography and history (they are closely linked) it is almost incredible that men with no ties at all with the county should have been so resoundingly received by it. Perhaps the explanation is that the shrewd Clare-man can spot a future leader; at any rate it has made leaders of its members.

Political meetings in Ennis are invariably held in the square, with the speakers on a platform (perhaps a scaffold would be more apt) placed directly under the tall steepled statue of Daniel O'Connell. There have been many incidents there but probably the pleasantest concerns the amply built, very intoxicated lady of middle years who was engaged in periodic, good-natured heckling. This was tolerable, but suddenly spreading out her arms and looking up – not to heaven but to the figure of Daniel O'Connell – she broke into song in a voice so loud and clear that it would have done him credit. And the song she chose was – "Danny Boy". Many came to usher her away. She would not have it. As a last fling she shouted out, "Come down outa that, me Danny Boy, and we'll knock the divil outa this lot."

It is perhaps hard to see O'Connell, for all his roles, in that of a banker, but strangely enough it is, I think, an appropriate role in which to take leave of him.

In his time banking in Ireland was either in the hands of big corporations of English influence or those of unsuitable companies. The ordinary people mostly had nothing to bank, but those with some savings had seen a number of small banks collapse. This was sometimes, but not always, as a result of fraud. At least as often it was due to rumour causing a "run" on a bank and the bank not having sufficient financial resources to weather the storm.

This example led several people, particularly in the Western counties like Kerry and Clare, to hide such money as they had, not so much in and under beds as under grates, in the sides of chimneys and in holes in the ground. Demolitions still sometimes strike gold; literally gold – because in it there was the greatest faith.

Daniel O'Connell saw that the ordinary people needed a strong, trustworthy bank of their own. He had a considerable battle to enter the banking world but he achieved it with the National Bank, which he founded in 1835. It attracted the custom he expected and branches quickly grew up all over the country. It eventually opened some branches in England, principally in centres of Irish population. With an English head office in the banking area of the City of London it achieved the distinction of becoming one of the clearing banks.

The National Bank was a success and yet a further tribute to the initiative, force and energy of Daniel O'Connell. Then some twenty years ago it was taken over – its Irish business by the Bank of Ireland, its English by Williams and Glyn's. It sank without trace and its branches soon bore the titles of their new owners. There was no collapse in its case, just a takeover.

A spirited man by the name of O'Connell moved heaven and earth – and the Courts – to try to prevent the takeover, but he failed.

A witness as to character in County Galway called on behalf of an Accused gave a glowing account of him. Counsel unfortunately saw fit to ask him a fatal final question – "Would my client be the sort of man to steal money?" The witness did not answer at first, then he said, "How much?"

John Mitchel
 1848

DANIEL O'CONNELL, WHO won Catholic Emancipation for Ireland in 1829, believed strongly that further concessions could also be won by peaceful means, but found that circumstances, including in particular the Irish Famine of the late 1840s, drove some adherents into a rival, militant, association. These included, most militant of all, John Mitchel.

John Mitchel was born in November 1815 at Camuish, near Dungiven, in County Derry. His father was the Presbyterian Minister at Dungiven and a United Irishman of the 1798 period. His mother came from a County Derry Presbyterian family also.

In 1823 the Reverend John Mitchel was transferred to Newry, in County Down, and young John went to school there until he entered Trinity College, Dublin, in the early 1830s. At the same time, he became apprentice to a solicitor in Newry.

In 1837 he married a sixteen-year-old girl named Jane Verner and their love affair continued until his death, over a period when both had much to suffer, including the deaths of two sons in the American Civil War, fighting on the Southern side.

Jane's father, a military officer, tried everything to prevent the marriage, and when they eloped to England he caught up with them before they could arrange marriage and, on their enforced return to Ireland, had young Mitchel charged with abduction, of which he was cleared. They were married in County Armagh on 3 February 1837.

After marriage, John Mitchel completed his apprenticeship

in Newry and became a solicitor in 1840. He then entered into partnership as a solicitor at Banbridge, a town about eleven miles from Newry. He continued in practice there until 1845 when he went to Dublin to take over the editorship of the republican paper the *Nation*, to which he had been a regular contributor, whose Editor, Thomas Davis, had died.

The next two and a half years saw the Famine (The Great Hunger) at its worst and Mitchel wrote strongly on the subject. Finding his colleagues, as he believed, too pacifist in their attitude, he broke away from them and the *Nation* and collected a team of like-minded men around him. He then founded a newspaper called the *United Irishmen*, which first appeared in February 1848 and which made the *Nation* seem to be a paper for pacifists. People were incredulous that it was allowed to continue. Not only did it contain seditious matter, it was all of it seditious. Mitchel was a great writer and a master of invective. He proclaimed that only a packed jury – that is to say one specially chosen for their political beliefs – could convict him of any crime. He attacked the woeful conditions prevailing in the country and gave a regular series of specific examples. He drew attention to the many revolutionary movements current in Europe and incited his readers to be ready to follow suit.

This could not go on and he and certain colleagues were arrested on 21 March 1848, all for sedition. He was given bail. Then, shortly before he was due for trial, a newly created offence, Treason-Felony, was charged against him, an offence directed to render unlawful all forms of critical writing and such activities as his.

He was tried at Green Street Courthouse for a full week in May 1848 before Baron Lefroy and a jury. He was defended by Robert Emmet's brother-in-law, an elderly, very able counsel named Robert Holmes. The defence was really a plea to the jury to look beyond the statute to freedom of speech and to justice. Although the jury was a packed one, they paid the defence the compliment of being out for two hours before convicting.

Mitchel said from the dock, "I have been found guilty by a packed jury obtained by a juggle – a jury not empanelled by a sheriff, but by a juggler."

The Judge was stern in his defence of the jury and the High Sheriff and in his condemnation of the prisoner. He said in effect that the prisoner's own writings had written his conviction.

The sentence was awaited with tenseness. It was greeted with shock – transportation for fourteen years. Mitchel made a short statement, including this: "Neither the jury nor the judges, nor any other man in this court, presumes to imagine that it is a criminal who stands in this dock."

He sought to create a demonstration in Court and partly succeeded, but Baron Lefroy sharply ordered the warders to remove him and he disappeared below. He was leaving behind a wife of twenty-six and five children.

At four o'clock that afternoon he was escorted out of the Court cells in fetters and put in a heavily guarded prison van. He had to be assisted into the van and again out of it when it drew up by a government steamer at the North Wall in the Port of Dublin. He was put aboard the steamer, later transferred to a man-of-war and brought first to Bermuda, where he spent some ten months on a prison ship. He was then taken on to another convict ship which travelled to the Cape of Good Hope. The ship's captain apparently found the Cape unwilling to accept his cargo of convicts. The vessel accordingly proceeded to Van Diemen's Land, now Tasmania, where it arrived on 7 April 1850. Mitchel and others were, after a time, given comparative liberty by a parole of honour.

It was possible at that time for a wife and family to join a transported prisoner where he had been settled. The plight of Jane Mitchel and the children in Ireland had been a sorry one, particularly as they found that all his assets were forfeited as a felon. They were reduced to living upon charity and the provision of a home by his mother in Newry. John Mitchel was at first opposed to bringing his family out to Tasmania, but he relented and, after a five-month journey, they were reunited with him in the summer of 1851.

With money from Irish and American sympathisers they managed to buy a farm and stock it, but Mitchel found the restriction on movement and intercourse with his friends increasingly irksome. Then, early in 1853, a man named

P. J. Smyth came from America to Tasmania to help transportees, especially Mitchel, to escape.

Mitchel had pledged his honour when given parole, and when he decided to attempt to escape he wrote a letter to the Governor of Tasmania revoking his promise and delivered it to the local magistrate. He did not delay when delivering the letter to the magistrate at the local police office. He came and went by fast horse. It seems likely that the message had not properly sunk in before he was miles away. But the delivery of it added to his risks in attempting escape because all likely ports in Tasmania were put on special alert.

The delay was longer than expected and Mitchel had to stay in hiding and on the run for over six weeks. Then, the rumour being that he had made good his escape to America, his family embarked on a passenger frigate at Hobart bound for Sydney, and some miles beyond the bay John Mitchel himself was put on board. There were problems to be faced at Sydney, which, of course, was also within British jurisdiction. However, a safe landing was achieved and he went into hiding there for a short time.

He had to split from his family for the next stage of his journey, which was to be to Honolulu via Tahiti. Becalmed at Tahiti an American ship was sighted and it sent a boat ashore for John Mitchel. It was the *Julia Ann* and, to his delight, had on board his wife and (as there now were) six children.

He received a tremendous reception in America in October 1853 and quickly got down to journalism again. He founded a paper called the *Citizen* in New York, and later founded at Knoxville, Tennessee, the *Southern Citizen*. He wrote books, articles and pamphlets in profusion.

He also ran the *Richmond Enquirer* and the *Richmond Examiner* and, during the American Civil War, made them eloquent voices in the Southern cause.

Three of Mitchel's sons served with the Southern Army: William was killed at the battle of Gettysburg and John, who had become an officer, at Fort Sumter. James, the only remaining son, survived the war. John Mitchel himself volunteered for service to Jefferson Davis personally, but, because of defective eyesight, had to be content with city guard and ambulance duties.

108

When the Civil War ended, Mitchel found himself once again in conflict with the law. Editing the *Daily News* in New York, he appealed for a fair and just attitude to the South. He was arrested by the Federal Government as a prominent and powerful supporter of the now suppressed Southern rebels, and this was done on the direct orders of Ulysses S. Grant. What he would have been charged with, and what might have happened to him, must remain the subject of conjecture. It is quite possible that he would have faced charges in the nature of treason and would have been sentenced to death. As it was, after some five months' imprisonment, he was released by order of President Johnson. Clearly, considerable Irish influence had been exerted on the President. Then, in 1867, returning once again to journalism, he founded the *Irish Citizen* in New York.

He worked with and for Irish organisations throughout, but did not venture into Ireland until 1874, when – as he correctly judged – the authorities would be unlikely to take any action against him. It was twenty-six years since he had been transported, but he was well remembered and greatly welcomed as he went around the country.

Not long after his return to New York, he was asked to contest a parliamentary election in County Tipperary and accepted the offer. He travelled to Ireland, taking his son James to help him. He found the electioneering too much for him and had to go to stay with his sister in Newry to rest. He was clearly very ill and could not be present to hear his success at the election announced nor to greet his constituents. On 20 March 1875 he died in Newry, where his career had begun and in whose countryside his heart lay.

Counsel was presenting the case of clients who had suffered a fire and who were painting a worse picture of it and the resultant damage than their insurers thought right. The case was being tried by a jury, and counsel, getting a little carried away, said, "Volumes of smoke, gentlemen; did I say volumes? Nay – whole encyclopaedias."

In County Tyrone a man charged with a serious offence was quickly and surprisingly acquitted by the jury.

The Judge said, "Mr Foreman, I have no right whatever to ask you but would you mind telling me why you acquitted the Accused?"

"Insanity," replied the foreman – to the astonishment of everybody.

"What," said the Judge, "all twelve of you?"

Re Peter Mulligan
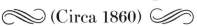 (Circa 1860)

ADVOCACY HAS FASCINATED people through the ages. Great speeches in Court have been listened to with admiration and read and re-read with pleasure and enjoyment. Many books have been written on the subject, examining and giving examples of "the art". There undoubtedly is an "art" about it but in essence it is a gift – a gift for words and situations. To my mind, advocacy just means being able to say the right thing, in the right way, at the right time.

Despite the classic examples which are so often quoted, the one I find most telling is a speech by a counsel named Dr Webb, who later became County Court Judge of Donegal. He was appearing before the Recorder of Dublin for Peter Mulligan, a respectable young man of twenty-five, who was applying for a licence for a public house in the city. It was a wholly unlikely occasion for brilliant advocacy. The whole incident arose because the police objected on the ground of the applicant's youth. The learned Recorder echoed the objection, saying, "He is very young for such a responsible position."

"My Lord," said Webb, "Alexander the Great at twenty-two years of age had crushed the Illyrians and razed the city of Thebes to the ground, had crossed the Hellespont at the head of his army, had conquered Darius with a force of one million in the defiles of Issus and brought the great Persian empire under his sway. At twenty-three, René Descartes evolved a new system of philosophy. At twenty-four, Pitt was Prime Minister of the British Empire, on which the sun never sets. At twenty-four, Napoleon overthrew his enemies with a whiff of grape-shot in the streets of Paris. Is it now to be judicially

111

decided that Peter Mulligan, at the age of twenty-five, is too young to manage a public house in Capel Street?"

There could be no answer to that; the licence was granted.

Was the speech extempore or prepared? With a great speech it does not really matter, because preparation does not detract from it. My own feeling is that, as with most advocates, the structure of the speech was already there, stored away in counsel's computer ready for use if opportunity should arise. Not specially prepared but available – capable of use in full or in part or in adapted form.

A splendid description of a man charged with stealing the Lord Lieutenant of Ireland's dog appeared in the *Freeman's Journal* of 7 July 1862. He was James Morris of Manchester, who, in view of the nature of the charge, gave himself the rather unfortunate description of "dog-fancier".

Reporting his conviction and fine of £10 (four months in default) the paper said, "James Morris' abdomen was by far the most remarkable feature of his person. It reposed in front of him as if it was very well pleased with the usage it had received from its proprietor."

Travers v. Wilde

 1864

IT IS FITTING that Oscar Wilde's parents should have been talented, literary and very unusual.

The father, Sir William Wilde (born in 1815, knighted in January 1864), was a leading eye and ear specialist in Dublin and enjoyed a world-wide reputation. He lived latterly in the Harley Street of Dublin, Merrion Square, and perhaps appropriately at Number One. As well as his medical writings, which were highly regarded, he wrote historical and archaeological books and articles, and admirable accounts of Irish localities.

He was thirty-six when, on 12 November 1851, he married Jane Francesca Elgee. She was ever-reticent about her age and about the occupation of her father. It is probable that she was only a little younger than her husband, possibly the same age. It seems reasonably clear that her father was a Dublin attorney (as solicitors were then known). She had a great dislike for attorneys.

Before marriage Miss Elgee had been active in the Irish republican cause in the years after the disastrous famine. She wrote inflammatory articles and verse for its leading publication, the *Nation*, which was a weekly paper costing 5*d* and had a large circulation throughout the country. The verses were written under the pseudonym "Speranza", and became well known. The identity of the author was not long a secret, and indeed in the course of a prosecution against the Editor she interrupted the proceedings to announce that she and not he was responsible for them.

The Wildes had three children: Willie (born in 1852), Oscar

(born in 1854) and Isola, who was born in 1857 and died when she was only twelve.

It is known that Dr Wilde had three illegitimate children, all born before his marriage. The first, Henry Wilson, was born in about 1838 and followed in his father's footsteps, becoming a well-known eye and ear surgeon. He died when he was thirty-nine. The other two were girls, Emily and Mary Wilde, born in about 1847 and 1849 respectively. They lived with their father's clergyman brother in County Monaghan. They died tragically in November 1871 when, ready to go to a ball, the skirt of one caught fire and ignited the clothing of the other.

It was in 1854, the year of Oscar's birth, that Dr Wilde had the misfortune to meet in a doctor-patient relationship a nineteen-year-old girl named Mary Josephine Travers, the daughter of the Professor of Medical Jurisprudence at Trinity College, Dublin.

A curious relationship developed between the girl and the thirty-nine-year-old doctor, involving her friendship also for a considerable time with Mrs Wilde. What the true relationship was it is impossible to know because when she brought her proceedings ten years later in 1864 her allegation was of one act of rape, eight years after the original meeting, in October 1862, and a couple of attempts later. In a dramatic opening of the case her second leading counsel, Serjeant Armstrong, spoke of a rape in the consulting-room – "She went in a maid. But out a maid she never departed."

Sir William Wilde (as he then was) did not give evidence, and accordingly the only account of the sexual aspect of the affair is that of Miss Travers – one act of rape. It is hard to credit that allegation. But she did not make – nor was there put to her in cross-examination – any allegation of an ordinary sexual relationship. It is possible there was and that that explains everything, including the absence of Sir William from the witness-box. It is equally possible that either or both of them wanted and enjoyed an affectionate relationship without sex.

Mary Travers lived with her parents at Blackrock, some five miles along the coast south of Dublin. It was on a direct line to Westland Row railway station, her station for the city, a couple of minutes from where the Wildes lived. Her home was not a happy one; she had a sister at home but her two brothers had emigrated to Australia.

During the five years after their meeting Mary Travers was often with the Wildes, calling on them, going out with them on occasions and being helped by Dr Wilde about her reading. He was treating her as a protégée and his wife appeared to accept this. In 1859 Wilde brought her to the Dublin Exhibition and she accompanied the family to a pantomime. Whenever he was away he wrote to her.

From at least 1859 he pressed money on her; not by way of gift but as loans, which she usually repaid out of her quarterly dress allowance of £4.

In October 1861 he invited her to the distribution of prizes at the Queen's University, held in the impressive vice-regal state apartments at Dublin Castle. Next day he told her that Mrs Wilde was keeping observation on them.

She dined with the Wildes on Christmas Day 1861.

In February 1862 (as she described in Court) when she called, he clasped her to him and there followed a series of letters of apology.

In April 1862 she said she was going to Australia and he gave her £40, but she went no further than Liverpool. Once more that year the same, except she did not even go to Liverpool that time.

In March and again in May 1862 she dined with the Wildes, and in June Mrs Wilde asked her to take the three children to a service in the Chapel Royal in Dublin Castle, but unfortunately she arrived late and the party left without her. Mrs Wilde was evidently very annoyed, and it was from about that time onwards that a rift between them became apparent.

The allegation of rape which Miss Travers made was in respect of an afternoon in mid-October 1862 in the doctor's consulting-room, outside which in the hall-way there were several patients waiting. Her allegations about the attempts first came out under cross-examination and related to two subsequent incidents in the same place and under the same circumstances. Miss Travers was by then twenty-seven and Dr Wilde forty-seven.

They continued to meet, but at first after that autumn not so frequently because we find him writing letters to her, including one which said: "Can't you come or answer? Don't you want something – boots and underclothing for winter?"

He gave her presents and she continued to seek small loans from him.

She was, however, plainly working up to a crisis because she started sending letters which he wrote to her on to his wife – who returned them to her. And she created a scene in his study one day by drinking four pennyworth of laudanum in his presence. He shouted out, "Revenge! Revenge! Everyone will say I poisoned you!" – and promptly got her to a nearby chemist for an emetic, which worked.

1863 was an eventful year in this extraordinary affair. First of all Speranza published a three-volume novel said to be "from the German" and called *The First Temptation*. Almost unbelievably Mary Travers managed to review it in no less than two separate papers, and the reviews were naturally in the slashing terms which she was by then adopting against the Wildes. In October she wrote a pamphlet herself under the name of Speranza and in it told the story of a Dr Quilp who chloroformed a female patient in his consulting-room and then raped her; significantly there were no waiting patients. The chloroform had been administered via a scent bottle.

Early in 1864 when Dr Wilde was giving an important public lecture in the Metropolitan Hall, Dublin, she and a group of boys employed by her distributed outside the hall the pamphlet, leaflets and copies of letters from Dr Wilde.

The Wilde children were at that stage twelve, Oscar ten, and the little girl seven. The boys were at the well-known Royal Portora School at Enniskillen.

Their mother went for one of her first summer visits to Bray, a seaside resort about twenty miles from Dublin. There she found herself besieged by boys dispensing pamphlets and leaflets and copy letters. Also by other boys with offensive placards.

She then wrote to Mary Travers' father the letter which became the subject-matter of Travers v. Wilde. It read as follows:

117

From Lady Wilde to Doctor Travers.

Tower, Bray, May 6th.

Sir,

You may not be aware of the disreputable conduct of your daughter at Bray, where she consorts with all the newspaper boys in the place, employing them to disseminate offensive placards in which my name is given, and also tracts in which she makes it appear that she has had an intrigue with Sir William Wilde. If she chooses to disgrace herself, that is not my affair, but as her object in insulting me is the hope of extorting money, for which she has several times applied to Sir William Wilde, with threats of more annoyance if not given, I think it is right to tell you that no threat or additional insult shall ever extort money for her from our hands. The wages of disgrace she has so largely treated for and demanded shall never be given to her.

Jane Wilde

A solicitor's letter was sent to the Wildes demanding £2,000 for libel. A settlement at that figure would have been a cheap price, but the offer was refused and the stage begun to be set for the *cause célèbre* which was in fact heard on 12 December 1864 before Chief Justice Monahan and a jury. Isaac Butt QC, the famous lawyer-politician, and Serjeant Armstrong led for Miss Travers. The Wildes were represented by the then Serjeant Sullivan and Michael Morris (later Lord Killanin).

The reason that Sir William was sued as well as his wife was the now discarded principle that a husband was responsible for his wife's torts (civil wrongs). Attempts were made by their counsel to have the letters written by Sir William to Miss Travers excluded from the evidence, but these were unsuccessful, and this would appear to be right.

Another handicap to their case was the fact that a close study of Lady Wilde's letter will show that her charges against Miss Travers went further than blackmail of the Wildes; they also asserted that she was "consorting" with newspaper boys. It may well be that it was the insinuation of general bad character which got her the verdict – the nominal verdict – she eventually obtained.

In evidence Miss Travers told her story of rape, saying that she was momentarily unconscious at the time, but not from any drug. This enabled Isaac Butt to end his examination of her in splendidly Victorian fashion by asking: "Are you now able to state, from anything you have observed or known, that in the interval of unconsciousness you have referred to, your person was violated?" A demure but positive "Yes" was the answer.

Cross-examined by Serjeant Sullivan she admitted that after the occasion she complained about she visited Sir William Wilde at his home, borrowed money from him and accepted presents.

Coming to the vital incident he asked, "Nothing of the sort occurred before or after?"

"Not before."

"Did it after?"

"I consider . . ."

"Did it after? Answer me yes or no."

"I cannot say yes or no."

"You cannot say yes or no?"

"No, because it was attempted."

Thus for the first time was introduced the matter of the attempts. Even when elaborated they did not amount to much. There had been advances which she had repelled.

Lady Wilde gave evidence but Sir William did not. His absence from the witness-box created much comment from the crowd in Court and, when it became known, from the thousands who were following the case with close interest.

In his final speech to the jury Isaac Butt made much play of the fact that Sir William Wilde had not given evidence. "If her story is not true," he said, "why did Sir William Wilde not come to contradict it? Will you convict her while the man who asks you to believe she is perjured shrinks from coming in here and pledging his oath to which he asks twelve Irish gentlemen to pledge theirs?"

The Chief Justice in his summing-up (or Charge to the Jury as it has always been called in Ireland) did not comment much or strongly on Sir William's absence from the witness-box. He did, however, say that if the alleged rape had been the subject of a criminal charge it would have been quickly thrown out.

After a retirement of an hour and twenty minutes the jury

119

returned with a verdict for the plaintiff, Miss Travers – for a farthing damages. This however carried an order for costs against the Wildes, making the total expense more than the £2,000 originally sought; and there was now in addition the publicity, which proved in fact very damaging. The case was widely reported in the newspapers and must have been all too well known to the Wilde boys at school in the North.

Some six months later, Miss Travers sought to revive the whole matter by another action, this time against *Saunders' Newsletter* in respect of their comments on the original trial. This action was fully fought out and she lost completely.

Sir William Wilde had undoubtedly lost caste. As with many prominent people who litigate, this possibility had no doubt never occurred to him and when it happened he felt confident of overcoming it. In fact he did go a long way towards redeeming his reputation but he was never quite the same man again.

Sir William lived for nearly twelve years more; he died in April 1876. Despite the high standard of life which he and his wife had enjoyed he left her in poor circumstances. She moved to London and eventually, incongruously for Speranza, received a pension from the Civil List of £70 per annum. Oscar helped her financially when he could – which was not always. She saw him married and with children and she died when he was in prison, in February 1896.

It would have been impossible to invent two parents for Oscar Wilde anything like the ones he had.

Mickie Morris, later Lord Killanin, Lord Chief Justice of Ireland, had a ready wit. A prisoner at Cork Assizes was found Guilty of taking part in a vicious attack on the police. "God Save Ireland," he shouted after he was sentenced. "Now look here," said Lord Killanin, "you are just one of those people who make it impossible for God to save Ireland."

He was, unexpectedly for a Catholic, opposed to Home Rule and he used to say, "Here we are, a very poor country, in partnership with a very wealthy kingdom, having one hand in the till, yet we want to get away and start a little shebeen of our own."

He was often asked what the Irish Question was about. "Ah," he used to say, "it is the difficulty of a solid and simple people to govern a clever and cute one."

In an abduction case which was not very serious, Lord Morris in summing-up said, "The father was not averse, the mother was not opposed, the girl was willing and the boy was convaynient." When the boy was found Guilty, the Judge sentenced him to be imprisoned until the Court rose – and then rose.

Peter O'Brien and
Mr Justice Keogh
 1877

PETER O'BRIEN, KNOWN to Irish history as "Peter the Packer" because, when he was Crown Prosecutor and later Attorney-General, he allegedly packed juries to gain convictions, was born in County Clare in 1842 and from that County took his peerage as Lord O'Brien of Kilfenora when he became Lord Chief Justice of Ireland in 1889. He was Lord Chief Justice for twenty-four years and died in 1914, the year after his retirement.

As assistant or "devil" during the 1880s he had young Edward Carson, whom he affectionately referred to as "Bon Diable".

Peter O'Brien was called to the Irish Bar in 1865 after education by the Jesuits at Clongowes Wood College and then at Trinity College, Dublin. He naturally joined the Munster Circuit, where not only were his family known, but where the name O'Brien was of great historic affection.

After twelve years' call, in 1877, at Cork Assizes he clashed in an important criminal conspiracy case with the presiding Judge, Mr Justice Keogh, a man of known quick temper. O'Brien interrupted him in his summing-up to the jury to dispute his definition of conspiracy. The Judge turned on him angrily and said, "Resume your seat, Mr O'Brien, and if you stand up again I shall have you removed from the Court." Peter sat down, and after the jury had retired he got up and referred to the incident. "I rose to suggest an alternative definition," he said. "I did so most respectfully. I should perhaps have waited until the jury had retired. But your Lordship said if I did not resume my seat you would have me removed from Court." "Yes, I did," said the Judge. "Well," continued Peter O'Brien, "on behalf of the Bar of the Munster Circuit, I strongly protest against such language being addressed to any member. If such language can be used by the Bench, we may say farewell to the freedom of the Bar."

It was then 7 p.m., and the Judge looked and sounded gruff as he said that he would retire for dinner and return at 9 p.m.

At 9 p.m. the Court was crowded. The doors were left open and more poured in. It was over an hour before the Judge arrived. He held up the recall of the jury. Then, turning to Peter, he said, "Mr O'Brien, I said something to you this evening which I regret and you very properly resented. I fully withdraw it. That statement was made in the presence of a crowded Court and so I sent word that the doors of the Court were to be left open so that as many might be present while I withdrew those words as were here when I uttered them."

There are not often cheers in Court, but there were then and Peter O'Brien could hardly be heard as he rose to acknowledge this *amende honorable*.

In this unhappy (but happily ending) incident, both counsel and judge were wrong. Peter O'Brien, youthful enthusiasm or not, should not have interrupted the summing-up. On a matter of substance, as distinct from a trivial error, he should have waited until the end of the summing-up. The Judge, however, should never have reacted in so extreme a way, with the threat of removal from Court, a threat which is only made in the event of a disturbance of a contemptuous nature.

The picture of a clash between counsel and judge is much enjoyed by public and press. Fortunately it is now extremely rare. There certainly was rudeness in the old days, but now the happy fashion is that you can have fearless advocacy and strong judges whilst having courtesy and politeness. There is a marked contrast between London's Old Bailey or Dublin's Green Street now and even fifty years ago.

A young lawyer from Cork was short-listed for a first-rate post in Belfast. The interview went splendidly. At the end the Chairman, in a friendly and conversational way, said, "By the way, what religion are you?" The young man paused for a second and replied, "Did you have any particular religion in mind, sir?" He got the job.

The Twoheys

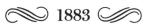 1883

P ETER O'B RIEN, THE later Attorney-General and Lord Chief
Justice of Ireland, was a fervent Catholic and Irishman, but,
in a small minority of such, anti-Nationalist. He was a strong
Unionist and it was his politics that got him his offices, starting
with Junior Crown Prosecutor in 1881 and Senior Crown
Prosecutor in 1883. This is not to say that he was undeserving
of his promotions; he eminently deserved them. But it is to
recognise the dreadful connection between politics and legal
preferment, which lingered on in Ireland until very recently,
but has wholly gone in England these sixty years or more.

There was a great deal of political or so-called political crime
in Ireland when Peter O'Brien was prosecuting in the 1880s.
Landlordism, evictions, the entry of others in place of evicted
tenants ("grabbers") and multifarious agrarian disputes gave
rise to criminal charges.

Peter O'Brien earned his famous nickname of "Peter the
Packer" by doing all he could to secure what were called
"packed juries", meaning juries packed, or picked, for convicting. His method was by challenging questionable jurors,
and, his opponents said, by otherwise fixing the jury lists.

He did not resent the nickname at all, indeed enjoyed it as a
mark of distinction, and perhaps enjoyed best its abbreviation
on occasions to just "The Packer".

On one occasion his brief was stolen and was later referred to
in the House of Commons by a Nationalist MP, who said that it
contained a long list of prospective jurors and that O'Brien had
put the letter "C" – obviously standing for Catholic – beside a
number of them. "C", explained O'Brien, was not for

Catholic at all, but for Challenge. Was that the same thing? In the nature of things at that time it often was. But one thing is certain, O'Brien was sincere. He wanted, and was determined to get, convictions where there should, in his view, clearly be convictions. The most one can say is that he may not have been as infallible as he thought he was in his prosecutions.

One case he brought home against the Accused was proved in a strange and interesting way. Two men named Jeremiah and James Twohey (pronounced Toohee) were indicted for breaking and entering the house of an old widow, Mrs Fitzgerald, threatening her, assaulting her and beating up her daughters. She lived at the foot of Mushera Mountain in County Cork. The motive was some agrarian grievance against her and her late husband.

The main witness for the prosecution was a man named Connell, who in modern language would be called simply "an informer", but was in those days called "an approver". In short, he turned Queen's Evidence and purported to give all the details about the Twoheys' preparation for and participation in the raid.

Then – as now – there was by law an almost absolute requirement of corroboration for an accomplice; that is to say, independent supporting evidence. There was precious little other evidence in respect of the Twoheys. Mother and daughters were too shaken to identify their assailants. A servant did.

What really clinched the case was this. A strange dog was found round the Fitzgeralds' place. It was taken to the police station, but no one claimed it. Acting – as the phrase has it – on information received, Sub-Inspector Starkie and Captain Plunkett took it in a bag to a point near the house of the Twoheys and there let it loose. It made straight for the house and although the whole Twohey family tried to shoo it away, it jumped up on them in greeting, furiously wagging its tail. It showed particular affection towards James. A close inspection of the Twoheys' house revealed some hidden ammunition and some disguises. The dog – Sam – was produced in Court – and even there appeared to recognise the prisoners!

Both prisoners were found Guilty and each got seven years' penal servitude.

Sir Peter O'Brien had a pronounced lisp. Thus, in one great judgment he gave the true transcript was: "But thath case was not of course thitsh case. They are really as dhifferent as thalk and thcheesthe."

Charles Stewart Parnell

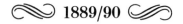 1889/90

B ETWEEN ABOUT 1875 and 1890 a Protestant landowner from County Wicklow named Charles Stewart Parnell, born in 1846, was virtually the "uncrowned King of Ireland". With a substantial Irish Party behind him in the House of Commons he pressed fervently for Home Rule for Ireland. He was in many ways an incongruous leader for the Irish at that time, being a Protestant, a landowner, a landlord, and a man of no obvious humour.

In the end it was a divorce case, O'Shea v. O'Shea and Parnell, which brought about his downfall (just as a divorce case shattered the career of his brilliant contemporary, Sir Charles Dilke).

Parnell (he was generally known by his surname alone) had other legal experiences before the divorce case. On 6 May 1882 there took place in Dublin the dreadful Phoenix Park Murders when two very prominent officials, Thomas Henry Burke (being Permanent Under-Secretary in the Irish Office) and Lord Frederick Cavendish (just sworn in as Chief Secretary for Ireland) were mercilessly slashed to death by a knife-gang.

Parnell spoke out in condemnation of the crime. Some five years later, in the course of a campaign against Parnell, *The Times* published on 18 April 1887 the facsimile of a letter purporting to have been written by Parnell nine days after the murders apologising for having had to denounce them.

Parnell was an odd person and never reacted violently to anything. In this instance he simply quietly told the House of Commons that the letter was a forgery.

The Times developed its attack and relied on other similar letters. Parnell then requested that a select committee of the House be appointed to enquire into the matter. The government refused but appointed instead a special commission with far wider terms of reference.

The Parnell Commission sat through the winter of 1888–89, and Parnell was fortunate enough to have the services of his fellow-countryman Charles Russell QC, later Lord Russell of Killowen, Lord Chief Justice of England.

The original source of the vital letters obtained by *The Times* was a Dublin journalist, Richard Pigott, who said he had bought them. Charles Russell broke him in cross-examination, most strikingly by asking him almost casually to spell the word "hesitancy". The witness wrote down "hesitency" and that mis-spelling occurred in one of the letters. He subsequently confessed to having forged the letters, ran away and committed suicide in Madrid. Parnell was cleared and in an action against *The Times* for libel got £5,000 damages.

The divorce case swung the pendulum back against Parnell in a devastating way. In December 1889 Captain O'Shea MP, whose political career had been helped by Parnell, presented a petition for divorce in London against his wife Katharine O'Shea (Kitty O'Shea as she was widely called) on the ground of her adultery with Charles Stewart Parnell, whom he cited as Co-respondent.

There was little divorce in England in those days and none in Ireland, where it was against the belief of all Catholics and most non-Catholics.

Mrs O'Shea put in a strong combative answer alleging connivance, condonation and adultery by her husband with her sister, Mrs Steele.

Parnell treated the pending case almost with nonchalance and assured everyone that he had nothing to worry about and would be completely vindicated. The London Editor of the *Freeman's Journal* was fined for contempt of court in publicising that point of view. Other papers with solely Irish circulations said the same, but there is no doubt that the very fact of the petition had alienated a substantial part of the Irish press and the Irish people from Parnell.

Parnell's confidence may be explained on the basis that he

thought O'Shea would never go through with the case, but whatever the reason the confidence was genuine and strong.

Parnell and Kitty O'Shea met in 1880, when both were thirty-four years of age. Captain O'Shea was six years older, the son of a Dublin solicitor. He had been in the Army and was a Member of Parliament for County Clare. At the time of the meeting they had been married for thirteen years and had three children.

Mrs O'Shea was English, the youngest of thirteen children of a former Chaplain to Queen Caroline, Sir John Page Wood. One of her uncles had been Lord Chancellor, Lord Hatherley.

Mrs O'Shea has given a romantic story about the first meeting, with Parnell kissing a rose which she dropped. Matthew Kenny, who practised as a barrister on the Munster Circuit, told later generations of barristers quite a lot about Parnell and can be regarded as particularly reliable because he was Parnell's Secretary and a fellow-MP. He said that Mrs O'Shea was a frequent visitor to the House and one afternoon asked Justin McCarthy, a prominent member of the Irish Party, for an introduction to Parnell. This he duly effected at tea on the Terrace. When she left, McCarthy told Parnell that he regarded her as a rather tiresome woman. Parnell would not have it. "I think she is the most interesting woman I've ever met," he said.

The history of the O'Shea affair was in any view an unusual and a protracted one. At the time of the meeting in 1880, Mrs O'Shea was living in a house at Eltham in Kent provided for her by her wealthy, elderly aunt, Mrs Benjamin Wood (Aunt Ben), who lived opposite and wanted somebody available to give her companionship and, when necessary, active help. Captain O'Shea was not living at home regularly and by reason of Parliamentary duties and business ventures had a small flat in London, which was apparently also paid for by the aunt. The aunt gave Mrs O'Shea an allowance of about £4,000 a year. Parnell commuted between London and the estate he had in County Wicklow, spending long periods elsewhere in Ireland as political meetings required.

Mrs O'Shea's house at Eltham was called Wonersh Lodge and Mrs Wood's simply The Lodge.

By the latter part of 1880 Parnell was addressing love letters to Mrs O'Shea, and soon afterwards was staying when in England at her house at Eltham – and that was the position during the ensuing eight years before the Divorce Petition was filed, except that Parnell's periods in Ireland grew shorter.

The history has some very odd features. First of all there was a quarrel between O'Shea and Parnell in 1881 as a result of which O'Shea challenged Parnell to a duel, but though the challenge was accepted the duel did not take place because the parties made up their differences. There have been a number of versions of this incident but no satisfactory explanation. The most one can say is that it had something to do with Parnell's association with Kitty O'Shea but that the compromise did not contain anything to support the plea of connivance.

Far more extraordinary are the facts that Mrs O'Shea gave birth to children in February 1882, March 1883 and November 1884. The child born in 1882 only lived a couple of months. It is widely held that all these three children were Parnell's, but in the divorce case Captain O'Shea claimed them as his, and he claimed that he became truly suspicious only in 1886. The natural questions which arise are (i) was Captain O'Shea having relations with his wife at about the time each of these children was conceived, or (ii) did he know in respect of each that he was not the father but that Parnell was?

Parnell and Mrs O'Shea liked seaside resorts, particularly Brighton. Undoubtedly they used false names at times. One piece of evidence by a servant was that when they were staying at a house in Walsingham Terrace in Brighton in 1893, Parnell avoided detection by Captain O'Shea by escaping by the fire-escape and then presenting himself as a caller. In the Munster Circuit Bar Mess Matthew Kenny said that that was the evidence which hurt Parnell most; he could brave hatred but not ridicule.

In Court, Captain O'Shea claimed that by 1884 he had protested to both his wife and Parnell about the scandal that would arise if Parnell continued visiting his wife in his absence.

In 1886 and 1887 there were various references in newspapers to Parnell living at Eltham. In each instance Captain O'Shea telegraphed or wrote to his wife asking for an explanation and forbidding her to have anything more to do with Parnell.

Oddly, perhaps, in December 1886 Captain O'Shea assured W. T. Stead, the Editor of the *Pall Mall Gazette*, that he had not the least cause to suspect his wife.

In May 1889 Mrs O'Shea's aunt died, leaving everything (over £140,000) to Mrs O'Shea absolutely. Other relatives disputed the Will.

In the Parnell Commission hearings, 1888–89, Captain O'Shea gave evidence against Parnell on the general allegation of criminal incitement in Ireland.

The Divorce Petition as we know was presented in December 1889. The plea of connivance made by Mrs O'Shea stretched right the way back to 1880.

In November 1890 the divorce case came on for hearing before Mr Justice Butt and a jury, trial by jury being the normal course then for defended cases. But, at the last moment, Mrs O'Shea and Parnell did not turn up to defend. It was they, and not Captain O'Shea, who backed out. This is said to have been Parnell's decision rather than Mrs O'Shea's. He had taken no active part in the proceedings apart from accompanying Mrs O'Shea to see her leading counsel, Sir Frank Lockwood QC. When there was no defence on the day the real damage occurred. By reason of the serious cross-allegations Captain O'Shea was enabled – perhaps it is fairer to say indeed required – to deal with his case in detail, un-trammelled by cross-examination of him or his witnesses. His leading counsel was the famous Sir Edward Clarke QC, who made the most of the unopposed "contest".

There was no prohibition then as there is now against publi-cation of counsel's speeches and of the evidence given in a divorce case. Accordingly, all the details of O'Shea v. O'Shea and Parnell received extensive – for Parnell ruinous – coverage.

Captain O'Shea gave evidence in detailed denial of the charges of connivance, condonation and adultery made against him. His case was that he suspected nothing until 1896, and by that evidence he went further than necessary to negative the allegations of connivance and condonation.

There were witnesses as to the adultery between Kitty O'Shea and Parnell, including the maid from the house in Brighton. Mrs Anna Steele, Mrs O'Shea's sister, gave evidence in denial of the charge of adultery against her and the Captain.

She said that the charge arose because she had quarrelled with Kitty over the aunt's Will.

Captain O'Shea won the day all along the line. The cross-charges being rejected, he was granted a decree nisi of divorce with custody of the children under sixteen and costs against the co-respondent; costs were ordered against the wife, too, in so far as she had separate estate. Parnell duly paid the costs, which amounted to £700.

When the decree was made absolute Parnell married Kitty O'Shea on 25 June 1891 at the Register Office at Steyning in Sussex, and they made their home in Brighton at 10 Walsingham Terrace.

The scandal of the divorce and in particular the details of it shocked Catholic Ireland and many others as well. Parnell, at forty-four years of age, was finished as an Irish leader. He made a gallant effort to retain his position and, in Committee Room 15 of the House of Commons, there were stormy sessions of the party. He had support there and in Ireland, but not enough; not enough to preserve an idol or an ideal.

In one session in Committee Room 15 Parnell used the phrase that he was determined to remain master of the party. T. M. Healy (Tim Healy) shouted out bitterly, "And who will be mistress?"

In 1891 Parnell continued his battle to remain as the Irish leader and he took the battle to the people, fighting his cause at public meetings. At Creggs in County Galway on 27 September he said at a meeting how much he admired the courage of his friends, "and I will not leave them until they get a better leader".

Travelling back from County Galway, far from well, he rested in Dublin for several days. He arrived back to his wife in Brighton on 2 October. On 6 October 1891, shortly before midnight, he died. He was only forty-five.

On 11 October 1891 Charles Stewart Parnell was given a huge funeral through Dublin to Glasnevin Cemetery, where he was buried near the O'Connell Monument and tomb.

A Dublin jury returned to Court to say, "We are unanimously of opinion that we cannot agree." This was on the twentieth day of the trial of Parnell for seditious conspiracy in 1880.

A jury in the West of Ireland returned to Court without a verdict but simply to say that they did not believe any of the witnesses on either side – or either of the barristers.

Oscar Wilde

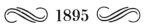 1895

OSCAR WILDE WAS born in Dublin on 16 October 1854, son of Dr (later Sir) William Wilde, a famous eye and ear specialist, and remarkable wife Jane Francesca Wilde. He died on 30 November 1900 in exile in Paris, just forty-six years of age. Poor Oscar: Reading Gaol killed him, but he immortalised it. His literary greatness survives his Court appearances. Indeed, in more tolerant times they assume an historical rather than an over-riding interest.

The infant Oscar was inflicted on christening with no less than four Christian names, and he left the font as Oscar Fingal O'Flahertie Wills Wilde. He often joked about the number of his Christian names and used to say that real fame only came when one was known by one's surname alone, like Parnell. It was by his own choice that he dropped three and became known as just Oscar Wilde. It is indeed odd how men and women shape their names, some using a second forename, others using just initials.

Oscar Wilde was educated at the Royal Portora School in Enniskillen, and then at Dublin University and Magdalen College, Oxford. At Dublin University he came very much under the influence of Dr Mahaffy, already famous and later Provost. Professor Mahaffy was a great classical scholar, wit and socialite. His epigrams and his love of social life and of sparkling conversation left an obvious mark on the young Wilde.

Oscar Wilde's plays, prose and verse have shown an enduring quality. They are appreciated as much now as when they were first written. But his way of life was as much a part of him as his literary work, and it is that which led him to the Courts.

He married Constance Lloyd in 1884 and they had two sons, Cyril Wilde (born in 1885), who was killed in action in the 1914–18 War, and Vyvyan (born in 1886), whose surnames were changed to Holland.

Oscar Wilde had three public trials. The first – from which the others stemmed – was his impulsive, ill-conceived private prosecution of the eighth Marquess of Queensberry for criminal libel, which he dropped, on advice, in the middle of the hearing. The second was of him and a man called Taylor for homosexual offences. This ended in disagreement of the jury. The third was a repetition of the second but against him separately, and it resulted in a verdict of Guilty and a sentence of two years' imprisonment. Taylor in his trial was also found Guilty and got the same sentence.

It is tragically clear that had he not instituted his own private prosecution he would never have been prosecuted himself. It is difficult now to understand how he allowed himself to proceed and how he was allowed to. It is equally clear that he could readily have fled the country before he was prosecuted himself. Many advised him to do so, some (his mother included) begged him to stay. It is commonly supposed that he dithered until the opportunity had gone. The fact seems to be that he stayed because he fully decided to, knowing what would be likely to happen.

It all started in 1891 when Oscar came to know Lord Alfred Douglas, the twenty-two-year-old third son of the Marquess of Queensberry. A close and enduring friendship developed between them which many thought became a homosexual relationship at Wilde's instance. Lord Alfred's father was one who fervently believed that there was such a relationship and he fulminated against it at every opportunity, even going to the length of trying to create a disturbance at the first night of *The Importance of Being Earnest*.

It is worth remembering that a homosexual relationship between consenting male adults in private is now lawful, but that such has been the law only since 1967.

Queensberry brought matters to a head on 28 February 1895 by leaving a visiting card for Wilde at the latter's club, the Albemarle Club, with written on the back "To Oscar Wilde posing as a somdomite". When he called at the club ten days later Wilde was given the card by the porter, who had tactfully put it in an envelope.

It will be noticed that Queensberry mis-spelt the word "sodomite", writing it as "somdomite". The general belief is that it was a genuine mis-spelling, the Marquess perhaps thinking it the correct one, or else just making a mistake. But it has always seemed to me possible that it was deliberate and that the Marquess thought perhaps that this and use of the word "posing" would avoid any legal action against him. No such technicality could have been raised or was raised. There is nothing to suggest positively that he was courting proceedings; he certainly had no legal advice before doing what he did and his defence had to be prepared hurriedly and from scratch when he was arrested.

Oscar Wilde's was a private prosecution for criminal libel. Truth alone is not a defence to such a charge and to succeed the defendant has to show additionally that the publication was for the public benefit. Hence the rather puzzling legal maxim: "The greater the truth the greater the libel".

Sir Edward Clarke QC undertook the prosecution, leading Mr Mathews and Mr Travers Humphreys. Before undertaking the case Sir Edward apparently asked his client if he would give him his word of honour as an "English" gentleman that he was not guilty of the charges made against him, and Wilde readily gave such assurances. It is most unusual for a counsel to call for any such assurances, but no doubt Sir Edward felt that the position was different where he was asked to undertake a prosecution and not a defence, and a private prosecution at that.

Edward Carson QC led for the defence. His juniors were Charles Frederick Gill and Arthur Gill. He had been doubtful about accepting the brief because he had been a direct contemporary of Oscar Wilde at Dublin University and had known him there. They were not, however, in any sense friends, and Wilde's observation that "he will cross-examine me with all the venom of an old friend" is only another Oscar epigram with the literary – and literal – leave that that allows. Carson did think about the matter and consult others in the law before finally taking the case.

137

At the time when the Marquess was arrested it seems that the only ammunition which the defence had was Wilde's literary writings and two unhappy letters from Wilde to Lord Alfred which had fallen into the hands of the Marquess.

By the time of the trial his solicitor, Mr Charles Russell, junior, had obtained as potential witnesses a number of young men prepared to say that Wilde had solicited them to commit sodomy with him and had, in fact, committed various acts of indecency with them.

As the rules required, these allegations had to be set out in writing as Particulars of Justification. They were accordingly seen by Wilde and his advisers before the trial started – and yet the case was allowed to go on.

The trial opened at the Old Bailey on 3 April 1895 and, by a further coincidence, the Judge was another Irishman and graduate of Dublin University, Mr Justice Henn Collins.

Sir Edward Clarke opened the prosecution and, after formally proving the note through the club porter, called Oscar Wilde and examined him in chief quite shortly. Then, still in the morning of the first day, Edward Carson rose to cross-examine.

Carson's cross-examination of Wilde is a classic. Although he had a good deal of ammunition he embarked on a war of attrition and, despite Wilde scoring off him several times, he gradually began to wear him down and to pounce in deadly fashion on unfortunately phrased answers. To achieve the withdrawal of the case shortly afterwards – during his opening of the defence – was a tremendous feat.

A few words about counsel's various tasks in asking questions are appropriate here. Examination in Chief, the bringing out of one's own client's evidence by question and answer, can be very difficult because one is not allowed to ask leading questions (questions which suggest their own answers) and the witness unaccustomed to telling a story by way of question and answer may well not be forthcoming. To get one's own witness to come up to proof over a long history I regard as the most potentially difficult of all counsel's tasks. Cross-examination is a wholly different art. Basically, I consider that it will only succeed if (a) the witness is not telling the truth, or (b) he/she has something relevant to hide or (c) he/she is being thoroughly unreasonable. Every counsel has his own particular style of cross-examination – some believe in being short, others in being long – but the style naturally varies a great deal with the case. Some plan to go through the witness' evidence chronologically, others prefer to skip around, so as to put the witness off his stride or to probe the weaker spots in his evidence. Yet again, others attach particular importance to the first question or questions.

As we will see Carson adopted with Wilde two of the techniques just mentioned: importance attached to the first few questions and a long cross-examination, a war of attrition. Wilde committed the litigant's greatest folly – to answer back instead of to answer; to score instead of to answer shortly and simply. It is a mistake to try to play counsel at his own game: he has the experience; he is the professional; he has his own lines of retreat and counter-attack.

There are witnesses who can fool anybody. I have come across a few, a very few. But fundamentally, as I say, the honest witness cannot be broken by cross-examination – however bad he is as a witness.

Re-examination is the opportunity for a party's own counsel to clear up points which arose during cross-examination. It is usually either a hopeless or an unnecessary task. Rarely does it contribute much. There are cases where it helps, but they are few.

Counsel's first question in cross-examination exposed a stupid lie by Wilde. "You stated that your age was thirty-nine. I think you are over forty? You were born on the 16th October 1854." This made him forty and a half, but Wilde tried to shrug the matter off.

Carson then elicited that Wilde had stayed with the young Lord Alfred Douglas, then twenty-four, at various places in England and abroad.

On literary matters Wilde seemed to score.

"You are of the opinion, I believe, that there is no such thing as an immoral book?"

"Yes."

"May I take it that you think *The Priest and the Acolyte* was not immoral?"

"It was worse. It was badly written."

Taking a quotation from *Dorian Gray*, Carson asked: "Have you ever adored a young man madly?"

"No, not madly. I prefer love – that is a higher form."

"Never mind about that. Let us keep down to the level we are at now."

"I have never given adoration to anybody except myself." (Compare his remark when landing at New York: "I have nothing to declare except my genius.")

Reading from one of Wilde's letters to Lord Alfred Douglas, which were in the possession of the Marquess, Carson took the phrase "Your slim gilt soul walks between passion and poetry". "Is that a beautiful phrase?" he asked.

"Not as you read it, Mr Carson. You read very badly."

A little later: "Have you often written letters in the same style as this?"

"I don't repeat myself in style."

Wilde was asked about the other letter, which, amongst other things, said: "You are the divine thing I want, the thing of grace and beauty." "Is that," asked Carson, "an ordinary letter?"

"Everything I write is extraordinary," replied Wilde. "I do not pose as being ordinary. Sweet heavens, ask me any question you like about it."

"Is it the kind of letter a man writes to another?"

"It was a tender expression of my great admiration for Lord Alfred Douglas. It was not, like the other, a prose poem."

Carson then asked him about a whole series of young men whom Wilde admitted he had gone about with and given presents to. When pressed as to why he went about with young men of such a different class ("grooms and coachmen"), Oscar Wilde replied: "The pleasure to me was being with those who are young, bright, happy, careless and free. I do not like the sensible and I do not like the old."

"Do you drink champagne yourself?" he was asked.

"Yes. Iced champagne is a favourite drink of mine – strongly against my doctor's orders."

"Never mind your doctor's orders, sir."

"I never do," replied Wilde swiftly.

Despite Wilde's successes in the witness-box, judge and jury were obviously getting a very unsatisfactory picture of him as an associate of and benefactor to a string of unsavoury young men.

One question about one young man broke through Wilde's armour, and no one could safely give chances (even half-chances) to Carson.

The young man was Grainger, who was a servant of Lord Alfred's at Oxford.

"Did you kiss him?" Carson asked.

"Oh dear no," replied Wilde. "He was a peculiarly plain boy. He was, unfortunately, extremely ugly. I pitied him for it."

Carson was through the gap in a flash. Why, why, why add what he did? Wilde was stung and shaken – and finished.

During Carson's opening of the defence it emerged that he intended to call a number of the young men he had asked Wilde about. This appears to have come as a surprise to defence and public alike. Why it should have is hard to imagine. The Particulars of Justification could not have been taken as bluff – especially by Wilde himself. It is very difficult to understand how he – even he – could ever have thought that he would survive against these Particulars.

As Carson developed his opening on the third day of the Wilde trial Sir Edward Clarke, after a few moments out of Court, returned, spoke to Carson and announced that the prosecution would accept a verdict of Not Guilty – Not Guilty, he added, "having reference to the word 'posing' ".

That evening, Wilde was arrested at the Cadogan Hotel.

Shortly afterwards, Wilde and Taylor were prosecuted. The jury, after a five-day trial before Mr Justice Charles, disagreed on 1 May 1895. Carson did not prosecute then or at the re-trial.

At the re-trial, which began on 20 May 1895, of Wilde separately, Sir Frank Lockwood QC, the Solicitor-General, prosecuted. After a four-day trial before Mr Justice Wills, and a jury retirement of two and a half hours, Wilde was convicted and got the maximum sentence of two years. Then, after various London prisons, he was transferred to Reading Gaol on 30 November 1895.

His mother died while he was in prison and he was made bankrupt. Subsequent royalties paid all debts and left a surplus for his family.

Exactly two years after the commencement of his second trial, on 19 May 1897, he was released from Reading Gaol. A year later his wife died. With the help of friends he got to France. There he got just sufficient money from friends and admirers to keep body and soul together. He was a broken man and a sick one. "I am dying," he said, "as I lived – beyond my means." On 30 November 1900 – three and a half years after he had left prison and Britain – he died. Poor Oscar, a genius whose trials will unfortunately be remembered – but never as well as his works.

> "And the wild regrets, and the bloody sweats,
>   None knew so well as I:
> For he who lives more lives than one
>   More deaths than one must die."

(from "The Ballad of Reading Gaol")

Edward Carson's first cases were in the area of Waterford. A lady named Miss Anthony can truly be said to have launched herself and young Carson into legal and public prominence. In her first case, against a railway company for personal injuries, she retained him, and the case not only attracted great local interest but went to the Court of Appeal and became of great legal interest. Carson and Miss Anthony won. Thereafter they went their separate ways; she to become Ireland's most famous litigant in person; he to be a famous advocate and politician. Her speciality was claiming penalties as a "common informer". Her usual ploy was to borrow £5 or so from somebody – often clerical – and to insist on leaving a token (once five sheep) for repayment. When repaying she would then serve a Writ, claiming that the poor unfortunate lender had taken a pledge when not a licensed moneylender or pawnbroker. She became so feared that she got free transport from virtually every railway and newspapers were afraid to report her death in case it was not true.

McCartney v. Londonderry and Lough Swilly Railway Company Limited

 1904

RAILWAYS HAVE BEEN lawyers' friends ever since they first began. They have litigated almost as much as they have been litigated against. They have fought hard for the best interpretation of the statutes which gave them authority; they have defended stoutly all manner of claims against them – accident claims by passengers, claims of all sorts by railway employees and even delightful claims such as the ones about sparks from their engines burning down thatched cottages.

Ireland has contributed liberally to railway cases. One which I often think of as I go by train to the West of Ireland is an enormous case in Company Law which arose because the line authorised for Mullingar to Galway ran out of money when it was laid as far as Athlone, which is about half-way and is (though few realise it) the geographical centre of Ireland. There was a great fuss about making calls on shares and so forth. It would really have been rather a disappointing and frustrating line if it had not managed eventually to push on.

In the North of Ireland an unusual case showed, by going to the House of Lords, how bitterly contested a comparatively small matter could turn out to be. There was a natural stream crossed by a railway line and, further down, a Mr McCartney had a corn mill, which was old and required a great deal of water to operate. The railway crossed the stream by a culvert, and the company owned about eight feet of land at each side of the culvert and abutting the stream.

In 1901 the Railway Company inserted a three-inch pipe into the stream at the side of the culvert and abstracted water through the pipe along the railway line for about half a mile into a tank which stood on land they owned there. From the tank they watered their engines.

Mr McCartney stopped up the pipe.

The Railway Company sued and claimed a watering right. They said that they had a right to what the pipe would take, 15,000 gallons a day, but that their present need was only 5,000 gallons a day.

There is a good deal of learning on the question of rivers and streams, what one can take out and for what purposes and what one can and cannot put in (under which comes pollution).

Lord Justice Holmes, sitting alone, tried the action at Derry Assizes and dismissed the Railway Company's claim. No water for the engines.

There were two appeals in Ireland, first to the King's Bench Divisional Court, which reversed the decision with costs (making two lots of costs), and then by Mr McCartney to the Irish Court of Appeal, who agreed with the Divisional Court (three lots of costs against Mr McCartney now). In the Court of Appeal, the Lord Chancellor, Lord Ashbourne, and Lord Justice Walker formed a majority; Lord Justice FitzGibbon dissented.

Then came the appeal to the House of Lords. Two points which greatly impressed their Lordships were that the water was moved away from the stream for half a mile and was then fed to engines which had a track length of forty miles; but, more than that, the system was connected with other systems which allowed the engines a far larger range.

The Railway Company, as well as arguing a right to take the water because they were riparian owners, said that Mr McCartney was being quite unreasonable because the flow was over half a million gallons a day, their 15,000 gallons would mean hardly anything to the mill and, anyway, their present needs were only 5,000 gallons.

The Law Lords spent a lot of time worrying about the fact that before the trial Judge the case appeared to have run mainly on the footing that the "stream" was an artificial watercourse. The Judge had, however, held that artificial watercourse or natural stream, the result was the same. They felt rather aggrieved that the artificial watercourse had gone, and a good deal of time was spent in trying to find out how,

145

where and why it had gone. This surprisingly defied explanation and in the end they said that the case must go forward on the natural stream basis. This and the two appeals in Ireland led Lord McNaghten to say that he preferred "what now remains of the judgment of Lord Justice Holmes".

The Earl of Halsbury, the Lord Chancellor (after whom the famous Laws of England are called), turned the Railway Company's plea of reasonableness neatly against them. He thought it was most unreasonable that "the use of a stream passing through a very small area of riparian land should be made to extend to forty miles of country, or wherever else the exigencies of the railway service might require". It conjures up a rather pleasant picture of reluctant water being taken away from home for the benefit of far-away engines.

But, he held, reasonableness did not come into the matter at all, nor quantity. The question was whether there was a right or not. In his judgment there was not. This was not within a riparian owner's right at all.

Lord McNaghten, after his pleasant observation about what remained of Lord Justice Holmes' judgment, put the ultimate point very clearly when he said that there were three ways in which a person whose lands are intersected or bounded by a running stream may use the water: (1) for ordinary purposes such as domestic use or for watering cattle, (2) under certain conditions for other purposes connected with his land or (3) for foreign or unconnected purposes. He had rights in the first two classes, no right at all under the third. He had no sympathy with the Railway Company: they would not be returning any of the water to the stream: they were taking the water for their own gain "to save themselves the expense of paying for the water required for the purposes of their business or gathering it for themselves". He went on, "It seems to me that they might just as well claim to sell the water. And, indeed, Mr Ronan, in his able argument, did not shrink from that position. He baldly contended that they would be perfectly justified in selling the water or doing anything they pleased with it, provided the lower proprietor was not practically injured." He ended with a delightful *coup de grâce* in saying that the Railway Company could not establish that its system and the lines of connected companies were "a single riparian tenement".

Lord Lindley said that by buying the small piece of land necessary for the crossing of the stream they bought only the water rights which it conferred, and that did not include taking a large quantity of water for consumption away from the land. He said that no doubt they could take the infinitesimal quantity of water needed to cross the stream!

Mr McCartney's appeal was accordingly allowed and the trial Judge's verdict in his favour restored. The appeal was allowed with costs all along the way, making four lots of costs in all which the Railway Company had to pay.

The greatest pleasure I get out of the case is the sense of judicial shock at the use of the water along the forty-mile system but – worse still – on connecting lines. Their Lordships' observations conjure up a picture of engines travelling far beyond Derry or Lough Swilly, to Belfast perhaps, or Dublin, or even to Cork, consuming Mr McCartney's water – without payment.

Edward Carson's first ambition was to be an architect. And it so happened that one of his first cases at the Bar was about buildings. The County Court Judge was very old and appeared to be taking copious notes, but was observed at one stage by both counsel to be "writing" with the wrong end of the pen. He reserved judgment and a few days later asked counsel for their notes in order to "check" with his own. Carson's note was the better – and he won!

In a Dublin Magistrates' Court, Carson was briefed to defend some Trinity College students who were charged with assaulting a bookmaker. They suspected him, with some reason, of being about to welsh. They were about to throw him into the sea when apprehended by the police.

"How did you know they were going to drown you?" asked Carson.

"I knew right enough. Didn't they hold me by the leg over the sea wall!"

"Which leg?" said Carson. "Was it your black leg, by any chance?"

Patrick Pearse
 As an Advocate, 1906

PATRICK PEARSE, PADRAIG PEARSE, was the acknowledged leader of the Easter Week Rising of 1916. It was he who signed in first place, and read in front of the GPO in Dublin the Proclamation of an Irish Republic. He gave the eventual order to surrender, was made prisoner, put before a court martial, sentenced to death and shot. So was his brother and close supporter, William Pearse.

The Pearse brothers remind one in some ways of the Sheares brothers of the 1798 Rebellion; they were barristers also, in their case members of the Munster Circuit, and were defended by their fellow-circuiteer, John Philpot Curran.

It is not of Patrick Pearse – or his brother – *qua* accused that I write. But of a case which, trivial in itself, illustrates their philosophy and that of their opponents.

Both the Pearse brothers were qualified barristers and practised a little. Their hearts, however, were in education on strictly Irish lines; the Irish language (which is not called Erse but Irish), Irish literature and Irish history; and all other subjects against that background. Both were avowed Nationalists.

Patrick Pearse ran a small school at his home in Rathfarnham, then a rural suburb of Dublin, and he ran it on the lines mentioned.

At the time of the case in question, 1906, the position about the Irish language in the country was this. Everything official and virtually everything commercial was transacted in English. The great majority of the country used English as their ordinary language. There were areas, particularly

149

in the West, where Irish was spoken as the sole or the main language. Through the country many people understood Irish and some spoke it on occasions. The Irish language was very far from dead, but years of Anglicisation had made the country predominantly English-speaking, and the best that could be said was that it was to some extent bi-lingual. The Irish language was taught in the schools, but there were no incentives for it either in the schoolroom or in the outside world.

It is against that background that one looks at the case of Mr McBride, a small farmer in County Donegal.

There was (indeed, I think there still is) an Act of Parliament of 1851 which requires the owner of a cart to have his name and address painted upon a conspicuous part of the off-side of the cart in legible letters. Mischievously, one wonders why on the off-side only and why not on all vehicles, including nowadays motor cars? That could be embarrassing.

The reason for this somewhat odd enactment was stated rather grandly by one of the High Court judges who eventually dealt with it to enable persons injured by the cart to ascertain the name and address of the person responsible for it. After all, carts did not have number-plates or licences or insurance.

The picture of somebody actually consulting the off-side of a cart, either in the presence or the absence of its owner, is a delightful one.

Mr McBride, whatever he thought of this law, considered that he had complied with the letter of it. He put his name and address on the off-side of his cart, conspicuously, but in the Irish language – which was what he and his friends spoke. Moreover he did so in Irish character letters, not just the Irish language in English letters.

A police officer, whose political and general views were not those of Mr McBride, summoned him (or, as Irish people commonly and probably correctly say, summonsed him). At the Dunfanaghy, County Donegal, Petty Sessions he fought the case but lost. He was fined one shilling and ordered to pay one shilling costs, a total penalty in modern money of 10p.

Exercising his legal right Mr McBride called upon the Court to state a case in writing for the opinion of the High Court. The case was well and fairly stated, recording everything that

Mr McBride could want, including a finding that in the area three-quarters of the population were Irish-speaking.

Before the High Court in Dublin Mr McBride had the advantage of three counsel, including Patrick Pearse. It was Pearse who made the most impression of all.

The Appellant's case was, of course, that his name and address in Irish complied with the statute and that, accordingly, he had committed no offence.

Patrick Pearse was armed with much historical and linguistic material. My uncle, Michael Comyn KC, was in Court during the hearing and was very much impressed by him. He was quiet in delivery, careful and cogent in presentation; obviously intense in his feelings but managing to suppress them. Michael Comyn was far from impressed by the way the judges reacted to him. They were Lord Chief Justice O'Brien, Mr Justice Andrews and Mr Justice Gibson. They seemed to treat it all as rather a joke – but a joke at the expense of Pearse and his client.

Pearse did have humour amongst his characteristics, but it surfaced only occasionally and when it did, with effect. He certainly never exercised it in matters upon which he felt deeply. It was a sense of humour wholly different from the rough, tough, loud humour of the kind the judges showed. But he kept his head.

Mr Justice Gibson, in particular, seemed determined literally to laugh Pearse out of Court. He asked Pearse to render a series of names into Irish, the name Gibson included, and then to say what the Irish names meant. Pearse complied earnestly but was obviously genuinely puzzled by the judges' attitude.

The theme of his argument was interesting. After dealing with the history of the Irish language, he stressed that his client lived in an area (comparable to a state or a province) where Irish was the language. The stranger must take an area's language as he finds it. Moreover Irish was a used language throughout the country and a lawful one. Letters addressed in Irish were carried and delivered. A man could properly and lawfully use an Irish name and an Irish address and use no other. Ireland was a bi-lingual country.

Their Lordships were unanimous in dismissing the appeal.

They gave longish judgments, but did not seem to acknowledge that the case had any real importance. Their attitude was that Pearse and his client and others like them were harmless fanatics, living in a twilight Celtic world of their own. To be quite fair my uncle and others who knew Patrick Pearse well saw him then as a dreamer of dreams and an intellectual, never as a possible military leader.

The Lord Chief Justice in his judgment completely rejected the proposition that Ireland was bi-lingual. Its language was English. The Courts were conducted in English. Parliament legislated in English. The statute was in English and plainly meant English writing when it provided as it did. He considered that the operative words were "in legible letters", and in his view Irish character letters or even Irish letters in English characters were not "legible letters". Mr Justice Andrews agreed and said that English was the only language for legal purposes.

Mr Justice Gibson said that any other conclusion would make nonsense of the countless requirements for the filling in of forms. Life would be impossible if people could fill in official documents in Irish. He was very solemn about the offence committed by the Appellant, saying that if such conduct were allowed it would be a facility for escaping identification. In lighter vein he made the startling suggestion that if the Appellant really felt so strongly on the subject there was nothing to stop him putting his Irish name and address on the near-side of the cart, provided that they appeared properly in English on the off-side.

Passing reference was made in the case to the Welsh language and to Scottish Gaelic. It is interesting to note that for Wales now there is special legislation enabling Welsh to be used officially. And, of course, in present-day Ireland (except the North) Irish is one of the officially recognised languages.

In Ireland now the Irish language is a compulsory subject in the schools, but (to be Irish) not as compulsory as it was in de Valera's day. Proficiency in it is required for many public appointments. And it is given considerable financial and other assistance. However it has, as always, the formidable opposition of an English-speaking outside world. And a TV home intruder at that.

Irish will now survive; of that there is no doubt. But its progress is debatable and, with some, controversial. George Bernard Shaw is credited – or debited – with the observation that it is very useful at the Arrivals part of Euston Station. But he, of course, was obsessed with a new alphabet of his own, which has not been as successful as *Pygmalion*.

The case against Mr McBride might well have been left unbrought. Having been brought it looked pretty trivial then – but oaks from little acorns grow.

When Edward Carson was at the English Bar, he attended a wedding with some of his legal colleagues.

"How I wish," he said , "that I had a shoe to throw at the bride."

"Well," said a colleague, "there's always your brogue."

In one of his early cases in Ireland, Carson was subjected – as the Court was subjected – to a long and tedious final speech by his opposing counsel. It wandered wearily through the facts and the law and then back to some of the facts and a different view of the law. When it came to Carson's turn, he smiled slightly at the Judge and jury and said, "I think I will follow my learned friend's example and submit the case to you without argument."

At a trial in Dublin, a judge asked Carson about the discrepancy between the evidence of two witnesses, a carpenter and a publican.

"It is, my Lord," replied Carson, "only the difference between Bench and Bar."

Big Jim Larkin

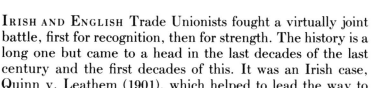 Cases between 1907 and 1914

IRISH AND ENGLISH Trade Unionists fought a virtually joint battle, first for recognition, then for strength. The history is a long one but came to a head in the last decades of the last century and the first decades of this. It was an Irish case, Quinn v. Leathem (1901), which helped to lead the way to the Trades Disputes Act of 1906: a North of Ireland grazier (sometimes described rather vulgarly as "a flesher") held a verdict in the House of Lords against union officials who sought to compel him to employ only union labour, and persuaded his biggest customer, a meat retailer named Munroe, to give up dealing with him. The House of Lords found the combination unlawful and the result actionable conspiracy.

There is, of course, a long history of Trade Unionism in both countries. As far back as 1781 when the great English architect James Gandon was constructing his magnificent Custom House in Dublin (he was also the architect of the Four Courts) he was faced with the demand that only union labour should be used, and he readily complied. In the last century there were several examples of unions fighting against any invention or practice designed to reduce employment – a situation familiar today.

The great names in Irish Trade Unionism in this century, where so much has happened, were James Larkin and James Connolly. Many would give pride of place to Connolly, as being the producer on whose stage Larkin played the leading role. Certain it is that Connolly had his horizon very far beyond the Trade Union movement, on a Marxist-socialist future. He founded a Citizens' Army, which fought with him in the 1916 Rebellion. When it ended he, as one of the leaders, was executed. His movement is still alive and many think that his name and writings will survive those of all his contemporaries.

James Larkin was Liverpudlian Irish and came to Ireland in 1907 as organiser for the National Union of Dock Labourers. He was over six feet tall, tough in physique and character, a fighting speaker of powerful voice and aggressive spirit.

By then Connolly had been on the Irish scene for eleven years, having come from Scotland to manage the Socialist Club in Dublin.

Both men found Belfast and Dublin employer strongholds. In Belfast in the summer of 1907 dockers struck because of the use of non-union labour. Larkin advised them to go back but they found that specially imported "blacklegs" from Liverpool had taken their places and they were turned away. A belligerent four-month all-out strike developed; other industries joined in or were forced in, and even the Royal Irish Constabulary based in Belfast staged a short-lived mutiny. The police found a surprising and unlikely advocate in Larkin, who publicised their grievances about pay and hours of duty and blasted the authorities in his own characteristic way.

Larkin, who once declared, "I recognise no law but the people's law," had a number of clashes with the Law of the Land.

On 31 May 1907 he was arrested for an assault on a "blackleg", who used a knife on him. Violence had by then become a commonplace in the strike. He was acquitted of the charges on 24 July and the verdict was received by the employers and their supporters with great indignation.

Since the passage of the 1906 Act and the leave given for peaceful picketing, Larkin had made great play and great use of this valuable right. He ran into difficulties, however, when a case against him by Belfast Harbour Commissioners about picketing on the quays was lost. It was decided that picketing on private property was a trespass and therefore unlawful. Ironically, he was using the dock at the time to persuade the dockers to go back to work.

As the violence of the strike grew, union authorities in England became alarmed and, over Larkin's head, settled with the employers in August 1907 with the workers gaining very little and – most important of all – failing to get any assurance that non-union labour would be prohibited. The police strike, or mutiny as its opponents liked to call it, was quickly quelled by the dismissal of certain ringleaders and the mass transfer of police officers.

The end of the Belfast affair may appear as a defeat for Larkin and the Trade Unions, but it is generally accepted now that it marked a turning-point which led on to the unions' subsequent successes. People became aware of the solidarity of the workers, their militancy and their grievances.

Larkin was dismissed as organiser of the National Union of Dock Labourers in Ireland by the higher-ups in England, ostensibly for disobedience. He retaliated by founding with Connolly in 1909 the eventually famous and powerful Irish Transport and General Workers Union. The philosophy behind it was a single general union for workers in all trades.

Meanwhile, while still with the dock union, Larkin had been to Cork to aid dockers who were in dispute with the Cork Steam Packet Company. He had some success there but later ran into trouble when accused of misappropriating contributions paid by the workers. He was tried for this in 1910 and was convicted. Mr Justice Boyd sentenced him to twelve months' imprisonment, with – ironically – hard labour. Finances had certainly gone wrong, but it was widely believed that Larkin was guilty of carelessness and muddle but not crime. A petition was presented to the Viceroy, Lord Aberdeen, and Larkin was released after serving three months of his sentence.

This conviction, though for as heinous an offence as a trade union official can commit, did not hinder Larkin's progress in the movement. Those for whom he worked knew the courage and integrity of the man. However, his enemies, and he had some within the movement as well as outside it, never let it be wholly forgotten and sought to build on it other alleged irregularities.

The years between 1909 and 1913 saw much industrial unrest and many strikes throughout the country. Conditions were appalling. In Dublin alone 100,000 people lived in tenement rooms and the average income was about £1 a week.

In 1912 Big Jim was in legal trouble again. He and other officials of his new union were sued by a Dublin stevedore named Long for damages for conspiracy and an injunction. What happened was that an Association of Stevedores had been formed, and because its aim was to get better rates from shipowners and thereby better pay for dockers Larkin and his colleagues had weighed in with all their support. In particular they had warned dockers not to work for any stevedores who were not members of the Association. Mr Long was a stevedore; he employed union labour but did not want to join the Association. As a result Larkin and his friends exerted pressure and a number of dockers gave up their employment with him. He sued, alleging that there was a conspiracy to procure breaches of contract with him and for an injunction against such interference.

The case was hard fought before Lord Chief Baron Palles and a jury and Mr Long won £250 damages and the injunction he asked for. No less than three Appeals were brought by Larkin and the union against that decision. The first was to the Divisional Court of the High Court and was lost. Then to the Court of Appeal in Ireland – lost again. Finally, three whole years after the original decision, the case went to the House of Lords, which again found in favour of Mr Long. Unions were prepared to fight hard in the Courts, but at that time they plainly had little sympathy from the general public or the judiciary. A lot of people saw no need for change in the social order.

In the middle of 1913 there came the great employers versus unions confrontation in Dublin. William Martin Murphy, a powerful employer with many business interests, reacted to constant union irritation by leading a band of employers into open battle with the unions, particularly with Larkin and his union.

Murphy controlled, amongst other concerns, the *Irish Independent* newspaper and the Dublin United Tramways Company. All were strictly non-union but they had been infiltrated. He issued a proclamation that any of his employees who were union members were to resign their membership at once or be dismissed; and on pain of dismissal no one was to join a union. Larkin promptly retaliated by calling strikes in all the businesses which adopted this attitude.

During the Great Strike, Larkin was arrested twice: once for seditious libel and seditious conspiracy; the other time for holding a banned meeting, at which he had arrived dressed as a clergyman. The British TUC subscribed thousands of pounds to a fighting fund and Lenin wrote in praise of "Comrade Larkin" and the Irish proletariat.

In October 1913 Larkin was tried on just the first of the two charges. He was convicted and sentenced to seven months' imprisonment. A campaign in Britain succeeded in the government freeing him after a few weeks.

Eventually, after some five months, the Great Strike in Dublin finished. Again, the workers only gained small concessions and the employers refused to grant the principle of non-union labour. But again, too, the struggle showed clearly the union successes that were to come.

It is a strange thing that although the Trade Union movement in Ireland and in England was socialist-inspired and has gained an enormous number of adherents over the years, Ireland has never had a large or strong Labour Party. There is undoubtedly Communism in the country, North and South, but religion is a powerful block to it. One might, however, have expected a stronger Labour representation in politics.

Just before the outburst of war in 1914, Jim Larkin went on a lecture tour of the United States, fund-raising for his union. He did not return to Ireland until 1923. As usual his views brought him into conflict with the authorities. He preached against the war, even when America was joining it. He laid down Trade Union law in a bellicose way. And then, further to invite governmental disapproval, he campaigned in favour of the Soviet Union. In 1919 he was charged with criminal anarchy. Found guilty, he was sentenced to five years' imprisonment and was sent to Sing Sing.

Larkin had luck with his imprisonments. He never served a full term. In this instance Governor Al Smith gave him a free pardon in 1922 saying that it was wrong to punish a man for his beliefs.

When Big Jim Larkin returned to Ireland he found himself irrecoverably replaced in his own union. He continued in active Trade Unionism but was never the force he had been. His work – the pioneering – was done. He died in 1945. At his funeral all Dublin's workers turned out to honour him.

159

Lord Russell of Killowen, the first Catholic and Irishman to be Lord Chief Justice of England, was a strong and brilliant leader at the Bar. On one occasion at the end of the day, he had a passage at arms with Mr Justice Denman, later Lord Denman, and almost certainly over-stepped the bounds. The Judge rose in annoyance saying that he would deal further with the matter in the morning.

Next morning, when he took his seat, Mr Justice Denman began, "I have been thinking deeply about what happened last evening."

Charles Russell interrupted him, and with a disarming smile said, "Please, my Lord, think no more about it. I have, I can assure you, put it right out of my mind."

The incident closed with a ready laugh by the Judge.

Irish Workmen's Compensation

 1908 and 1914

THE WORKMEN'S COMPENSATION Acts of 1897 onwards sought
to produce for Britain and Ireland a simple code of informal
procedure whereby claims in respect of workmen's accidents
would be expeditiously dealt with on a liability without fault
basis. Instead they led over the ensuing fifty years to a flood
of litigation, to a considerable body of specialist lawyers, to
numerous textbooks and to a special set of Law Reports dealing
with nothing else.

All this sprang from the three essentials laid down for a
claim: (1) an injury caused by an accident, (2) arising out of
and (3) in the course of, the employment. No few expressions
have been more litigated – and, of course, Ireland contributed
its share of cases.

Every workman however injured at work considered that
all qualifications were automatically fulfilled. Every employer
or insurer regularly questioned whether the occurrence was
properly speaking "an accident", and even if it were whether
it arose "out of" the employment and "in the course of it".

I have chosen two Irish cases on the subject which went
right up to the House of Lords and became leading authorities.

In ISMAY, IMRIE & CO. V. WILLIAMSON (1908), Mrs Williamson
claimed in respect of her husband's death. It appears that he
was a brass finisher by trade but went to the United States to
try to better himself. Having failed and being in a very run-
down state he sought the help of the Seaman's Mission in New
York and, with their help, got a passage home, shipping as a
trimmer on the appellant's steamship the *Majestic*.

161

A trimmer's work was to rake out the ashes of the furnaces, and they worked in shifts of four hours on and eight hours off.

On his third shift Mr Williamson suffered a "heatstroke". He was found to have a temperature of 106°. In the ship's hospital ice was applied and the temperature was brought down to 101°. He then became violent and two hours after collapsing at work he died from heatstroke and exhaustion.

The County Court Judge in Belfast found that what happened was "an accident" and awarded the widow compensation. By a majority of two to one the Irish Court of Appeal agreed.

In the House of Lords counsel for the shipowners argued: "The man died by disease, not by accident . . . An accident must be something external which supervenes in the conditions of the work, not the man . . . An accident may be an unexpected event but not every unexpected event is an accident."

Their Lordships, again by a majority of two to one, held that the occurrence was "an accident" and accordingly dismissed the shipowners' appeal.

Lord Loreburn, Lord Chancellor, said that the event in question was "an unlooked for mishap in the course of his employment. In common language, it was a case of accidental death."

Lord Ashbourne in agreeing said that he saw no room for serious doubt. "Everything was in the course of his employment and arising out of it. But for the boiler and the heatstroke, and the speedy exhaustion it caused, there would have been no accident."

Lord McNaghten dissented. He could not see how the heatstroke could be regarded as "an accident", any more than would be an attack of bronchitis or pneumonia brought on by a sudden chill and disregarded or neglected at the outset.

There was a great deal of learning expounded in that case but one cannot help feeling that the judgment was right in common-sense and in law. It is very interesting to see the word "accident" so carefully analysed, but I believe that the Act in question (the 1906 Act) was intended to cover such a situation bibliotheca SelfCheck System

Customer name: Allannah Curran
Customer ID: L00181496

Items that you have checked out

Title Irish at law :
D: a50012427
Due: 21 November 2023

Total items: 1
Account balance: 0.00 EUR
Checked out: 1
Overdue: 0
Hold requests: 0
Ready for collection: 0
7/11/2023 09:41

Thank you for using the bibliotheca SelfCheck
System

as Mr Williamson's – extremely unusual though it was and extremely unlikely as it would have been in the case of a fully fit, experienced man.

In BOARD OF MANAGEMENT OF TRIM JOINT DISTRICT SCHOOL v. KELLY (1914), the claimant was the mother, as sole dependant, in respect of the death of her son John Kelly. He was an assistant master in the Trim, County Meath, industrial school for boys under fifteen. It was part of his duty to supervise the boys in the school and the playground.

The boys were angry with Kelly because he stopped them playing the national game of hurling in the school yard and because he had caught one of them misbehaving. On 12 February 1912 a group of the boys attacked him with hurley sticks, brooms and scrubs (heavy blocks of wood with a handle). He sustained a fractured skull and died the same day.

The County Court Judge found that the occurrence was "an accident" and that it arose "out of and in the course of the employment". He awarded the mother £100 – a pathetic sum.

No doubt it was a matter of principle rather than the amount which led the Board of Management to bring no less than two appeals. The first was to the Irish Court of Appeal, which unanimously supported the County Court Judge.

The House of Lords had to be convened twice to deal with the matter. The first tribunal was obviously equally divided. The second, larger, tribunal by four to three dismissed the appeal.

The Board of Management took two points: (1) that what happened was not "an accident" and (2) that anyway it did not arise "out of and in the course of" Mr Kelly's employment.

They argued that a planned assault cannot be an accident. They challenged an Irish decision that a gamekeeper injured by poachers suffered "an accident" and an English decision that a cashier who was robbed and murdered was the victim of "an accident". They relied on a Scottish case which held that somebody taking over from a striker who was then beaten up by the strikers had not suffered "an accident".

On the other limb they contended that it was not incidental to the employment of Mr Kelly that his pupils should conspire to assault him.

The mother's side argued that an intentional act could be "an accident" to the victim. The case was a typical one "arising out of and in the course of the employment", because the injury occurred while the deceased was discharging his duty and was caused by those he had to control.

Viscount Haldane (the Lord Chancellor), Earl Loreburn, Lord Shaw of Dunfermline and Lord Reading held that the appeal should be dismissed. Lord Dunedin, Lord Atkinson and Lord Parker of Waddington dissented.

Viscount Haldane said that the object of the statute was wide and that an accident must include any injury not expected or designed by the workman himself. In so finding he (and the majority) over-ruled the Scottish case. He found evidence to support the other finding.

Earl Loreburn held that there was no single rigid meaning of the word "accident" and it applied to the circumstances here. That the event was unlikely and unprecedented did not prevent it "arising out of and in the course of" the employment. Lord Shaw and Lord Reading delivered speeches to like effect.

Lord Dunedin said it seemed clear to him that in ordinary language the injury in this case was not caused by accident. Mr Kelly was killed – as was found in the criminal trial – by manslaughter. Why should the matter be viewed from the point of view of the injured man? Why not from the employer's point of view? And anyway, anybody's "point of view" was irrelevant. On the second point – it could not be right to regard a conspiracy to assault as a risk of the employment, arising out of it.

Lord Atkinson considered that a "premeditated crime, deliberately committed, in pursuance of a conspiracy" could not reasonably be called "an accident". The injury was neither the effect of an unknown cause nor the unusual effect of a known cause. Further, he would not have regarded what occurred as arising out of or in the course of the employment.

Lord Parker of Waddington said that by no stretch of the imagination could the events here be described as "accidental". He considered that it would be equally artificial to hold that what happened arose out of Mr Kelly's employment.

By such a narrow margin, and after the display of such learning, Mrs Kelly held her £100 award.

If I have done nothing else by referring to these two cases and showing the conflicts of judicial opinion, I think I have certainly shown how the Workmen's Compensation Acts produced such work for judges, counsel and solicitors. Also two other things: how much lawyers had cause to bless "matters of principle", which spur litigants on from Court to Court; and how we never learn – because after the example of the Workmen's Compensation Acts we have had the Rent Acts and others which, intended to simplify, have in fact complicated.

An American at the beginning of this century whose Presidential candidate had been defeated largely by the Irish vote, greatly interested Lord Russell of Killowen by saying that he was going to take his holidays in Ireland.

"Why Ireland?" asked Lord Russell.

"Because," was the reply, "it's about the only country in the world where the Irish don't rule."

Cooke v. Midland Great Western Railway of Ireland

 1909

MASTER COOKE, AGED four at the relevant time, is ensured a place in legal history by this leading case, but I think it is right that history should not regard him as a ragamuffin as some of the legal textbooks suggest – a sort of aggressive hooligan, seventy years ahead of his time – or regard him, despite the harsh description of those non-legal-aid days, as being truly "a pauper". He was in fact the perfectly respectable son of a perfectly respectable chemist in Navan, the county town of County Meath. (Crossword devotees will no doubt have noticed the palindrome.)

Master Cooke became famous because his case laid down that where a railway company's servants knew that children were in the habit of trespassing and playing with a turntable on the company's land, to which they obtained ready access by a well-worn gap, there was evidence of actionable negligence fit to go to a jury.

The decision of the House of Lords is to this day a leading authority on this point concerning children (frequently referred to as "allurement"), and also in certain respects concerning adults.

Master Cooke sued by his father and "*in forma pauperis*", as it was in those days. He nevertheless had the fortune to secure the services of Mr William D. Sullivan, Solicitor of Navan, and no less a team of counsel than the Solicitor-General for Ireland (Redmond Barry), Dudley White, both of the Irish Bar, and Stebbing. In winning the appeal he got what were described as "pauper costs here and below".

The case went through no fewer than four courts. At the trial before Lord Chief Justice O'Brien and a jury the plaintiff won and got £550 damages. The King's Bench Divisional Court in Ireland, presided over by Chief Baron Palles, affirmed that judgment (Mr Justice Kenny dissenting). The Court of Appeal in Ireland unanimously reversed the judgment; the House of Lords unanimously restored it.

Lord McNaghten said that the true question was substantively that put to the jury by the Lord Chief Justice: would a person of common sense and intelligence placed in the position of the railway company and possessed of its knowledge have recognised the danger of injury to children playing with the turntable, and would he have stopped the practice or taken precautions?

He pointed out that the turntable was unfenced, unlocked and unfastened and that the ground where it stood was half-derelict – "devoted or abandoned to the sustenance of the railway-inspector's goat and the diversion of the youth of Navan".

Lord Atkinson, an Irishman, spoke of the propensity of children, particularly boys, to meddle with things which attracted or allured them, and said that if people left such things in a dangerous state and knew the likelihood of trespass they were liable. And he pointed out that in spite of "No Trespassers" notices, as here, they were of no avail where the practice was known and nothing was done.

Lord Collins, also Irish, said that the facts were such that no jury could properly infer leave and licence, even invitation, to the children to enter upon the land. However, the company's inactivity was "a form of benevolence which ought not to be encouraged".

The Lord Chancellor, Lord Loreburn, gave what can only be regarded as a grudging assent. With no pun intended he said, "I think this case is near the line."

Master Cooke, therefore, held his verdict, substantial damages in terms of seventy years ago, for a seriously injured leg.

There have been many allurement cases since, but this is the leading case in the field. "Allurement" is not of course a word applicable in this context to adults but the case has adult importance. It establishes that if a person has a tacit licence or invitation to enter upon land or to make use of an object then the owner of the land or object must take reasonable care to avoid danger or injury.

It would be nice to think that the youthful Cooke had blazed a clear trail for all subsequent mischievous children, but that alas is not so, because the numerous allurement cases since do not (I say it with respect) show complete consistency. Thus, amongst the things not found to allure children are a swing, a chute, a scaffold with a rope coiled round a pulley, a trench, a hole and a pile of mortars. Those regarded as allurements included a bomb-damaged house in course of demolition, waste ground containing glass, a moving staircase, a paddling pool and a tree close to a footpath, which apparently called out to be climbed by little boys but which had above it a live electric cable.

There was a well-known and well-liked member of the Munster Circuit during the period before the 1914–18 War named Paddy Fleming. He was not exactly an epigrammatist in the Wilde tradition, nor exactly a Dr Spooner. He was just Paddy Fleming, whose style of language became known as Flemish. On one occasion when a judge, whom he did not particularly like, corrected him on some point, and was correct in his correction, Paddy Fleming bowed and said, "Your Lordship is right and I am wrong as Your Lordship invariably is."

Roger Casement
 1916

FOUND GUILTY OF High Treason during the First World War, his appeal dismissed, Roger Casement was hanged at Pentonville Prison, London, on 3 August 1916. He was fifty-two.

In Casement, Britain found an unlikely traitor and Ireland an unexpected martyr.

He was a strange, solitary man, fervent in all he did, dignified in appearance and manner, difficult to work with but a prodigious worker, talented and courageous. He was also a prolific writer of letters and memoranda of great length and (to his cost) a compulsive hoarder of documents.

Were it not for his trial and execution and for the use or abuse of the controversial Black Diaries, as they came to be called, he would have a far smaller place in British or Irish history and memories. That place would have rested upon his splendid work in exposing colonial abuses in the Belgian Congo and in South America. Although still young when he died, he would not have been likely to accomplish anything more of a noteworthy kind, if only because his health was in decline.

For Britain, Roger Casement had done valuable work in the Foreign Service and had been knighted in 1911. In Ireland his name was, of course, known for his great work abroad, but few ordinary people knew of any activities of his for Ireland until his arrest, which coincided with the period of the 1916 Easter Rising. He has become associated with the Rising and regarded as one of the men of Easter Week.

In many British eyes Casement came to be seen not only as a traitor but as a pervert, too, whose exploits (real, imaginary

171

or a mixture of both) with boys and youths were fully recorded in diaries found on his arrest in luggage left by him at a previous lodgings in Ebury Street, near Victoria, in London. To many Irishmen the suggestion of immorality derived from the Black Diaries was a vile calumny on an honourable man and the Diaries were in their relevant parts forged or, as some maintained, genuine enough but merely copies made by Casement in the course of duty of material he had found when on service abroad.

It is right to say that nobody who had known or dealt with Casement over the years ever suspected, or had reason to suspect, that he was a pervert. It was the Diaries and the then construction put upon a later friendship which first suggested that he was a homosexual and/or compiler of erotica. I deal with this friendship later.

The suggestion of homosexuality, be it true or false, has no place in modern thinking but it was a very important matter in 1916. The Diaries remain important still because of the use made of them.

From what has been said above it will come as no surprise to find that a lot of what has been written about Roger Casement is violently partisan one way or the other. Two books from the same publishing house, Odhams, in 1961 and 1966 respectively, illustrate this graphically. In the first, *The Judges and The Judged* by Edgar Lustgarten, the treatment is bitterly hostile to Casement. In the other, *World Famous Trials* by Charles Franklin, it is strongly sympathetic. He seems destined for rival approaches forever.

Quite a literature has been built up about Casement, and there are a number of full-length books which deal with the Diaries and the question of homosexuality from rival points of view.

Roger Casement was one of four children (three boys and a girl) of a Protestant North of Ireland couple. It was a true accident of birth that he happened to be born in the South in 1864 in a seaside village near Dublin called Sandycove. The parents died when the children were still small and they were brought up by relatives – Roger in Ballymena (a large town north of Belfast), where he attended the local academy.

172

After leaving school, Roger Casement got a clerkship in a shipping firm in Liverpool and then a position with the Elder Dempster Line, which first introduced him to West Africa.

In West Africa, the Belgian Congo, then being exploited, was his immediate and intense interest. In 1892 he got appointed to the British Foreign Service (perhaps a more accurate description is attached himself to and became adopted by the Service). In between important postings connected with the developing South African crisis and eventual Boer War, he researched the Congo and sent voluminous reports to London revealing atrocities and cruelties against the natives. He was never given to brevity and was a prolific incessant writer.

It is ironic that during the period of the Boer War he reported on the activities of a Major MacBride and a Colonel Lynch, who were seeking to form an Irish Brigade from prisoners of war taken by the Boers. Being Irish was an advantage, but not an essential, for this force, which, in fact, achieved neither the membership nor the success hoped for by its promoters. It is ironic for four reasons. Firstly, because it was a similar activity which led to Casement's own trial less than twenty years later. Secondly, because Lynch was tried and convicted in England for High Treason in the same circumstances and under the same 1381 statute as Casement. Thirdly, because their subsequent histories were markedly different – Lynch was reprieved, released within a few months and lived on to become a respected and strongly loyal MP at Westminster. And fourthly, because Major MacBride became one of the leaders of the Easter Week Rising in Ireland and was executed for his part in it.

Roger Casement's final report on conditions in the Congo was issued by the Foreign Office in February 1904 and its catalogue of cruelty had a profound and international effect. His report was rather unexpectedly corroborated in some important respects by a Commission set up by King Leopold of the Belgians, which reported at the end of 1905. A grateful government rewarded Casement by making him a Companion of the Order of St Michael and St George.

It appears to have been from about 1904 and on his periodic

visits to Ireland that Casement became progressively interested in the cause of Irish Nationalism. If during the next nine
years British Intelligence knew anything of this it was not
treated at all seriously, and in 1911 he was knighted.

By then he had served as Consul at various places in South
America and in 1910 and 1911 he headed, as a natural choice,
the British mission of investigation into allegations of inhuman
treatment of natives in the Putamayo basin, adjoining the
borders of Peru, Colombia, Brazil and Ecuador.

This was another task of Congo proportions and meant two
years' hard work in trying conditions. There is no doubt that
Casement's health suffered as a result of both expeditions.

When informed of his knighthood he wrote a very fulsome
letter of thanks and appreciation to Sir Edward Grey. It was read
and strongly relied upon at his trial and left a bad impression.

In June 1912 the Putamayo Report was published. Again it
revealed extensive cruelty, again it received wide and favour-
able publicity at home and abroad. Casement had repeated
his previous success and was rightly regarded as an outstanding
humanitarian.

In the middle of 1913 he resigned from the British Foreign
Service giving as his ground ill-health, which was certainly
present although nothing precise or specific existed. It may be
that in part, even in large part, his object was to devote himself
to Irish affairs. He was granted a pension of a little over £400
a year, which was his right. It was one which was not paid
automatically but had to be applied for quarterly. There was
nothing sinister in that; its purpose was the cautious and
mundane one of making the applicant show that he was still
alive. The last pension he drew was in June 1914.

For at least two or three years before then he had been in
contact with members of the militant Irish movement. It does
not seem, however, that he ever held any recognised position
in any of the militant Irish organisations.

Whether he was an official, semi-official or entirely unofficial
emissary of Irish Republicans it is impossible to say but, on
4 July 1914, exactly a month before war was declared, he
travelled to America. There he met Irish-Americans and with
their help canvassed for money, arms and war supplies for
Ireland.

Through the German Ambassador he was invited to Germany and sailed for there on 15 October 1914, under a false name in a Norwegian ship. Although the Royal Navy made a routine interception and examination, he got through.

When he went to Germany Casement was fifty years of age. He was accompanied by a curious character named Adler Christensen, who was a Norwegian sailor of about twenty-four. They had met casually in New York. Whatever the circumstances of their coming together they were in fact together for some eighteen months, until Casement left Germany for Ireland with other companions but not Christensen. During that eighteen months Christensen acted as a general assistant or secretary to Casement. For a considerable part of it there was, on Christensen's account, a quite absurd episode when the British Minister in Norway was trying to bribe him to get Casement into British hands. The allegedly continual efforts to do this enraged Casement but obviously caused Christensen some amusement.

Few who knew Christensen had any good to say of him. Thus the fairly obvious inference of a homosexual relationship was subsequently made, but beyond the fact of the association, a strange association, there is no evidence of any immorality. Casement held him out as a young man whom he had befriended and who did useful work for him. It was an odd association but Casement was an odd man and Christensen just the sort of person to attach himself to somebody who had some money, the entrée to high-up people in Germany and the prospect of importance. And when Casement went to Ireland he left Christensen behind.

Other theories about Christensen include the one that he was in reality a British spy placed literally at Casement's elbow and that he was a potential witness for the Crown at Casement's trial. Spies are notoriously improbable, and anything is possible in love or war, but if Christensen were a spy he would achieve a new high (or a new low).

If, on the other hand, Adler Christensen were a homosexual partner and companion then he is the first and only one traceable to Casement. And it was a fully open association – whether that signifies one way or the other.

In Germany, Roger Casement received neither the welcome

nor the help which he had expected. In particular, there was no inclination on the German side to supply men or arms for a revolt in Ireland. He proposed the formation of an Irish Legion from the Irish prisoners of war in German hands and for this purpose he was, after difficulty, given facilities. He was not proposing – as Lynch had been – that the Legion should fight against their old companions in the trenches; he stressed all the time that it was to fight for Ireland in Ireland – but, of course, against the Crown. And what he continued to hope for was a hefty supplement of German soldiers and a good supply of arms.

During the remainder of 1914 and in 1915, he addressed Irish prisoners of war, specially assembled in certain camps (particularly one at Limburg) along these lines. He received in general a hostile reception, and of a total of some 2,500 prisoners it is thought that he recruited no more than about eighty and that many of these quickly recanted.

Two things have been said which call for comment. One is the assertion that prisoners of war who did not co-operate were punished by being put on poorer rations. The other that Britain arranged with Germany to exchange prisoners of war who would be able to give evidence against Casement at his trial. It seems probable that neither suggestion is correct, but it is impossible to be dogmatic. The probability is that rations were improved for those who were assembled in the special camps and then reverted in respect of those who did not volunteer to the meagre, progressively deteriorating, rations of ordinary prisoners. So far as exchange is concerned, it is quite clear that a number of men who had heard Casement in the eighteen months or so of his active recruiting were received back in England on exchange in the ordinary course.

Casement was becoming very disillusioned with Germany and the Germans. They, for their part, were becoming increasingly sceptical about him as an Irish leader who could effectively help them. He was, as many had found, a difficult man to deal with. He had his own ideas and did not take kindly to contradictory ones.

He was joined in 1915 by a man called Robert Monteith, who was sent from Ireland via New York to help to get arms and men from Germany. Monteith was a former British soldier who had fought in the Boer War. He was no more successful than Casement.

By early 1916, the Germans knew that a Rising in Ireland was planned for Easter of that year. There was no offer of men and only a small offer of light arms and ammunition. In the end the latter turned out to be only 20,000 or so out-of-date rifles and they were sent in a ship called the *Aud*, which was scheduled to land them on the coast of County Kerry just before Easter.

Casement and two other men decided to go to Ireland in advance of the Rising and accompanying the *Aud*. Casement was by now disgusted with the Germans and it has been said that he was minded to try to get the Rising stopped for want of German support. The two men going with him were Monteith and Daniel Bailey, one of the recruits. They travelled by train from Berlin to Wilhelmshaven and Roger Casement characteristically retained his sleeping-berth ticket, which then became an important exhibit against him.

At Wilhelmshaven, they joined the submarine U 20 and set off for Ireland. However, she broke down and they had to return to port. There they were transferred to the U 19, which made the journey to Ireland. When off the Irish coast, she signalled but got no response, and the Commander eventually ordered Casement and his colleagues ashore by dinghy. They each carried revolvers. The place of landing was Banna Strand, a remote part of County Kerry.

The *Aud* had arrived off Tralee Bay on the previous night, but got no response to her signals either. She tried again, without success, on the Good Friday. She was then challenged by a British ship, which knew what she was despite her Norwegian pose, and the Captain scuttled her.

Monteith and Bailey left Roger Casement near the point of landing while they went off to get help. The landing party had been noticed and within a few hours he was arrested by the police. No special precautions were taken then or until he was put on the train at Tralee next day bound for London. He was indeed walked through a crowded Tralee in handcuffs on his way to the station. At no time was any attempt of any sort made to rescue him; it would not have been difficult.

In London, Roger Casement was first put in Brixton Prison,

then in the Tower. In explanation of the latter, it was emphasised that he was being treated as a military prisoner.

However, the authorities decided to proceed against him under the ordinary criminal law for High Treason committed in Germany. No charge was made in respect of the landing in Ireland, none in respect of the Easter Rising, and accordingly there was no question of a trial in Ireland.

Meantime, the Easter Rising had taken place and had been quelled. The leaders of it had been executed. The Rising was not as extensive as originally planned because last-minute orders had been given to call it off. Casement might have advocated calling it off, but his voice could not be heard.

In London he retained as his solicitor George Gavan Duffy, who was then practising there. Gavan Duffy was bearded like his client, and so was the leading counsel eventually chosen. Gavan Duffy was later an Irish delegate to the Treaty negotiations and a signatory of the Treaty. He was subsequently a barrister in Dublin and then President of the Irish High Court.

There are indications that at the outset and at many stages during the period before the trial, Roger Casement was minded to conduct his own case. One who urged him to do so was George Bernard Shaw.

It is quite clear that Casement believed from the very beginning of the war that he was committing High Treason according to British Law, and that as a British subject he would be tried for it and sentenced to death if captured. He had no faith or hope in the defence eventually put forward on his behalf. His attitude was that he was an Irishman acting for Ireland.

On 15 May 1916 Casement was committed for trial from Bow Street Magistrates' Court on the charges of suborning or attempting to suborn the Irish prisoners in Germany, contrary to the Statute of Treason, 1381.

Bailey appeared with Casement in the dock on similar charges, but no evidence was offered against him. He seems to have adopted the line that he only acted as he did in order to be released from German custody and enabled to get home.

Monteith was never caught and subsequently went to live in America. He wrote a book about the whole affair which was published in Dublin in 1953.

In Britain, then two years through a war of heavy casualties, feeling ran high against Casement. He had served under the Crown, he had accepted honours from the Crown, he was, as the ordinary man or woman saw it, an obvious traitor.

In Ireland, on the other hand, and in America too, angry about the executions after Easter Week, he assumed the mantle of a hero. He became and remains one of the men of Easter Week, though in strict fact, of course, he took no part in the Rising. Nor was any charge in respect of the Rising made against him.

A junior counsel was readily chosen: Artemus Jones, who was afterwards a County Court judge, but whose fame rests upon his having been the successful plaintiff in libel proceedings which became a leading case in the House of Lords under the name Hulton v. Jones. A fictional story in a paper figured a character called Artemus Jones as being seen abroad with a woman who was not his wife. It was held that the reference was defamatory of this Artemus Jones however much it was intended and believed that the choice was an imaginary name and character.

A distinguished constitutional lawyer, Professor Morgan, was an additional junior counsel. But there was urgent need for a leading counsel capable of matching the Attorney-General, F. E. Smith. It is said that Sir John Simon was approached and refused, and that the famous Irish advocate Tim Healy also refused. The choice, then, fell upon a distinguished counsel of the Irish Bar named Serjeant Sullivan. There had for many years been in both countries a rank between Queen's or King's Counsel and the Bench known as Serjeants at Law. The rank was abolished in England before it was in Ireland and there were by 1916 a dwindling number of Serjeants left, all of the Irish Bar. Sullivan was at the time about fifty and he lived on to be the last of the Serjeants. He was married with twelve children, and a few years after the Casement case, with his large family and little money, he bravely transferred practice to the English Bar, to which he lent great distinction.

At the time of the Casement trial, Sullivan did not have the precedence of a Serjeant, or a King's Counsel, at the English Bar, except before the House of Lords and the Privy Council.

Accordingly, he appeared in his role of an ordinary barrister of the English Bar.

The Attorney-General led distinguished counsel: Sir George Cave (the Solicitor-General), Travers Humphreys (later a High Court judge), Bodkin and Branson. The two last-named became respectively Director of Public Prosecutions and a High Court judge.

Something of the order of £1,540 was raised for Casement's defence. £700 of that sum was contributed by Sir Arthur Conan Doyle and £200 by Mr William Cadbury.

The trial was fixed for 26 June 1916 and was to be that rare occurrence, "a trial at bar", that is notionally a trial before all judges of the King's Bench Division but in practice before three judges, instead of one, plus a jury. No longer being in military custody, Casement was not in the Tower but in the civilian remand prison, Brixton. The trial was held at the Law Courts in London and not at the Old Bailey. The celebrated Lavery painting of it shows the trial in progress in the Lord Chief Justice's Court.

There is no doubt that copies of the Black Diaries had been circulated before trial because they had been referred to in the press. It is also quite plain that the prosecution wanted the defence to see them; Serjeant Sullivan, who has spoken and written about the case to a quite remarkable extent, has said that the prosecution persisted in attempts to get the defence to see them.

He believed that the prosecution, sensitive of American opinion at a crucial time in the war, wanted him to base a defence of insanity on the Diaries and that they would co-operate.

In practice, Casement's lawyers would not look at the Diaries and Casement would not tolerate a plea of insanity.

I find the Crown interest in insanity a fascinating one because I cannot see how it could have been raised in any shape or form.

To state the conclusive point first: Roger Casement was not and never had been insane in any legal sense of the word. If, in a colloquial sense, "he must have been mad to do what he did", it was only in a colloquial sense. He knew perfectly well what he was doing at all times, intended to do it and, far from not knowing whether it was right or wrong, firmly believed that it was right. He was not insane when captured or when awaiting trial. He gave full instructions for his defence, he spoke at his trial in clear terms, and it is to be assumed beyond argument that he would not have been executed if there was any doubt as to his sanity because it was, in the days of capital punishment, the long-established practice in England to have detailed medical examinations between verdict and execution date and to reprieve in the case of insanity, indeed if there was even real doubt about the question.

That disposes of insanity as a question in the case, but it leaves a huge question-mark which I have never seen dealt with in any detail as to what the prosecution had in mind.

Was it to be a submission of Unfitness to Plead? This, if successful, would have meant remand at His Majesty's pleasure at Broadmoor.

Or was it to be a plea to the indictment of Guilty but Insane? This, if successful, would have meant the same result.

On either it would not suffice for the Crown to accept the plea. It would be a matter for the Court and it would require evidence.

For Unfitness to Plead it would have to be shown that Casement had such illness of mind that he could not properly instruct lawyers to defend him or properly defend himself. This would have been ridiculous to suggest.

For a substantive defence of Guilty but Insane the Court would have had to be satisfied under the old, much criticised, McNaghten Rules that at the time of the acts alleged against him Casement did not know the nature and quality of such acts or that they were wrong. It is to be remembered that the acts in question were over long periods in 1915 and 1916.

Homosexuality or the making or keeping of erotic material are not, any of them, insanity. Nor are they, without more, even evidence of it. They might become evidence of it, and even strong evidence of it, if there were something else to support them.

The Black Diaries could, therefore, have been a step towards proof of insanity, but only a step. Much more would have been necessary.

A point which seems to me deadly against their having any

value at all is that they related to a period years before the crimes alleged. Moreover, for a plea of insanity to succeed it would have had to cover the whole long period of Casement's stay in Germany in 1915 and 1916.

What, then, had the prosecution in mind? Did they not see that a Court could not possibly be satisfied of insanity on the material available?

There can be no question of the prosecution seeking to trick the defence or lead them into some trap. That is inconceivable. But what did they think as they pressed the defence not once, spontaneously, but frequently, deliberately, to consider the Diaries?

The problem is a most interesting one. It goes to the very root of the planning of the prosecution.

I think the only possible explanation is that the prosecution were serious (but wildly in error) in floating the idea of accepting a plea of Guilty but Insane; that they had no evidence of it apart from the Black Diaries; and that their co-operation would consist of seeking medical evidence. The fatal objection was that no Court could possibly accept the plea unless there was very strong evidence apart from the Black Diaries, which there was not.

In the event, the ultimate question of insanity never arose. Casement would not hear of it, his advisers would not consider it, and he was not insane.

According to Serjeant Sullivan, in his book *The Last Serjeant* (Macdonald 1952), written in his retirement, the last approach was made just before the trial began. Presumably, if favourably reacted to by the defence an adjournment – a sensational adjournment – would have had to be sought.

As it was the case went on and the defence as planned was two-fold: mainly, that the Statute of Treason 1381 did not apply, and secondly, that intention was a necessary element and Casement had only an intent to aid his fellow-Irishmen. The second ground had in it a pointed comparison with F. E. Smith himself and Carson having sought before the war to arm "Ulster" in favour of continued Union even against the wishes of the United Kingdom government.

The main point turned on the meaning of the Statute of Treason 1381, which was in Norman French. A translation will suffice to illustrate the point. The translation is given with punctuation, but should be re-read omitting all punctuation in order to see if there is any difference. The relevant provisions were that it was treason where there was "Levying war upon the King within his realm: Being adherent to the King's enemies within his realm, giving them aid and comfort within the realm or elsewhere."

Serjeant Sullivan's point was that adhering to the King's enemies outside the realm was not within the statute. A superficial impression that this would be very strange was in his argument readily explicable by having regard to the history of the time when the enactment was made and by noting that treason outside the realm could within strict conditions be otherwise dealt with under procedure then available but now disused.

The trial Judges were Lord Reading, Lord Chief Justice (Rufus Isaacs), Mr Justice Avory and Mr Justice Horridge. Avory, J., had experience of the main point having, as counsel in the Lynch case, unsuccessfully raised it then.

At the very beginning of the trial Serjeant Sullivan sought to quash the indictment on the basis that it did not disclose a crime. This would seem to have been the right course, taken at the right time, but the Court ruled that the submission should be made at the end of the prosecution's case.

Then came the swearing-in of the jury. Challenges by the defence, stand-bys for the Crown, were not well known or much practised at the English Bar at that time, but in Ireland they had been a regular feature for years. Serjeant Sullivan caused considerable surprise by copious challenges. When challenging "for cause" after his peremptory challenges were exhausted, he was not, in fact, called upon to show the cause. Not to be left out, the Crown took to requiring prospective jurors to stand-by. Seventy-one prospective jurors were dealt with by challenge or stand-by.

The Attorney-General, F. E. Smith (Sir Frederick Smith KC), opened the case for the prosecution and did so in deadly fashion. He stressed Casement's links with the Crown, dwelt on his fulsome knighthood letter and outlined the evidence that would be called to prove the events mentioned above. At the end of his speech he said that the prisoner "was blinded by hatred of Britain as malignant in quality as it was sudden in origin [and] has played a desperate hand. He has played it and lost it. Now the forfeit is claimed."

Getting on for thirty witnesses were called in support of the various matters to be proved, including the landing, the arrest and interrogations. The most striking were the Irish ex-prisoners of war who deposed to Casement's attempts to get them to join an Irish Legion. In cross-examination of them Serjeant Sullivan simply sought to emphasise that Casement tried to recruit them for an Irish Legion for use in Ireland and not as part or an ally of the German forces. The Easter Week Rising did not come into the case at all because, of course, no Irish Legion took part in it and Casement arrived in Ireland with only two companions only a few days before it and took no part in it.

At the end of the prosecution case Serjeant Sullivan renewed his submission. It was dealt with at length by both sides. The Crown submitted that logically and naturally the words of the statute covered treason beyond the realm. Where the defence contended that the relevant part required two things (i) adherence within and (ii) giving aid and comfort within or without, the Crown submitted that (ii) alone was sufficient.

The Court rejected the defence submission – as did a five-judge Court of Criminal Appeal later. Lawyers and others have often rehearsed the point since. For a full appreciation of the rival submissions it is, of course, necessary to read them closely and to study the judgments. This author respectfully feels that although Serjeant Sullivan's point was ingenious, the statute really covered treason within and without the realm. It would be strange if only those within the realm could commit treason; stranger still if they could commit it without but only provided that they were within. Punctuation would seem to assist the prosecution's interpretation, but even without it the meaning would seem to be clearly that way.

Roger Casement himself, I believe, did not set any real hope on either of the defence points. He seems from his letters and statements always to have appreciated that his relevant actions were treasonable under English Law. His great argument was that to him and many of his fellow-countrymen

184

they were far from being treasonable and were in fact praise-worthy. He saw nothing odd or wrong in having served Britain and then for the sake of Ireland turning against her.

When the main point failed, the defence began its case. No witnesses were called and Roger Casement made a short and forceful statement from the dock. This is a familiar alternative to not giving evidence or giving evidence on oath and being open to cross-examination. In his statement he strongly refuted some suggestions which had been expressly or impliedly made against him. He said that the pension he had received had been earned, the honours he got were not in his power to refuse, he had never asked anyone to fight for Germany, there was no German money behind him nor behind any of his activities, and that it was untrue that any of the Irish prisoners of war had had their rations reduced. He was a tall, dignified figure, who spoke clearly and well, and undoubtedly made a certain impression on a largely and naturally hostile audience.

Serjeant Sullivan then began his final speech to the jury. It was an eloquent speech which dwelt largely on the Irish aspect of the prisoner's actions and sought to show that they were not intended to be treasonable and should not be held to be so in the particular circumstances. When dealing with the Ulster situation, he came in for interruption from the Lord Chief Justice and the Attorney-General, both of whom said that there was nothing in the evidence to support his incursion into that sphere. He was put off his stride and shortly afterwards said that he could not continue. The Lord Chief Justice readily adjourned the case until the next morning, 29 June. The Serjeant had collapsed completely (the strain had been very great), and he was unable to be present next day. Artemus Jones finished the speech for the defence.

The prosecution had the right to the last word and their speech reiterated the points made in evidence and said that intention was irrelevant but could, in any case, be inferred from the prisoner's very actions. The Attorney-General made much play of a German code found on Casement, and by reference to specific parts of it showed how it could be used for German purposes. In fact, Casement came by the code quite casually and not only had not used it but was most unlikely ever to use it. He was simply a hoarder. The prosecution's

185

point was, however, a perfectly fair one and, in the particular context of the case, a telling one.

After a short summing-up by the Lord Chief Justice, the jury retired just before 3 p.m. They returned after fifty-five minutes with their verdict – Guilty.

Casement was asked if there was anything he had to say why sentence of death should not be passed upon him. The speech from the dock is an old Irish tradition and intended by the speaker in no way for the Court but for the people and posterity. I have often wondered how Courts through the years have allowed speeches of the kind which Casement in fact made. His was an hour-long speech of a clearly political, Irish nationalist, character. It was impressive and made plain how Irish nationalism had, for a long time, been at the forefront of his mind. In one passage he said, "The Unionist champions chose a path they felt would lead to the Woolsack, while I went a road I knew must lead to the dock."

His speech was not interrupted at any stage by the Bench, but F. E. Smith walked out of Court during it.

At the end of it, Roger Casement was duly sentenced to death. He was thereupon removed to the condemned cell at Pentonville Prison.

On advice, but without any personal hope, he appealed to the Court of Criminal Appeal. The appeal was heard on 17 and 18 July 1916 before Mr Justices Darling, Bray, Lawrence, Scrutton and Atkin. The point taken was the one about the interpretation of the statute. The appeal was dismissed.

For a further appeal, to the House of Lords, the leave of the Attorney-General was required. This legal anomaly was particularly unfortunate in this case where the Attorney-General himself was the main prosecuting counsel and had a personal record and political view very antipathetic to Casement. It was even more unfortunate that he should have refused his leave. An appeal to the highest tribunal never took long to come on for hearing in a capital case, the point in question had never been before the House of Lords and the whole case merited the view of being particularly important. The refusal of leave could only bequeath some residual doubt about the law and a feeling that the Accused had been finally judged by his principal Accuser. It would have been wiser to have given leave, but it should be realised by critics that the final appeal would have failed.

After the appeal to the Court of Criminal Appeal had been dismissed, there were strong representations made for a reprieve. There was considerable actual and potential sympathy in America, not then in the war, and it is said that copies of the Black Diaries were extensively used to stifle sympathy. If it were so, it is a sad commentary on all concerned, not least on the recipients. The Diaries had no relevance.

A reprieve was refused. Many believe, for varying reasons, that it should have been granted. The scaffold makes martyrs.

Roger Casement was received into the Catholic Church shortly before he was executed. He was stripped of his honours.

In 1965, forty-nine years after his death, Roger Casement's remains were exhumed from his grave within Pentonville Prison and sent to Dublin. They now lie buried in Glasnevin Cemetery, Dublin, near the O'Connell Monument and tomb. A space had been reserved for them there for years.

Roger Casement will ever be an odd character in English and Irish history, one whose immortality really rests on his trial and execution. He was by all accounts a brave man throughout. From what I can judge, he was a very solitary, very fervent man – probably always a very sad and lonely man. In history, he is an accident.

A judge in Cork once did that most dangerous of all things: he chided a jury for not agreeing on a verdict. This was too much for one of the jury, who with the forthrightness of a Corkman, said, "Steady on, Me Lord, I agreed with you."

Tim Healy – Advocate and Politician

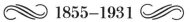 1855–1931

THE HEALYS AND the Sullivans from County Cork have provided several prominent politicians and lawyers in Ireland and England. Much inter-marrying has made them seem one family and it is far from easy to disentangle the relationships.

Taking the great Tim Healy as the centre-point, one finds that he married T. D. Sullivan MP's daughter, and that his brother Maurice Healy, who became a solicitor, married a daughter of A. M. Sullivan MP. Those Sullivans were brothers. The Serjeant Sullivan so well known at the Irish Bar and at the English Bar was a son of the A. M. Sullivan. Maurice Healy, author of that delightful book, *The Old Munster Circuit*, was Maurice Healy's son.

To add to the confusion, one of Tim Healy's daughters married a Sullivan, who was I believe not related to the other family. He was Timothy Sullivan, who became Chief Justice of the Irish Free State as the new state was first called.

When it is noted that Serjeant Sullivan had no fewer than twelve children the intricacies of tracing the combined family can be appreciated.

Tim Healy was an extraordinary man; for over forty years he was an Irish Member of Parliament at Westminster and a leading advocate. He tried, like his old friend and political opponent Edward Carson, to make a career at the English Bar; the general opinion at the Irish Bar was that he would succeed but Carson not. The reverse proved to be the case and it was in Ireland that Tim had his big legal successes. Politics played some part in this, for Healy was a fervent Nationalist and Carson an equally fervent Unionist.

As a young man, Tim was jailed for the prevalent offence of holding a banned meeting. The penalty imposed was a fine with six months' imprisonment in lieu. Tim enthusiastically chose the alternative, which greatly increased his support in Ireland. Gaol had a touch of martyrdom about it. In fact he confessed that it was boredom.

He had great facility for speech, and at times great felicity, too. But he had a bitterness of tongue which could outrival even Carson's.

In the Westminster Parliament he was christened Tiger Tim. Lord Curzon of Kedleston described him as being "the most talented member of the Irish Party, with an unsurpassed gift of corrosive humour and almost diabolical irony".

F. E. Smith (Lord Birkenhead), not himself wholly lacking in those commodities, again used the word corrosive in respect of him, saying, "He possessed a power of corrosive sarcasm the like of which I have never met elsewhere. I can still see him standing up to address the House, his chin aggressively protruded, his expression one of melancholy gravity, pouring out a long succession of bitter and wounding insults. His wit was as extraordinary as his invective."

In Parnell's heyday Tim Healy was a strong and prominent supporter of his, but after the O'Shea affair he broke with Parnell.

In the Parnellite days, Tim harboured a grudge against Joseph Chamberlain for having let down the Irish Party. On one occasion, when Parnell was absent from the House, Chamberlain was incautious enough to say of the boisterous Irish Party, "When the cat's away the mice will play." Healy quickly cried out, "And what about the rats?"

One Irish newspaper described him as "a volcano in constant eruption". And of his political career he once wrote, to his brother, "The hissing of the mob is music in my ears."

There were various splits in the Irish Party after the Parnell débâcle, and at one particular stage it split 83–1. "There are, Mr Speaker," said Healy, "two united Irish Parties in this House and I am one of them."

A silly, schoolboyish story of him is when a pompous member speaking in the House said of him that his rhetoric was all very well but when it really mattered he wouldn't say boo to a goose. He paused for breath and Tim popped to his feet, stuck out his head and neck towards his opponent and said – "Boo."

The splendid satirical magazine *Private Eye* is not, in fact, the originator of connecting Uganda and Ugandan affairs with other things. In 1902 the Prime Minister, Mr Arthur Balfour, introduced as urgent business the matter of making a railway in Uganda. This involved passing over a lot of Irish business. Tim Healy suddenly intervened to speak as "a native of Uganda" and made all the references he wanted to about Irish affairs relating them to Uganda.

At the Irish Bar, too, he was a master of sarcasm and ridicule. On one occasion a polite old Chancery judge said to him in a kindly way, "I'm afraid, Mr Healy, I do not understand that point." Tim replied, "I never thought for one moment your Lordship would, but I had to mention it in case I needed it on appeal."

He once asked a witness in cross-examination, "In your view is truth a virtue or a vice?"

He disarmingly, and successfully, submitted to one judge that both sides were lying (his own side as well as the other) and that since his side were the defendants they were entitled to judgment because the opponents had not proved their case.

He referred to a decision of the House of Lords as being "the Voice of Infallibility, speaking by a majority of 3 to 2".

I am indebted to Mr Justice James D'Arcy of the Irish High Court for important corrections in a Tim Healy story which I told elsewhere. The proper version is this. In a breach of promise action, Healy was faced with cross-examining a plaintiff who was heavily veiled, to conceal her age and her looks. Tim Healy's first question was to ask her to remove her "yashmak". When she expressed ignorance as to what he meant he said, "Kindly uncocoon yourself, madam." Eventually she had to. And in his speech to the jury he said, "Gentlemen, the sight you saw during my cross-examination has not been witnessed since the day the Board of Works stripped the ivy off the ruins of Muckross Abbey."

On another occasion, a judge said, "I hope, Healy, that my Charge to that jury did not seem too biased." "Biased," exclaimed Tim, "Your Lordship does not know the meaning of the word."

A barrister, whom he disliked, changed his name. I will disguise it. His name for years had been, say, Coonan. He put a prefix and a hyphen before it so that he became Cooke-Coonan. In the Counsel's Robing-Room in Ennis a colleague sought to warn Tim of this lest he should call the other man Coonan. "He's not Coonan any more," explained the barrister, "he's now Cooke-Coonan." "Ah," boomed Tim, busy robing for the Court, "Cook on the mother's side I presume."

He once led my father in a case about possession of a house. With leaders and experts on both sides the case was costing a fortune. Tim himself had a lovely house at Chapelizod on the edge of Dublin called Ardaulin. At the pre-trial consultation he said to my father when they were alone, "Litigation is a form of madness. If somebody claimed possession of Ardaulin from me I'd fight them until they issued proceedings, then I'd give it to them. It would be cheaper and less worrying in the long run."

A solicitor once asked him to reduce his fee because the case had settled and he had not had to do or say much in the end. "No," he replied firmly, "I spent a lot of time thinking about it."

To a solicitor who sent him endless further observations about a case he wrote, "Ammunition is what I want, not stores."

When the Treaty of 1922 came into force and twenty-six of the thirty-two counties of Ireland became a Dominion known as the Irish Free State, a first Governor-General was needed. Somewhat unexpectedly, perhaps, Tim Healy was chosen. He had mellowed a lot and turned out to be an excellent choice. He moved to live in the Vice-Regal Lodge in the Phoenix Park and, as if to signify the change from Tiger Tim, it became known as Uncle Tim's Cabin.

His epitaph he himself pronounced years before when he said, "I'm no man's man but Ireland's."

Tim Healy's opponent in a case, which was called on at about 3.15 p.m., asked the Judge for an adjournment until the next morning. When asked why, he said, "I have been on my feet arguing all day in the adjacent Court and I am, I confess, much exhausted." The Judge turned to Tim who said, "I would agree to an adjournment, my Lord. I too am exhausted."

"Good Heavens," said the Judge, "why should you be exhausted, Mr Healy?"

"I've been in the next Court also, my Lord, and I've been listening to my friend all day."

A judge told the Bar that he proposed to sit on the following day, Good Friday. "Very well, my Lord," said Tim Healy, "but you will be the first judge to do so since Pontius Pilate."

John Boyd Dunlop
 1920

DUNLOP OF THE tyres was a Scotsman who lived his life in Ireland, first in Belfast and then in Dublin. He was by profession a veterinary surgeon, and I have heard it said that the need for a pneumatic tyre was impressed upon him as he bicycled over the cobblestones on his rounds in Belfast. His friend Judge Bodkin KC (father of Professor Bodkin of the Barber Institute in Birmingham) says, however, that the invention was inspired by and intended for Dunlop's son Johnny. The father noticed that the son's tricycle with its solid rubber tyres cut into the ground and moved extraordinarily slowly. He considered that what was hard on the ground must be hard on the rider too.

Mr Dunlop was a man slow and deliberate in thought and speech. He had a special aptitude for science. Having had his attention drawn to the problem he thought about it deeply. He decided that the solution lay in compressed air.

On a wooden wheel, he explained to Judge Bodkin, he fitted a thin sheet of rubber, sticking on a bit of a baby's feeding bottle for a valve. Over it he put an outer covering of linen. Sticking down the sides to the wooden wheel he blew hard on the valve and produced the Dunlop pneumatic tyre.

The first "going concern" for the pneumatic tyre was little Johnny's tricycle. More work was then done to adapt the tyre for bicycles, eventually motor cars and then, of course, aircraft.

It proved difficult for Dunlop to get anybody interested in his tyre, even to the extent of using it. But patience paid and in 1889, when he was forty-nine, at the Belfast College Sports of all places, the Dunlop tyre proved itself. With misgivings, and for a consideration, a young Belfast cyclist was persuaded to ride a bicycle fitted with these tyres in the bicycle races at the Sports. His appearance for the first race was greeted with derision, but attitudes changed when he won it and when he won all the other four bicycle races on the day's card.

Success was now ensured, but here came the first of Dunlop's involvements with the law. Despite the best of endeavour and advice, it proved impossible for him to secure any really valid patent. The reason was the almost incredible one that somebody else had previously invented a pneumatic tyre, another Scotsman, a man named Thompson, some thirty years before. And although nothing had been done to develop it, it blocked Dunlop's way so far as patents were concerned.

Nevertheless the company which he formed thrived. (Poor Judge Bodkin was advised to withdraw his application for a hundred founder shares and was allowed to do so.)

It was John Boyd Dunlop's wish that his company should operate in Ireland, with its main manufacturing in Dublin. It duly set up to do so but reckoned without the Dublin Corporation.

The manufacture of tyres threw off a disagreeable but in no way over-offensive smell. The Dublin Corporation duly prosecuted the company for creating a nuisance, and as it happened thus prosecuted them out of the country altogether. Quaintly enough the Corporation lost the prosecution. But they notified their intention to appeal and that, unfortunately, was enough. The company emigrated to Coventry. It certainly seems a weak surrender by a strong man.

The achievements of the Dublin Corporation are many. Their mistakes, when made, are usually on a grand scale. This particular prosecution must rank very high in their list of mistakes. Ireland was wholly deprived of the development of an Irish invention of world-wide dimensions.

Mr Dunlop remained in Ireland and was, amongst other things, Chairman of the well-known drapers company, Todd Burns, which carried on business at the top of the Quays near O'Connell Street Bridge.

Mr Dunlop sold out his rubber company, and with it the right to the increasingly familiar portrait of him with flowing beard impressed on his tyres.

195

He had, however, two other incidents involving the law.

Famous inventors are naturally bombarded by claims from the crooked and the lunatic to be entitled to shares in the invention. Mr Dunlop was no exception but unfortunately one lunatic, a man called Prost, took the unusual course of a personal visit. Politely received and politely seen on his way, that seemed to be the end of Mr Prost. A few days later on returning home Mr Dunlop was met by his wife with the news that the man was waiting for him in the dining-room. She said that he should go for the police and she would keep the man engaged.

Mr Dunlop's suggestion that she should waste time by asking the man to set out his claim in writing was defeated when the intruder produced to Mrs Dunlop an already fully documented claim, which said ominously that it would be enforced at pistol point.

Mr Dunlop went on his way to the police and Mrs Dunlop spent a terrible time seeking to assure the lunatic that her husband would be home soon. After what seemed an eternity he returned – with four stalwart policemen led by a sergeant. As they entered the dining-room the man tried to get up from the deeply cushioned chair Mrs Dunlop had put him into. He made to pull out one of the two fully loaded revolvers he had on him but was overwhelmed. On being searched it was found that he also had a hundred extra rounds of ammunition and under his coat a dagger with an eleven-inch blade.

Prost was tried, convicted and committed to the Criminal Lunatic Asylum at Dundrum, County Dublin. From there he used to write to Mr Dunlop begging him to secure his freedom and at the same time asserting that Mr Dunlop had acknowledged his claim. But fortunately it all died down.

When he was approaching his eighties Mr Dunlop became incensed by the portraits of him which he alleged were being used in Ireland by the Dunlop Pneumatic Tyre Company Limited of London. They were, he claimed, advertisements and impressions of him placing his features upon the body of a very tall man dressed in an exaggeratedly foppish manner, wearing a tall white hat, a white waistcoat, and carrying a cane and eye-glass, none of which it was his custom to wear or carry.

In January 1920 Mr Dunlop got leave from the High Court in Dublin to serve a Writ out of the jurisdiction – in England – on the company, claiming damages and an injunction to restrict them from printing, publishing or exhibiting in Ireland any material containing pictures representing him in absurd or unsuitable costumes or attitudes or caricatures of him. He got an interim injunction and disclaimed any desire to press the claim for damages.

The company duly moved to set aside the Writ. The Judge who had first made the Order, Mr Justice Powell, dismissed their application. Their appeal to the Irish Court of Appeal (Lord Chancellor Campbell, Lords Justices Ronan and O'Connor) was dismissed.

They appealed to the House of Lords. The burden of their objection was that as a London-based company they would be embarrassed in time, expense, transport of witnesses and generally by having to fight a case in Ireland. Mr Dunlop's contention was that he was in Ireland and the mischief he wanted stopped was in Ireland. He was not alleging anything wrong in England or anywhere else.

The company had a formidable team: Sir John Simon KC, leading Tim Healy KC and the future Mr Justice Wrottesley. They said that the Courts below exercised their discretion in favour of an Irish forum wrongly, and they strongly questioned whether what was alleged was capable of being defamatory. Let the plaintiff come to England, they said, if he wants to sue on this dubious libel.

The then Lord Chancellor, Lord Birkenhead (the great F. E. Smith of the Bar and politics), was not, I feel, very gracious to the distinguished plaintiff when giving his speech, or judgment. He referred to him as "a Mr John B. Dunlop whose residence is in Dublin" and as "an old gentleman who resides in Ireland". None of their Lordships had a single word to say about his role in giving the world one of its greatest inventions.

The company's final appeal was dismissed, but the impression left in my mind is the rather sad one that they were saying that a silly old man should be allowed to sue in his own country if he really wanted to.

Nothing final was ever decided about this odd caricature case. Mr Dunlop died. He was eighty.

There has never been any requirement in Irish (or English) law that a witness should, on taking the oath, "kiss the book". It was, however, a practice that grew up in Ireland about 150 years ago and which has endured to a greater or lesser degree up to the present day.

Most Irish legal customs have developed their antidotes. Accordingly, the less scrupulous witnesses took to interposing a thumb between the cover of the book and their lips, thus avoiding – as they believed – the complete requirement of truth.

One such (a clumsy man) was detected in this trick by a County Court judge in Mayo at the beginning of this century. "Stop," he said. And, in stern tones, he addressed the witness, "You may try to deceive Almighty God, my man, but you won't deceive me."

Nearer home, I have, I regret to say, known of a witness at a Special Examination in Counsel's Chambers in London being "sworn" on a brown-paper-wrapped copy of the *Concise Oxford Dictionary*.

Erskine Childers

 1922

ONE OF THE strangest stories in history is that of Erskine
Childers.

Soldier, sailor, airman too; scholar, successful author and
Civil Servant; gun-runner before, and rebel during, the Irish
troubles which preceded the 1922 Treaty; close companion,
friend and aide of de Valera in the Treaty negotiations and
during the awful Civil War which followed it; caught and
court-martialled by the Provisional Government of the Irish
Free State; centre of widely publicised legal proceedings but
shot while his appeal was pending; father of a future President
of Ireland; he was all of these and much more. He is in many
ways one of the great mysteries of history. He was fifty-two
when he died. Had he lived he would have been sixty-two
when de Valera got into power and would have undoubtedly
held high office, probably that of Deputy Prime Minister. He
would have become well known as a top-class administrator
and probably have reached the indefinable rank of statesman.
But, on the other hand, he had enemies, many enemies,
everywhere. His tragedy was in the end not really being
accepted, truly accepted, anywhere – except by de Valera and
those close to him.

It was Childers' fate to be hated by many Irishmen and
Englishmen. They regarded him as a renegade, some of his
Irish critics openly regarding him alternatively as a spy. On
hearing of his arrest and court martial, Winston Churchill said,
"Such as he is may all who hate us be."

My uncle, Michael Comyn KC, who knew him well and who
defended him before the court martial and appeared for him

in the High Court, regarded him as an intense, utterly sincere man, a mixture of the academic and the propagandist, sensitive and brave, full of ideals and ideas. He always associated Childers with working at or carrying "his inevitable little type-writer". He had a neat, tidy mind and a flair for administration. He was well-spoken, highly intelligent and imaginative. He had a sense of fun and humour in private life, but they never surfaced in his work.

Erskine Childers was born in London on 25 June 1870 to Robert Caesar Childers and Anna Henrietta Childers, née Barton. There were five children of the marriage, which matched the five children of her brother in Ireland, who had married her husband's sister.

Childers, the father, had relations in influential positions in England. One had been Chancellor of the Exchequer and Home Secretary in Gladstone governments. He himself had been a Civil Servant in Ceylon, but had had to retire because of ill-health. Mrs Childers was a member of an old County Wicklow family, whose residence was Glan House, Annamoe – very near Parnell's estate.

When the parents died, Erskine and his brother and sisters made their home there. The head of the house was their uncle by blood, his wife their aunt by blood and the children their double first cousins. One was Robert Barton, destined to be a Home Ruler and a signatory of the Treaty in 1921. He and Erskine were close friends all their lives and, though opposed on the question of the Treaty, the relationship was such that on his final journey Erskine went to the family home and found his cousin away but instructions left behind that he was always to be received and made welcome there.

Erskine went to school at Haileybury and then went to Trinity, Cambridge. He read law and got First Class Honours, but he had no interest in and probably little aptitude for becoming a practising lawyer. He passed high into the Civil Service and was thus able to obtain one of the coveted positions of Clerk in the House of Commons.

He was a keen soldier and when the Boer War broke out he volunteered and saw active service. It is of interest that at the time and in the years after that war, he found none of the qualms about Imperialism and feelings for the rights of small nations which were later to become so much a part of him. Indeed, in the war he knew about and disapproved of the activities of John MacBride, who was prominent in the operating of an Irish-American Brigade on the Boer side. That was the John MacBride who married the great beauty Maud Gonne and who was one of the signatories to the Republican Proclamation in Easter Week 1916. He was executed.

In 1903 Erskine Childers brought out his famous novel *The Riddle of The Sands*. It was a great success on publication and ran into a number of editions long before he became famous in the wider field of politics. It is much read still and has been made into a successful film.

In the same year, on a British Army visit to America, he met and married a delightful American lady, Molly Osgood. Her father gave them the very suitable present of a large yacht, for both loved sailing and the sea.

He was very fortunate in his wife. She stood solidly behind him in all he did, even when he embarked on the troubled sea of Irish politics and later became involved in the pre- and post-1921 warfare in Ireland. She was behind him in everything. Once and once only did she even faintly question what he wanted; that was on his demobilisation from the British Navy in 1919 when she questioned the wisdom of their going to Ireland to live. When he decided that that was his life's ambition, she said no more and set about helping him in his work there. She took all that came her way with great courage.

They had two sons. One made his life in Ireland, although like his father educated in England (including the same college at Cambridge). He sided with de Valera in politics and became a much-admired President. His Presidency promised much in the cause of peace and justice. He was a highly cultivated, able and dignified man. Unfortunately he died suddenly after only a short time in office. He was President from May 1973 until November 1974. He was sixty-nine when he died.

The other son made his life in England and attained a high position with a newspaper group.

Erskine Childers showed his considerable ability as a writer in other books apart from *The Riddle of The Sands*. He wrote about the Boer War and contemporary warfare in several still available, knowledgeable books.

He always had a great interest in and deep affection for Ireland. He paid visits there and he kept in regular touch with his Barton cousins, particularly with Robert Barton. It is obvious now that he must always have had an underlying interest in Irish politics, but this did not show itself outwardly until about 1908. From then on he became an active participant in Irish affairs, first in peaceable support of Home Rule and later as an out-and-out militant Republican.

In 1911 he published a book called *The Framework of Home Rule*. By 1914 he was heavily involved with the Irish Republican movement. By then a strong contingent in the North-East of the country, led by Edward Carson and F. E. Smith, had shown that they would oppose, by force if necessary, any kind of break with England. They openly armed. The Republicans in the rest of the country did likewise, but not so effectively. The familiar misadventures dogged their efforts. Then in the spring of 1914 the opportunity arose for the Republicans to get arms and ammunition from Hamburg. The snag was that they had to be collected. Erskine Childers and his wife, with the help of friends, decided to use their wedding present, the large ketch called the *Asgard*, for the purpose.

It was an adventurous journey, first to the mouth of the Scheldt, loading up there, and then making for Howth, one of the land arms of Dublin Bay. The voyage is capable and worthy of a story all its own. Its significance here, however, is that the whole enterprise was, of course, illegal – avowedly so – and would have meant severe sentences for Erskine Childers, Molly and their friends if caught. But they were not caught and successfully landed in Howth harbour 15,000 rifles and a large quantity of ammunition.

That took place in June–July 1914. It seems odd that a few weeks later, just after war had broken out, Erskine Childers should have reported for service to the British forces. It seems odd both from the point of view of his doing so and from the point of view of his being so unquestioningly accepted. At any rate, he went to a Royal Navy Air Station in the middle of August 1914 and was put on active sea-plane duty with the rank of Lieutenant. His yachting knowledge of the North Sea and of German waters made him invaluable and his services were so recognised. He won promotion to Lieutenant-Commander and was awarded the DSC.

There was something about Erskine Childers that picked him out as an organiser – not an ordinary secretary – for anything of importance. No doubt it was his command of language, his orderly approach and his experience with Parliament. In any case, Lloyd George chose him as Secretary for the special Convention in 1917 which, as so often before, produced no answer to the Irish question. If it did nothing else, the appointment brought Erskine Childers' name before Irish politicians and public again.

On his demobilisation from the Royal Navy in 1919, Childers chose to make his home in Ireland and to take an active part in very active politics by joining the Irish Republican Party, Sinn Fein (which in English means Ourselves Alone). The War of Independence, as it was called, against the British was then in operation. The British were represented by a motley force which became known as the Black and Tans, because their odd uniform resembled that of a well-known County Limerick Hunt of that name.

Childers soon became aligned to Eamonn de Valera, a man who figured prominently in subsequent Irish history. De Valera had been one of the leaders of the Easter Week Rising, commanding the force which held Boland's Mills on the direct route from the port of Kingstown (now Dun Laoghaire) into Dublin. He had surrendered with the others, but although sentenced to death by court martial, had been reprieved. This was – and is – often thought to have been because of his American citizenship. It may be wholly or in part so, but two other leaders were also reprieved – the Countess Markievicz and Thomas Ashe. The reprieve of the Countess may well have been due to her sex (she survived to become the first woman MP elected to Westminster for Ireland and a Minister in an Irish government), but there was less logic in regard to the reprieve of Thomas Ashe than there was in the case of de Valera. The probable reason for the reprieve of the two men was that there had been a number of executions already and public feeling was running high.

The relationship between Childers and de Valera is very difficult to define. It would be quite wrong to regard the former as being subservient to the latter, although of course de Valera was the great leader and to his adherents was known as "The Chief" to the end of his life. But Childers was more than just a confidant and aide, more than just a right-hand man; they were a team. In many respects they thought alike, in many other respects they complemented each other. De Valera had a scholarly, mathematical, mind; Childers a literary one; both were great paper-workers, drafting and re-drafting, making and sending memoranda; Childers was the more fluent, de Valera the more decisive. If not a team they were a partnership. It was a very close relationship, which even many of de Valera's supporters disliked and distrusted.

With the Black and Tan war wending its weary way came the Treaty negotiations in 1921. Britain fielded a First Eleven, headed by Lloyd George and including such as F. E. Smith and Winston Churchill. It can only be said that Ireland fielded an under-strength First Eleven. The then acknowledged leader, de Valera, chose to abstain from membership of the Irish delegation and to remain in Dublin.

The question of de Valera's absence from the Treaty negotiations has often been discussed. Was it a clever choice, to leave himself freedom of movement whatever might be decided in London? Or was it because his presence was really necessary in Ireland? This is one of history's most intriguing questions. Because on it, of course, depends the whole question of the ensuing civil war.

There is no ready answer to the question. The two alternative answers have much to attract them. But, to broaden the first alternative, it would seem that de Valera felt that strategically he had more to gain for his course by refraining from being part of the delegation. It gave him freedom of movement. If he had attended, certain it is that he would have been a most awkward man to negotiate with.

Erskine Childers was, on de Valera's nomination, Secretary to the Irish delegation. None of the delegates on either side – except his cousin Robert Barton and Michael Collins – liked or trusted him. He was regarded as a renegade Englishman, though he was as much Irish as English. Worse still, he was felt to be de Valera's personal observer at the discussions, which was certainly true.

The Treaty, which partitioned Ireland and gave Dominion status to a twenty-six (out of thirty-two) county Irish Free State, was – strangely – quickly signed without reference back to Dublin or de Valera. The explanation given was that Lloyd George had given an ultimatum of outright war. It is difficult to understand why there was no reference back; the threat of war, at any rate any immediate war, cannot have been a real one, if only because of the likely reaction of America. Was it a case of bluff by Lloyd George paying off? Or was it that the delegation considered that de Valera, if consulted, would block the only peace that was obtainable? None of the Irish delegates wanted partition, but they clearly considered that they could get no better terms.

It seems, too, that some, if not all, of them set some hope on the Boundary Revision Commission which was provided for. It, in fact, flopped completely and there were no revisions.

Erskine Childers was seething at the signing of the Treaty and so was de Valera when he heard of it.

The craving for peace was great in Ireland and there were majorities, albeit narrow, both in parliament and in the country in favour of the Treaty. A few of the signatories, including Robert Barton, repudiated it in time.

A dreadful civil war of some eighteen months' duration followed the ratification of the Treaty. De Valera headed the Republicans, or Irregulars, against the Provisional Government, its army and police. Erskine Childers was his foremost man, in charge of propaganda and administration.

In the course of the civil war, Michael Collins, Chairman of the Provisional Government and Commander-in-Chief of the armed forces, was killed in an ambush. In their extensive coverage of this event, many of the English papers had a good deal to say about the remaining personalities in Irish affairs. The *Daily Sketch* published a photograph of Erskine Childers and said underneath, "Mr Erskine Childers, the Englishman, who on the very day before the assassination was engaged in a verbal contest with Mr Bernard Shaw, the Irishman, who urged that it was "better to live than die for Ireland".

The *Morning Post* had a piece which stated at the beginning, "The following message bore at the top of each page 'Passed by the Military Censor' and must be read with this reservation." Two parts referred to de Valera and Childers and the copy I have is marked by Childers and has his marginal note, "See unfortunate passage passed by F.S. [Free State] Military Censor."

The first passage read as follows: "What will happen next can easily be foretold. Erskine Childers, the one irreconcilable, will either escape to England, as he is reported to be trying to do, or he will be shot. De Valera will either escape to America or be shot, or, as is much more likely, will realise that Collins' death will be immediately avenged upon himself, and in sheer terror will shake off the sway which Childers now exercises over his mind and will make the gesture of surrender."

The second passage said, "Labour will, in the meantime, be given a hint that the opportune time has arrived for it to act as an intermediary between the warring factions and negotiations will be entered into, as the result of which either de Valera or, if he has bolted or been shot along with Childers, the Southern leaders will accept the Treaty as it stands or the pro-Treatyites will accept and will persuade the British Cabinet to accept document number two. There appears to be no difference between the existing Treaty and document number two, except that the latter is the offspring of de Valera's private brain, and its acceptance would save his egregious, but in certain quarters, still admired face."

The writer in the *Morning Post* was correct only in one thing – that Childers would be shot. Neither he nor de Valera ever contemplated running away or surrendering. And de Valera, though a wanted man, was never caught.

The assassination of Collins certainly increased the hatred and bitterness towards Erskine Childers which had always existed in the ranks of the Provisional Government. They were anxious to get him – and they did. They also got him in possession of a revolver, which sealed his fate. Without the revolver it would have been hard to put him on trial, much less execute him.

He was making his surreptitious way to Dublin to join de Valera at the latter's urgent request, when he stayed the last night of his journey at his old family home, the Barton house in County Wicklow. He was obviously betrayed by somebody local because two squads of Government troops arrived and went straight to where he was. He came out into a passage-way holding his small revolver. It had been a gift from Michael Collins. He later told Michael Comyn that he would have used it – against an armed force of some twelve men – but he was overpowered and arrested. That was on 10 November 1922. He was immediately transported to the forbidding Portobello Barracks in Dublin.

The news of Childers' arrest made world headlines. It greatly shocked de Valera and he immediately sent instructions for his defence.

The prevailing rule for Republican prisoners who were captured and put on trial was to refuse to recognise the Court. Their lawyers, who had to plead before the tribunal, did not always find this the most propitious way to begin, but the men themselves were, of course, speaking beyond their lawyers and the tribunal to their friends and countrymen.

It was also a rule for such men to claim prisoner-of-war status. This had, for more than a century, been the claim of those caught in the various risings. It had never succeeded, unless the Court order in Wolfe Tone's case could be called a success. The answer always was that the prisoner was not an enemy soldier, but a rebel against the lawful authority. However, the distinction is often not as clear cut as that.

In the detention-room in Portobello Barracks where they discussed his case, Erskine Childers said to Michael Comyn, "You know, there is no defence in fact. I did have a gun."

"That's as may be," replied Michael Comyn, "but you are too famous a figure to be condemned without due form and solemnity."

Childers went on trial in camera in that Barracks on Friday 17 November 1922 – on the charge that on 10 November 1922 without proper authority he was in possession of an automatic pistol when apprehended by a party of the National forces.

On the very morning of his trial four young men had been executed for similar charges. More awaited trial.

The Military Court consisted of two high-ranking Irish army officers and a legal adviser.

The objection to the Court and the claim for prisoner-of-war status were made by way of a written statement handed in at the outset. The statement went on in Childers' words to vindicate himself. He resented being regarded as an English renegade or an English spy. He declared that he was Irish by blood, choice and domicile. He denied that he had acted against Ireland in any way; he had acted on principle and firmly and conscientiously believed in republicanism.

The lawyers attempted to argue too that the small automatic pistol could not really be regarded as arms. They had this to say – and said it – that Childers was not really being tried capitally for just the possession of that pistol, but for being Childers; Childers, who had given a technical cause for being tried when little or nothing would have been done about it in the case of somebody else. Everyone in the Court knew that, and it is uncomfortable to hear uncomfortable truths.

The court martial ran on into the Saturday and it was then decided that the High Court would be moved on Monday 20 November for Habeas Corpus – that is to say for a Writ removing Childers' case to the High Court.

The same counsel appeared for Childers in the High Court – Michael Comyn KC, Patrick Lynch KC and Conor Maguire, who was later to be Attorney-General and Chief Justice. The solicitor instructing them was an intrepid man named John Woods, who was engaged in several such cases and stood no nonsense from military, police or Court officials.

There were a number of grounds put forward in support of the application for Habeas Corpus but the main ones were that for several reasons the court martial had no jurisdiction, that Childers was anyway entitled to be treated as a prisoner of war and that if any Court had jurisdiction to try him it was the ordinary Criminal Court of the land, with a jury.

The challenge to the court martial's jurisdiction was put this way: first, the alleged offence (and penalty) was created by nothing more than a so-called Rule, Regulation or Order of the Provisional Government, not by a statute; second, assuming an Order would suffice the Provisional Government had no power to make such a one as this; third, it only applied if a state of war was proved and the ordinary Courts could not function.

The prisoner of war point was that if a state of war existed then Erskine Childers was a prisoner of war and not subject to a court martial. There was an ancillary point, often made before, that as a rule of law anyone engaged in military combat should not be tried by representatives of the opposing military forces. This had not been accepted by any Court in respect of so-called rebels.

Wolfe Tone's case was relied upon as a precedent for Habeas Corpus in such circumstances as the present. The circumstances in the Wolfe Tone case were, however, not only different but special as readers of the chapter about that case earlier in this book can remind themselves.

The Habeas Corpus application began on the Monday before the Master of the Rolls, The Right Honourable Charles A. O'Connor. As the hearing began the Military Court announced its verdict and sentence – Guilty and Death by Firing Squad. The confirmation of the findings and sentence was also announced. This led the Master of the Rolls to grant a stay of execution pending his decision.

The hearing before him lasted until the Thursday. While it went on messages came from all over the country and all over the world calling on the Government to reprieve Erskine Childers. He, and those acting for him, knew there was no hope of that.

The Judge listened with patience and interest to all the points made. When the submission ended he gave his judgment, on Thursday 23 November, dismissing the application. He based his judgment on a finding that there was a state of war in the country, caused by "political malcontents and criminals and other dangerous adventurers". He instanced this finding by referring to his having to sit in a makeshift Court because "one of the noblest buildings in this country [the Four Courts] is now a mass of crumbling ruins", and to the destruction of the Public Record Office and other great buildings. He decided that in a state of war the Court could not, and would not attempt to, control the military authority. He held that there was no substance in any of the grounds put forward and that Habeas Corpus had no application.

An appeal was immediately lodged against the decision of the Master of the Rolls and lay as of right, without leave, to the Court of Appeal. But although this was publicly known, the authorities decided to go ahead with the execution. And they prepared for the next morning.

Erskine Childers was now in Beggar's Bush Barracks, a

cold, menacing-looking embattled building which stands about two miles out from the centre of Dublin on the Wicklow side.

In the early morning of Friday 24 November 1922 Erskine Childers was led out to the courtyard of the Barracks. He declined to be blindfolded and shook hands with each member of the firing-squad. The officer in charge marched him to the wall and as the men took up their positions, Childers called out to them, "Come closer, boys. It's easier."

Came the signal, came the volley and Childers slumped to the ground.

Army Headquarters in announcing the execution referred to the Military Court finding, but not to the High Court, nor the pending appeal. Informally, the rumour was circulated that the execution had taken place because plans to rescue Childers were discovered.

Michael Comyn used to say that in a long experience of the law – in peace, war or civil war – he had never come across such a travesty of justice, knowingly and deliberately to execute a man while his appeal was pending. When the matter was mentioned to them the Court of Appeal agreed, but that was little use then.

The finest advocacy does not require flights of rhetoric. It can be achieved with bluntness and brevity.

My father rated highly the small red-headed youth who came out to serve him with petrol at a two-pump filling station in the far west of County Clare.

"Five gallons, please," said my father.

"Will you have the good shtuff or the shtuff?" enquired the boy.

Hayes (Inspector of Taxes)
v. Duggan

 1929

THE IRISH HOSPITALS' SWEEP is now old in years, success and respectability. It is sanctified by statute.

It had many predecessors which ran only brief and troublesome lives. One which was markedly successful and which bequeathed to the Irish Sweep some of its more picturesque trappings, was a sweep organised by a well-known Dublin bookmaker, Richard Duggan.

The Mater Misericordiae Hospital in Dublin, more commonly known as the Mater, was and is a splendid hospital on the north side of the city run by the Sisters of Charity. In the period immediately before 1922, it had run sweepstakes for small prizes in aid of its funds. However, the response was not at all lucrative.

Consulted on the subject, Mr Duggan diagnosed the hospital's trouble – prizes not large enough. He accordingly agreed with the hospital to run a sweepstake. In respect of it, he would pay them the sum of £10,000 certain, but no more. He would provide the prize money and the organisation and would cover the expenses. What he got, apart from the guaranteed £10,000, was to be his.

He ran this first widespread sweep on the 1922 Manchester November Handicap, a popular gambling race at the end of the flat-racing season. Tickets were sold at ten shillings (that is to say fifty new pence) and each and every ticket counterfoil went into a draw to be held a day or two before the race. The prizes were £5,000 for the holder of the ticket which drew the winner of the race, £2,500 for the second, £1,250 for the third and £1,250 to be divided between the holders of tickets in respect of also-rans.

The Sweep was well organised and tickets were sold widely at home and abroad. Shortly before the race an elaborate ceremony was arranged for the draw at that splendid scene of so many divers Irish gatherings, the Round Room of the Mansion House in Dublin.

The stage was full of enormously important personages; invigilation and security were more elaborate than for the movement of bullion. There was the unpleasant – but apparently accepted – spectacle of two blind children drawing from two large drums, matching a horse to a counterfoil. There was a huge crowd and much publicity. (The Hospitals' Sweep has, suitably, nurses to do the actual drawing.)

The winners duly got their money in accordance with the fate of their horses in the race. The Mater Hospital got its £10,000. And Mr Duggan got for himself – £x. On counsel's advice he refused to disclose his profit to the Revenue. They assessed it at £40,000.

For the next big race, the 1923 Grand National, Mr Duggan ran an identical sweep. The charity in this case was not the same; it was for the Cancer Hospital jointly with a parish priest who wanted funds to build a parochial house.

This sweep, too, was a great success.

The Revenue claimed to share in these successes and sought tax on the profits. This Mr Duggan resisted.

The Special Commissioners held that no tax was payable because the enterprises in question were unlawful. On appeal to the High Court this bold (and, dare one say it, praiseworthy) decision was reversed. The two-judge Court was unanimous.

Then to the Supreme Court and three judges. Much learning was displayed, many cases (Irish, English and foreign) referred to. That familiar "unruly horse" Public Policy had a good run. Both sides claimed him as an ally; an instance, perhaps, of each-way betting. Mr Duggan's counsel claimed that it would be an affront to the law if income tax could be levied on the proceeds of crime. The Revenue retaliated by arguing that it was public policy that income should be taxed and what Mr Duggan received was income.

The Supreme Court unanimously held that, since the profits

in question were derived from a criminal enterprise, they were not assessable to income tax. Criminal enterprise seems a strong description of Mr Duggan's activities, even in the language and by the standards of those days.

Mr Justice Fitzgibbon was full of good observations on the appeal. He set his standard to the point that the enterprise was one "every step and act of which is a criminal offence". Thus was he able, he said, to distinguish the instant case from that of a publican who made part of his profits by sales out of hours; he could not be heard to dispute tax liability in respect of all his profits, nor could a pawnbroker (nor a marine store dealer!) part of whose profits were derived from unlawful dealing.

All has changed now. There are still occasional cases about the illegality of certain gaming and wagering, certain lotteries and betting. More usual, however, in the law cases of the present time are disputes about winnings, and by 1939 my father was applying to the Irish Court – successfully – for an infant winner of the Irish Sweep to have the winnings transferred out of the jurisdiction to the United States of America as "trust money".

"What has happened to the dog?" enquired counsel of an expert witness he was cross-examining.

"What dog?" enquired the witness, understandably you might think.

"The dog that Mr Justice Fitzgibbon said he would not hang upon your evidence."

Re O'Connor

 1930

Sir James O'Connor was many things in his time. He became a solicitor in Ireland in 1894. After six years he was voluntarily taken off the rolls and called to the Irish Bar. He took silk in 1908, became Solicitor-General and Attorney-General, was made a High Court Judge in 1918 and shortly afterwards a Lord Justice. When the new regime took over in Ireland he was put on the retired list. So he got called to the English Bar and took silk in England, practising there for a time.

In 1929 he got himself disbarred in England and Ireland and had his patent as a King's Counsel revoked. He then applied in Ireland for re-admission as a solicitor – to complete the circle.

The application had to be made under the Solicitors Act and necessitated taking the matter before the Court. The Court (Chief Justice Kennedy) did not like it at all. Eventually with ill grace he granted the application but imposed a condition that Sir James should not appear as an advocate in any Court.

The Chief Justice gave a clear indication of his own views in this passage: "I have no doubt indeed that many persons will be shocked by the idea of this application. Perhaps the absence of modern precedent is to be counted to that very fitness of things or good taste. However that may be, a sense of proper or good taste merely is . . . for the guidance of the individual in choosing a particular course but not a ground upon which the judicial determination of this case may be based."

In imposing the condition that Sir James must not act anywhere as an advocate the Chief Justice observed that otherwise, "As Campbell said of Pemberton he would still be regarded as laying down the law with judicial authority and he would tend to overbear inferior courts, while it would be a scandal were he to explain his own judgments for the purpose of advancing a client's cause."

In the years between the two world wars there was a great character named Alfie Byrne, who was sixteen times Lord Mayor of Dublin, having almost a freehold of that charming Mansion House, with its famous Round Room, at the top of Dawson Street.

Alfie was the soul of affability and his famous handshake (of crippling strength) plus his cheery greetings became bywords. In fulfilling his duties he never forgot the need to promote his own re-election. A familiar and shrewd piece of advocacy was to say to a group of children, "Now when you go home don't forget to tell your family that you've been speaking to Alfie Byrne, the Lord Mayor of Dublin."

A barrister friend accompanied him once on a visit to the Criminal Lunatic Asylum at Dundrum on the outskirts of the city. Towards the end of the visit Alfie spied a solitary figure sitting in the corner of a room. He went over to the man, pumped his hand, said a few words to him and, as he was going, remarked, "Now don't forget to tell your visitors when they call that you've shaken hands with Alfie Byrne, the Lord Mayor of Dublin."

The man looked up at him and shook his head sadly. "I'm not surprised you're here," he said. "When I was sent here first I thought I was Lloyd George – but they knock that sort of nonsense out of you in a week or two."

Miss M'Greene
 1931

I T WAS IN the days when there was no monopoly in respect of buses in Ireland; the days which some people would like to see again when competition provided rival services.

Miss M'Greene, a nurse, sought to travel on the bus of one such independent operator, called – oddly – The Hibernian Taxi Company. She said that she was just about to enter the bus (its entrance was at the front) when it suddenly moved off and threw her back into the road so that the end of the bus in fact ran over her. She suffered serious injuries. The defence of the bus company was that she tried to enter the bus when it was already moving off and therefore caused her own injuries.

Thus far there is nothing out of the ordinary about Miss M'Greene's case. What takes it right out of the ordinary is that she had two cases and both went to the Irish Supreme Court.

At the first trial before the President of the High Court (Sullivan, P.) and a jury, she was the sole witness on her side as to the accident and there were seven witnesses (three completely independent) against her, supporting the defence that she tried too late to board a moving bus.

The jury found for the plaintiff and awarded her £1,500 damages.

The defendants appealed to the Supreme Court, contending that the verdict was against the weight of the evidence and should not be allowed to stand. This is a point that has been taken countless times over the years in civil and criminal cases. It usually depends on the particular facts.

The Supreme Court were hesitant (Mr Justice Fitzgibbon described it as the most difficult case the Court had had), but considered that the weight of the evidence had been so heavily on the defendant's side that the verdict could not stand and there must be a new trial. Chief Justice Kennedy forecast that a second jury might produce the same result.

The second trial was before Mr Justice O'Byrne and a jury. The defendant's evidence suffered certain damage, two of the previous seven not turning up and one being discredited. This jury thereupon found for Miss M'Greene and awarded her £3,500 damages. This was a slight embarrassment in that her claim had only been for £3,000, but her counsel sought and obtained leave to amend to the amount awarded.

The Hibernian Taxi Company went to the Supreme Court again, identically constituted. Previous success may have given them encouragement and again they alleged that the verdict was against the weight (albeit the diminished weight) of the evidence. In addition, they challenged the making of an award in excess of the claim.

Mr Justice Fitzgibbon still felt difficulties, but he felt driven to agree with his brethren that enough was enough; there could not go on being re-trials until a result was reached which the appellate court liked.

None of their Lordships found any difficulty about upholding the extra £500. So Miss M'Greene vindicated herself and received more than twice the damages she was awarded in the original trial.

Dick Adams was a lively and humorous figure at the Bar in the early years of this century. He later became County Court Judge of Limerick.

He once described a witness he had cross-examined – a frail but untruthful man – as one "who got baptism and vaccination at the same time but neither took".

General O'Duffy
 1933/34

GENERAL EOIN O'DUFFY litigated certainly, but he will best be remembered as first a strict enforcer of the Law and later a persistent flouter of it. His career took him from one extreme to the other.

O'Duffy was a friend of Cosgrave and his pro-Treaty party, and when the Irish Free State came into being in 1922 Cosgrave headed the government. He had as an early task the creation of a new police force, called the Civic Guards or, in Irish, the Garda Siochana. After a short time General O'Duffy was appointed as Commissioner of this force; he was, in fact, the second Commissioner, the first having only held office for a short time. He started with just 4,000 men under his control.

O'Duffy proved to be an excellent choice. He built up the Guards to a strong, efficient and respected force. But in doing so he stood up to authority firstly as to what he needed, and secondly as to the rights of his men. What his men deserved he demanded; he did not just ask. And he did these things to a government whose employee he was and which consisted of his old friends and colleagues.

His ten years in office were turbulent years in Ireland, covering as they did the tragic civil war and its aftermath. He had to use his force on the government side and against fellow-countrymen under de Valera and his anti-Treaty group. But, despite everything, his force survived and strengthened.

When de Valera came to power in 1932 he decided to call another election and, when reinforced in office in 1933, he dismissed General O'Duffy, offering him alternative employment at the same salary, which the General refused. In view of past events the dismissal was inevitable. The reason given, unofficially, was that his judgment was unsound. But there were many who resented de Valera's action.

Had there been no dismissal the extraordinary subsequent events would undoubtedly never have occurred and O'Duffy would have had only a small niche in history, as a distinguished Chief of Police.

In his place as Commissioner de Valera appointed Eamon Broy, the head of the detective branch. His picked inner corps soon became known as the Broy Harriers. (The seaside resort of Bray had a famous park known as the Bray Harriers.)

General O'Duffy was a born leader and had no intention of fading quietly into the background. He began his resurgence by what sounded the soul of innocence – becoming head of the Army Comrades' Association. Few could imagine that it would soon be an actual Army and the introducer of Fascism into Ireland.

In April 1933 the Association adopted as a uniform the wearing of blue shirts and thus was born The Blueshirts, a paler version of the black and brown shirts then assembling on the Continent of Europe. Amusingly, but with deadly seriousness, de Valera actually banned the making, importing and selling of any shirts coloured blue.

In July 1933 the peaceful sounding Association with its suggestion of ageing veterans found new vigour by changing its name to the National Guard. In a short time it began to make its presence felt through the country, but at first did so peacefully. When O'Duffy announced a mass march through Dublin for 13 August de Valera's government acted promptly by banning the march and making the National Guard an illegal organisation.

The Blue Shirts were powerful by then, perhaps 30,000 strong, and knowing that they had access to arms some thought that they might attempt to carry out the march. But they were not – and never were – strong enough to carry out a coup, and with due protests about interference with the citizens' rights General O'Duffy in a dignified way called off the march.

The Blue Shirts survived under a succession of different names, duly altered as each new one was made an illegal organisation in turn. Thus we had the Young Ireland

223

Association, then the League of Youth, and so forth. From an Old Comrades' Association to a youth organisation was quite a move. Everyone smiled at the changes but many did so with a certain grimness and fear; the very names suggested force and trouble; the new emphasis on youth had a familiar and sinister sound.

General O'Duffy went to the Irish High Court to have a proposed newly named body cleared in advance – declared in advance not to be capable of being proscribed. He failed, the Court refusing to interfere until it had something concrete, not just theoretical, to deal with.

The Blue Shirt movement spread and strengthened. Like all such movements it struck hardest where government was weakest. In this instance it was through the farmers. There were Land Annuities, which Britain had been receiving under the Treaty; de Valera refused to pay them over saying that their payment was unjustified; mutual tariff-raising led to what became known as "The Economic War"; as the poorer contestant, Ireland fared badly and farmers in particular; they now saw calves sold for half-a-crown (about 13p); cows and bullocks for £3 and £4. The Blue Shirts stirred up the farmers and other discontented groups, and promoted, for example, a "no rates" campaign.

Blue Shirt activity continued throughout 1933 and well into 1934. De Valera took it seriously and, in an attempt to stamp it out, reintroduced a special Criminal Court in the form of a Military Tribunal, which Cosgrave had used for dealing with extremists. This controversial but, let it be said, entirely fair Court, consisted of three high-ranking military officers, sitting in uniform and usually at Collins Barracks in Dublin. It had unlimited jurisdiction in criminal matters, including the right to try for murder and to pass the death sentence. It had, of course, no jury. An Accused had the right to legal representation, normal rules of law and evidence applied, and there was a right of appeal to the Court of Criminal Appeal.

It is doubtful if the idea of a military court for civilians was ever a good one. The country had had through the years more than enough of Martial Law and courts martial. The original idea was Cosgrave's; de Valera merely reintroduced it, but he clearly preferred it to a court of lawyers, of whom he was never enamoured.

O'Duffy counter-attacked. He and a colleague were arrested at Westport in County Mayo for wearing blue shirts and attempting to address a public meeting of Blue Shirts. He was arrested by senior members of the police force he had so recently commanded.

The prisoners were lodged in Arbour Hill military prison in Dublin, for trial before the Military Tribunal.

They applied to the High Court for Habeas Corpus, challenging the provisions which had been enacted under a statute which amended the then operative Constitution, the Constitution brought in when the state had come into existence in 1922.

They succeeded and were released. It was a triumph for O'Duffy but, strangely, one which he found did not have the impact one might have expected. Perhaps he realised that his Blue Shirts had not won the country and would not do so.

He made a clever, democratic move; he merged his followers with the opposition political parties and became President of the combined party. Therein lay a legitimate, political path to eventual power. But it did not work. The combined party found it too hard to live married to its widely differing constituent parts. O'Duffy and his Blue Shirts were not made for politics. And he himself was a commander, not a political leader.

Suddenly, in September 1934, General O'Duffy resigned from his Presidency of the combined opposition party. He gave as the reason a fundamental divergence of views.

Though disillusioned with politics, he surprisingly soon formed a new political party of his own. It quickly failed and with it died the Blue Shirts. It is easy to say now that they never had any chance of success in Ireland, but to those who know Ireland that was and is a fact. The leaders and the parties that win favour in Ireland are not uniformed forces.

In 1936 the General turned his attention to recruiting for Franco in the Spanish Civil War.

In 1939 when war broke out, he grandly offered his services in any capacity to de Valera. They were very quickly and firmly rejected. O'Duffy's colourful, eventful career was at an end. The Civic Guards remain his best achievement.

The unusual, often devastating, turn of phrase is a characteristic of Irish witnesses. One spoken to my father, though not in Court, left him speechless – not an easy thing to attain.

After a long interval he met an old farmer in the market town of Ennistymon in County Clare. The farmer looked him up and down and noticed that he had put on a good deal of weight.

"My God," said the farmer eventually, "you're fit for killing."

Sinclair v. Gogarty

 1937

OLIVER ST JOHN GOGARTY (1878–1957) was one of the great
Irish characters of his time. He was a famous ear, nose and
throat specialist in Dublin, a wit and raconteur, a well-known
poet, a politician and a friend of the great Irish writers and
artists, a circle which included Yeats, James Joyce (in *Ulysses*
Joyce depicted Gogarty as Buck Mulligan), J. M. Synge, Lord
Dunsany, George Moore, A. E. (George Russell), Padraic
Colum, Shane Leslie, George Bernard Shaw, Lady Gregory,
James Stephens, and Sir William Orpen. He was a friend also
of the politicians Arthur Griffith, Michael Collins and Kevin
O'Higgins. A man he could never stand at any price was de
Valera.

After schooling with the Jesuits in England and Ireland he
went to Dublin University and then, briefly, to Worcester
College, Oxford. Like his twenty-four-year-older compatriot,
Oscar Wilde, he was obviously influenced by Professor
Mahaffy, the famous Provost of Trinity College, Dublin, who
was a master of the epigram. Mahaffy's frequent form was
either a play on words or the adaptation with subtle alteration
of well-known sayings or maxims. Thus: "In Ireland the
inevitable never happens but the unexpected often occurs."

In his young days Gogarty was a champion cyclist; and from
the early days of flying he was a daring aviator, who often
scared the living daylights out of friends whom he brought up
for "a flip"; he showed the same enthusiasm for large cars and
made full use of their improving capacity for speed.

In the *Oxford Book of English Verse* a few of his poems were
included, but in the *Oxford Book of Modern Verse*, published

in 1936 under the editorship of his friend Yeats, no less than seventeen were included, which brought a good deal of criticism.

He knew Dublin – history and legend – intimately.

His first book of reminiscences was called *As I Was Going Down Sackville Street*, the old name for what is now O'Connell Street in Dublin. It was a racy, rollicking book which was a potpourri of the Dublin Gogarty had known: its fun, its foibles, its characters, its street ballads and above all, of course, his own escapades and activities and those of his distinguished circle of friends. Unfortunately it led to a libel action, a very odd libel action indeed.

In 1937 a man named Henry Morris Sinclair sued Gogarty alleging that two passages in the book were libellous of him. The main passage was mostly in prose and was a conversation between Dubliners:

"Very well," said I, "you must know that George is not only the *arbiter elegantiarum* of Dublin, but a critic of the grosser forms of licence. Now there was an old usurer . . . The older he grew the more he pursued the immature, and enticed little girls into his office. That was bad enough; but he had grandsons and these directed the steps of their youth to follow in grandfather's footsteps, with more zeal than discrimination. I explained the position to George who, after due fermentation produced the following pronunciamento:

'It is a thing to wonder at, but hardly to admire,
How they who do desire the most, guard most against desire.
They chose their friend or mistress so that none may yearn to touch her,
Thus did the twin grandchildren of the ancient Butcher.'"

Later in the passage the woman asked, "Who are the great twin brethren?" and the reply was, "Consummations of the poet's dream shadows invoked by sound. Men who do not exist. I thought I made that clear."

The plaintiff was Jewish; he had had a twin brother whose

name was Willie, who had died. He proved in evidence that his grandfather, an antique dealer in Nassau Street, who had left the business to them, had been commonly reputed to interfere with little girls.

The second passage complained of was in a different, unconnected part of the book and consisted of a verse:

"And one thing more – where can we buy antiques?"
"Nassau Street, Sackville Street, Liffey Street, where Naylor's is, and all along the quays. Have you not heard?"

"Two Jews grew in Sackville Street
And not in Piccadilly,
One was gaitered on the feet,
The other one was Willie.

"And if you took your pick of them
Whichever one you chose
You'd like the other one more than him
So wistful were these Jews.

"They kept a shop for objects wrought
By Masters famed of old,
Where you no matter what you bought
Were genuinely sold.

"But Willie spent the sesterces
And brought on strange disasters
Because he sought new mistresses
More keenly than old Masters.

"Two Jews grew in Sackville Street
And not in Piccadilly,
One was gaitered on the feet
The other one was Willie.

"And if you took the pick of them
Whichever one you chose,
You'd like the other one more than him,
So wistful were these Jews."

The third and fourth verses were in the American edition only.

The trial was before Mr Justice O'Byrne and a jury, and the parties were represented as follows: for the plaintiff, Albert Wood KC, Joseph McCarthy KC, and Ernest Wood; for the defendant, J. M. Fitzgerald KC, Ralph Brereton Barry KC, and Gogarty's son Oliver.

The libels alleged did not on the face of them readily attach to the plaintiff and it needed rather special information to make them do so. This information, which the plaintiff gave, would not (one might think) be available to many of the readers of the book.

A short analysis, based on the plaintiff's evidence, amounts to this: his grandfather had been reputed to entice little girls; the narrator in the first passage said that the grandsons did the same; the verse identified them as being twins; the second passage linked up by showing that they were Jews and one was called Willie; they had inherited their grandfather's antique business in one of the streets named, Nassau Street.

Mr Fitzgerald's comment to the plaintiff was, "You have dug up your grandfather!"

Samuel Beckett, the famous writer, said in evidence that he had identified the plaintiff from the two passages. Under cross-examination he said his wife's aunt was Mr Willie Sinclair's aunt and that he had been introduced to the book through the plaintiff asking him to buy it.

There followed witnesses – all relatives, friends or employees of the plaintiff, or people who had bought the book at his suggestion. They included a Mr Murray, a well-known Dublin optician. All identified the plaintiff as being one of the twins referred to.

Finally, on the Judge questioning whether authorship had been proved, Albert Wood called Gogarty. It is rare indeed that a plaintiff calls his defendant as a witness. And it has great potential disadvantages; it means that the plaintiff's counsel cannot cross-examine him, for he is his own witness; but worse, the defendant's counsel can. In fact Gogarty's counsel did not cross-examine him at all.

Gogarty took responsibility for authorship of the prose and the verse, with the proviso that what was said was drawn from

230

Dublin lore he had picked up over the years. Two witnesses of his, well-known literary figures (R. M. Smyllie, Editor of the *Irish Times*, and F. R. Higgins, the poet), said that they would not identify the plaintiff from the passages complained of and also that the verses were Dublin folk songs.

Gogarty further testified that he knew the plaintiff and had known Willie Sinclair but that Willie had been known as "Boss". He did not know that the Sinclairs were twins, the passages did not refer to them, and the reference to twins was explicable from mythology.

In addition to R. M. Smyllie and F. R. Higgins, Gogarty called Professor Fearon of Trinity College, Dublin, who said that he had often heard similar verses in Dublin and he would not associate them with the plaintiff.

In presenting the case to the jury, Albert Wood for the plaintiff made great play of the fact that the plaintiff was a Jew and said he felt sure that a Dublin jury would give justice to a Jew.

Fitzgerald for Gogarty said in his speech that the plaintiff's witnesses were all partisans and described Mr Murray, the optician, as having apparently spectacles useful in finding libels.

The Judge summed-up and the jury retired. They were out for an hour and a half and came back with a verdict for the plaintiff – for £900 damages. Costs followed, and in those days they would have amounted to at least as much more.

The decision in favour of the plaintiff seems a surprising one; the award in terms of 1937 a very large one. There was no appeal; against a jury's verdict in such a case one would have little hope of success. The sale of an excellent and entertaining book was also seriously affected.

Gogarty took the decision hardly. He moved practice to London. But litigation pursued him there, or rather this time he pursued litigation. And again it was libel. What a fascination that cause of action has for people. The Irish writer Patrick Kavanagh, then at the start of his literary career, published a book called *The Green Fool*, which was largely autobiographical. In one passage he described calling at Gogarty's house in Ely Place in Dublin and finding the door opened by a woman in a nightdress whom he thought "must be either Gogarty's wife or mistress". Gogarty won his libel action, but got only £100 damages.

In 1939 he went to America on a lecture tour. He remained there for five years, living on journalism, lecturing and writing books.

In 1945 he returned on a visit to Dublin but went back to live in America and, apart from visits home, stayed there until he died on 22 September 1957. The sad thing is that he had decided that he would go home to Dublin for good later that year.

A lady in the witness-box was being cross-examined by counsel. "I believe," he said, "that you're a widow."

"Indeed I'm not," she said, "I'm completely the reverse." Then she added, with all the caution that a witness should show, "At least I was when I left home this morning."

A lady had been cross-examined by one of the leaders of the Bar, probably "Counsellor" Butt, whose eloquence was legendary. "I resented his insinigations," she said, "but my God isn't he a man with words to spare."

Bernard Kirwan

 1943

BERNARD KIRWAN, AGED thirty-seven, executed on 2 June 1943 at Mountjoy Gaol, Dublin, for the murder of his younger brother, was The Quare Fellow of Brendan Behan's play of that name.

The murder of which Kirwan was found guilty has no outstanding interest so far as its general circumstances are concerned. It was a nasty, gruesome affair but that is nowadays unfortunately often the case.

What makes Kirwan's case of particular interest are two peculiar features: one, the need the prosecution felt to prove a previous imprisonment of the Accused in order to establish their case of murder, and second, the question of proving that part of the torso which had been found was that of the allegedly murdered man. Apart from the partial torso there was no body.

Up to 1936 Bernard Kirwan had been living with his brother Laurence and their mother on a medium-sized farm which she owned and which was not far from Tullamore in County Offaly. In February 1936 Bernard Kirwan was sentenced to seven years' penal servitude for armed robbery. In 1937 the mother died and left the farm equally between her six children. As so often happens in Ireland the will was never proved and Laurence remained in undisturbed possession. None of the four children who were settled elsewhere objected. Bernard in prison was in no position to object.

In 1941 Bernard was released from prison on licence and soon afterwards resumed living at the farm with his brother. The only other resident was a farm labourer.

From the afternoon of 22 November 1941, Laurence was never seen again. He was last seen in the company of brother Bernard – by the farm-worker.

There was a great deal to cast suspicion on Bernard. He had, as is frequent in disappearance cases, told a lot of stupid lies. He had shown, and expressed, indifference about his brother's continued absence. Laurence's car had been left behind and his bicycle was found hidden in a neighbouring farm. Personal possessions, including Laurence's pipe and his wallet (empty), were found in the house and some items of his were being openly used by Bernard. There had been a stand-up fight between the two shortly before, in which a knife had been used by one or other of them. This was witnessed by the man. Bernard had spent quite a lot of money after the disappearance. Laurence was known to carry a lot of money on him.

But suspicion is one thing and proof another. There was no body – until part of a torso was found six months later in a bog some miles away. The finding was literally a chance in a million. It occurred when two men were doing some work in the bog.

The part which was found was alleged by the prosecution to indicate skilful butchery.

Three immediate questions arose: (1) what about the rest of the body? (2) was there any evidence of any butchery having taken place near the farm? and (3) since the bog was so situated that some form of transport would have been necessary for any part of a body to be taken there, was there any transport discoverable which would show signs of this?

Despite a most thorough search the answers to these questions remained all through that there was no sign at all of the rest of the body or its disposal, no evidence of any butchery having taken place at or near the farm and no transport (notably Laurence's car) giving any clues. In this connection it is important to appreciate that the police had in fact pursued all such investigations meticulously soon after the disappearance and long before the discovery of the body.

It is a fairly common belief that without a body there can be no murder charge. This is quite wrong as a couple of illustrations will immediately show. If a man is proved to have pushed a woman overboard in mid-ocean there will be no body but a charge of murder will obviously lie. Similarly, if somebody is proved to have thrown another into a furnace.

In Kirwan's case the prosecution problem was rather different – it was to prove that the part torso was that of Laurence Kirwan. There was no means whatever of telling from the gruesome discovery that it was identifiable as part of Laurence Kirwan. Hence the importance to the prosecution of having the various surrounding matters admitted in evidence.

Anticipating slightly, the prosecution had available as witnesses three doctors (including the noted pathologist Dr McGrath) ready to say that the part in question was that of a man, that it was of a man between twenty-five and fifty, that it was skilfully butchered and that it was in the state to be expected of a body of the relevant period. The defence had two medical witnesses. One was Dr Flood, a well-known surgeon, and he was prepared to say that the probabilities were that the part of the torso was female and that the dismemberment was not skilful.

Bernard Kirwan was charged in August 1942 with the murder of Laurence and his case came on for hearing in the Central Criminal Court, Dublin (Green Street, as it is generally known), before Mr Justice Martin Maguire and a jury on 18 January 1943.

The prosecution wanted to prove Bernard's previous imprisonment for three main reasons: (a) to show that when in prison he had worked in butchery, (b) to establish that he had no means and no livelihood for the five years when he was in prison and (c) to prove that he had been prescribed Luminal while in prison – in support of a suggestion that he had drugged the servant man on the vital night of the disappearance and had as well quite possibly drugged his brother preparatory to murder.

The general rule of law is that a man's criminal record must not be disclosed to the jury unless he himself puts it in either directly or through the method of his defence.

The defence, led by Mr Barra O'Briain, Senior Counsel strongly objected to the imprisonment being opened to the jury or put in evidence and objected at every appropriate stage The Judge ruled against them. The nature of the previou crime was never mentioned. The length of imprisonment, however, plainly showed that it must have been serious.

The three matters which the prosecution wanted to extract from the imprisonment were accordingly proved by prison officers.

After a sixteen-day trial with well over a hundred witnesses the jury took only a little over three hours to bring in their verdict of Guilty. In the appeals which followed, to the Court of Criminal Appeal and then to the Irish Supreme Court, one of the two main points taken on behalf of Kirwan was that the evidence of imprisonment should not have been admitted.

Mr George Murnaghan, senior counsel leading for the prosecution, took the stand that he had taken throughout – that the evidence of imprisonment was so interwoven with the case that it could only be right to admit it. The Court of Criminal Appeal and the Supreme Court shared that view and rejected the objection.

It is plain of course that there are numerous circumstances in which the fact of imprisonment must be admissible as being an integral part of the case. A crime committed within the prison is an obvious example.

In Kirwan's case, however, I have always respectfully wondered about two things. First, was it necessary to prove the three matters in question from a prison source? And second, even if that were necessary, could it not have been done without the prosecution referring in any way to prison or imprisonment?

On the first point, there was farming evidence that Bernard knew a lot about butchery through killing pigs, there was strong independent evidence about his poor finances (agreed not as strong as the prison evidence), and his possession of Luminal could be proved by several people.

The prejudice obviously engendered by the jury's knowledge of the previous imprisonment must have been great. Was it, therefore, in all the circumstances right to admit it in evidence? I have, with deference, always felt concerned about that. Nowadays in England the problem could probably be solved by asking the defence to make admissions as to the underlying facts.

On the second point (whether it could have been done without mention of imprisonment), theoretically it could. The prison officers could have stated their knowledge but refrained from giving the source of it. If the defence so cross-examined as to let the source in, then that would be that.

What concerns me on that eminently fair solution is how it could have been achieved without having the prison officers' tell-tale addresses disclosed. Their addresses, however given, would have shown the town in which a well-known Irish prison is located and if precisely given would have linked it almost conclusively to the prison. Any question of a false or artificial address being given is unthinkable. But would it not have been possible to have it given in some such broad terms as: "You live, I think, in a town in the midlands and have lived there over the past five years?" The occupation of the witness need not have been mentioned at all.

There was a strong case against the Accused on these problem points and generally, without the prison evidence.

The second great question in the case is the part of the torso. The learned Judge very fairly and rightly told the jury that they could not convict unless satisfied that this was part of Laurence Kirwan. He further directed them that they could take into account all the evidence in considering that question. And he properly directed them on the burden of proof.

By that time – the time of summing-up – the defence had failed in a submission of no case to answer and had called Bernard Kirwan and the medical evidence.

Bernard Kirwan was a bad witness. He was intelligent, well able to speak but truculent and on several matters obviously lying.

Dr Flood's evidence was very strong. The part torso consisted of the neck to the small of the back. Much skin had been cut off and there was partial decomposition. He was emphatic that it was 60 to 75 per cent probable that it belonged to a female. The dismemberment was not the craftsmanship that the prosecution alleged but was clumsy.

The point taken on appeal was that it was not satisfactorily proved that the part of the torso was that of Laurence, and that the Judge was wrong in saying that the jury could look at all the evidence – including, of course, that of the Accused – in answering that question. The point was rejected by both Appeal Courts.

It is a little surprising that the evidence of Dr Flood did not raise a reasonable doubt; also that the entire absence of any absolutely direct incriminatory evidence (blood, blood-stained clothes, blood in a vehicle) should not have done so.

It is, respectfully, difficult to fault the finding of the appellate Court on this point. A jury in such a situation must be entitled to take everything into account and to *infer* that part of the body is that of a particular person. Dr Flood and the absence of evidence of blood and blood stains were only two out of many factors to be weighed up.

The abiding interest on this point of the case is that the jury were asked to and did take into account all the evidence in deciding whether an otherwise unidentifiable torso was that of the allegedly murdered man – nothing found of the rest and nothing pointing to disposal of the rest by the Accused. It is an excellent example of a murder case being built up with tremendous care and detail to overcome its inherent difficulties.

There is no reason to believe that the verdict was wrong; the lies and such matters as the money were strongly against Bernard Kirwan. At the end, after protesting his innocence, on the death sentence being pronounced, he said, "I forgive my enemies."

He was The Quare Fellow.

The Irish witness is a law unto himself. The graphic or unexpected, unrehearsed phrase is frequent. One witness, a garage-hand, spoke only in his own metaphor when asked how a very old man was in health. "Not a bother on him", he said. "Every Sunday dinner-time he can eat a chicken down to the chassis."

Dr Paul Singer
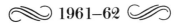 1961–62

PAUL SINGER, AGED forty-two, Doctor of Social and Political Science of Lausanne University, descended upon an unsuspecting Ireland at the beginning of 1954. In the time he was there he created a vast stamp auction empire and on its collapse created a series of Irish legal records. It is widely thought that the Irish legal system and its administrators come badly out of the story and that Dr Singer did all that clichés require, namely drove a coach and four through the law, showed it to be an ass, played ducks and drakes with it, etc. I take a contrary view over-all, but I do think that Paul Singer deserved an additional doctorate, a Doctorate of Laws, for his legal activities. Just as he learnt the stamp business from scratch so when the time came he learnt Irish Law, sometimes with the aid of solicitors and counsel, but often by acting in person with the knowledge acquired from law books specially kept for him in a separate cell, adjoining his own, in Mountjoy Gaol in Dublin. It is said that he found time to advise other prisoners about their cases – often successfully.

Singer had been born in Bratislava and brought up in Vienna until about ten years before the 1939-45 War, when his family fled as refugees from the Nazis to England. There he worked in a business run by his father and there he married an Englishwoman, Irma, by whom he had two children, a boy and a girl who were about eight and four respectively when he settled them all down in Ireland, in progressive luxury.

The vehicle he chose for his stamp venture was a small-sized, highly respected firm of auctioneers called Shanahans, which carried on business in Dun Laoghaire, a sea-coast township adjacent to Dublin. Shanahans was run by a father and son partnership – the father, Jerome, having served in the First World War in the British Army and the son, Desmond, in his late twenties, having qualified as a barrister but never practised.

The proposals which Dr Singer put to the Shanahans were quite modest but very attractive. He proposed a joint venture in the auctioneering of stamps principally by postal bidding. It was not a new idea but he brought new and grandiose ideas to it, including in particular the international circulation of a propaganda magazine and current sale catalogue (containing estimated prices and an order form).

A limited company was formed, Shanahans' Stamp Auctions Limited. The directors were Dr Singer and his wife, Mr Jerome Shanahan and his son. The latter's wife Diana – they eventually had five children – became the bookkeeper.

Shanahans' Stamps promised bargains, and gave them. Dr Singer went regularly round Europe buying at sales and securing collections at prices which enabled his customers to acquire stamps on very advantageous terms.

The business soon became a national success in Ireland and not long after a truly international success.

Singer then introduced a concurrent scheme, that of having investors who would put up anything from £5 for a fixed period (initially this was four months but longer periods were introduced). They would invest in stamps of Shanahans' choice and be virtually guaranteed a profit. It worked like a charm.

The next step was to have long-term investors grouped into syndicates made up at Shanahans' choice. On the part of the public it had become a matter of blind investment.

Business flowed – by 1959 five million pounds had been invested in a single year – and to keep the wheels turning the bearded Dr Singer had to secure bigger and better collections of stamps. This he managed to do on his extensive travels, buying amongst others the famous Lombardo-Venezia collection, and part of what was probably the most famous collection in the world, the Burnus Collection. Of the Burnus Collection, Dr Singer bought the section which included Great Britain for a reputed £½ million. In addition he got an option to buy the rest for, it was said, £2 million.

Such coups enabled the investors to be given satisfactory profits. And nobody lost out at all in the first five years of Shanahans' Stamp Auctions.

But the trouble was at the end of the five years that money was pouring in too fast – an odd, delightful situation one might think, but in this sort of business dangerous. It was becoming increasingly difficult to keep up supply of suitable stamps.

There is no doubt that Dr Paul Singer adopted many stratagems to keep the business running. Many of them were mentioned in the subsequent series of Court proceedings, and while the Doctor maintained to the end that he had not defrauded anybody, evidence was given of accounts in false names, of false figures being given and of massive buying in of stamps which were then given an invented figure for division between the syndicates.

The State when prosecuting and the critics when criticising said that the whole thing was a massive confidence trick, a "catch penny" except that here clients progressed from a few pounds to hundreds.

It was – so it was alleged – a less familiar method of collecting money from one to pay to another; if the phrase may be forgiven in relation to Dr Paul Singer, "robbing Peter to pay Paul".

The balloon burst in an extraordinary way. A burglary occurred at Shanahans' premises early one Saturday morning in May 1959 and stamps of a value between £¼ million and £½ million were taken; these included stamps of the famous collections mentioned earlier. About £5,000 worth was found in a lane near the offices and over £20,000 worth was later discovered in Geneva.

Dr Singer flamboyantly announced that all the stolen stamps were fully insured with Lloyds of London. They were not insured with anyone. He was still at the early stages of negotiating insurance.

There is no reason at all to believe that Dr Singer or anyone connected with him staged the burglary. He had nothing to gain by it, indeed everything to lose. This showed itself quickly as numerous rumours spread about the genuineness of Shanahans' Stamps and letters from investors started flowing in demanding the return of their money. To all the great man presented a front of assurance and confidence. If everybody just remained a little patient all would be well. Investors who sought their money back would get it back but they would naturally have to wait until he had a chance to straighten things out.

Within a fortnight of the burglary Shanahans' went into voluntary liquidation, and on 8 June 1951 a Winding Up Order was made in Court.

Meanwhile on 1 June Singer and his wife, Jerome and Desmond Shanahan, were arrested and brought before District Justice Reddin in the Dublin District Court on one charge – a holding charge pending the preferring of others. It was an allegation of conspiracy to cheat and defraud one named investor. Detective Superintendent Weymes, whose handling of the case throughout was superb, said in Court that he anticipated that a total of £750,000 or more might be involved.

All except Dr Singer were bailed. He spent the next two years in jail because the amount of the independent surety stipulated was always put so high as to be unattainable. Only towards the end of his long battle with the law did the amount come down to a sum – £1,000 – which a friend, a local publican, was prepared to put up.

In September 1959 committal proceedings started in the Dublin District Court against the two Singers and the two male Shanahans on thirty-nine charges of conspiracy and fraud. They lasted for over three months and involved calling more than three hundred witnesses. There were up to three thousand exhibits. The Justice presiding was District Justice Flynn.

There is no doubt that in Ireland, as in England, there has often been a tendency to overload prosecutions by having too many charges. A criticism of overloading in the Singer case is only one of many made against the prosecution and respectfully I feel it is unfair. This stamp empire which collapsed was colossal and it was necessary, at least in the committal stages, to get as much witness and documentary evidence on record as one could.

An extraordinary development occurred towards the end of the committal proceedings. The prosecution suddenly announced their intention of calling as a witness Mrs Diana Shanahan, Desmond Shanahan's wife. She was later to be made an Accused. There was general protest at the proposal to call her, based on the fact that she could not by law be called as a witness against her husband and in many of the charges he was joined with the others. The extraordinary proposal was then made by the State that he be sent on for trial alone and the proceedings against the others be adjourned and that she should give evidence in them. The District Justice refused this application by the State.

At the end of the proceedings in the District Court on 23 January 1960 District Justice Flynn found no case against Jerome Shanahan, the father, and discharged him. The other three he sent for trial. The Order was in common form "for trial to the next sittings of the Circuit Criminal Court".

Dr Paul Singer, a stranger to the legal system of these islands, was a quick-minded and astute student. The move he engineered next was only the first of many legal technicalities he turned to his own advantage.

In March he made an application to the Dublin Circuit Criminal Court to get his case on. It was explained (as he hoped and anticipated) that the State could not possibly be ready for some time; there was an enormous number of witnesses and large quantities of documents.

In April 1960, now retaining the well-known Sean MacBride, Senior Counsel (son of Maud Gonne MacBride and of one of the signatories of the 1916 Easter Week Proclamation, William MacBride, who was executed), and Noel Hartnett, he applied to the High Court for Habeas Corpus. The ground? That he had not been tried at "the next sittings of the Circuit Criminal Court" – even though he had tried to be tried!

A single judge and then a three-judge Divisional Court rejected the application but leave was given to appeal to the Supreme Court. There the matter was heard by five judges in early May and they reserved judgment. When this was given on 23 May it was found that he had succeeded – by a majority of 3 to 2.

There are in Irish and English law a number of cases where a slender majority in the final Court of Appeal wins the day against a total of twice that number all along the line. But as Arkle, the great Irish steeplechaser, is alleged to have known, you only need to be in the lead at the winning post. He was actually reputed to realise that the winning post first time round did not count.

The Judges in the Supreme Court divided as follows – Mr Justice Lavery, Mr Justice Kingsmill Moore and Mr Justice O Dalaigh (later Chief Justice and President) in favour of Dr Singer; Chief Justice Conor Maguire and his namesake Mr Justice Martin Maguire dissenting. Dr Singer also got an order for costs all along the line, which pleased him hugely.

His freedom was only momentary. On a fresh warrant he was arrested just outside Mountjoy Jail and he faced twenty-three new charges, together with his wife, Desmond Shanahan and now the unfortunate Mrs Diana Shanahan as well.

The proceedings on that warrant started before District Justice Farrell in the Dublin District Court. While they were proceeding the prosecution took another curious step: they arranged for the Accused to be brought before Mr Justice Walsh at the Central Criminal Court to see, as they said, whether any of them would plead to the original indictment. Sean MacBride on behalf of Dr Singer protested strongly and contended that his client had been brought unlawfully before the Court and was entitled to an Order of Habeas Corpus. The Judge accepted the argument but noticeably did not grant an out and out order of Habeas Corpus but merely discharged him from that Court. Only young Shanahan agreed to plead and his plea of Not Guilty was formally taken.

The proceedings in the District Court went on and Sean MacBride made a strong submission that in the events which had happened the case against his client had gone. This was rejected.

Meanwhile, Desmond Shanahan was tried before Mr Justice McLoughlin and a jury. Ironically, as later events showed, Mr Ernest Wood, senior counsel for Desmond Shanahan, asked that prospective jurors with any express interest in the case should not serve, and it turned out that a couple had an interest and were accordingly excused.

The evidence in the case was strong. None doubted young Shanahan's innate honesty. The question was whether he had allowed himself to be drawn into actual crime. The man whose name was freely bandied about as the evil influence was of course Dr Paul Singer – who was as yet untried.

In Desmond Shanahan's case after a long retirement, from about 6.00 p.m. until about 12.45 a.m., the jury convicted on sixteen counts, acquitted on five and were discharged from giving a verdict on others. They recommended the Accused to mercy. The Judge, again necessarily referring to the corrupting influence of the still untried Dr Singer, sentenced young Shanahan to a total of fifteen months' imprisonment, which (less remission) he duly served.

That Desmond Shanahan was a barrister, albeit an unpractising one, went against him but his leading counsel, Ernest Wood, showed eloquently how deficient the legal syllabus was in respect of Economics, Finance or Business Affairs.

As we shall see, the case as a whole attracted late sendings out of juries and very late returns. It has always been a feature of Irish jury trials that if at all possible a summing-up is completed however late and the jury sent out however late. This contrasts with the English practice of recent years of withholding the ending of a summing-up until the next morning.

Paul Singer was later to make great play of the point that certainly after this he could not be ensured a fair trial by any jury. To the nature of the publicity from the very outset and the publicity of his own court appearances now had to be added the repeated – and uncontradicted – assertions about him in the Desmond Shanahan trial. There was a good deal in the point because either consciously or unconsciously most people in Ireland had pre-judged Dr Singer. It was a more prejudicial position even than the Haigh, Christie, Moors Murders, Kray and Richardson trials in England. But nothing could be done about it, nor can anything be done about it in such cases. A case, if it attracts attention on an extensive scale, naturally carries with it its own handicaps. Juries and judges as a rule try their best to redress the balance.

Meanwhile, Paul Singer was fighting every inch of the way to being committed for trial on the second list of charges and a third lot which were preferred against him. His main ground was reliance upon his earlier release by the Supreme Court. This, argued MacBride on his behalf, had meant an end of the whole case; alternatively, he was being put in jeopardy a second time on substantially the same charges; further it was not possible for him in all the circumstances to get a fair trial.

MacBride was now opposed by Richard McGonigel SC, a well-known and well-loved leader, and James D'Arcy, now a High Court judge.

The application failed all along the line – before the District Justice, the Divisional Court in July 1960, and the Supreme Court in August 1960.

Accordingly, Dr Paul Singer at last came to trial at the Central Criminal Court in Green Street on 17 October 1960 before Mr Justice Haugh and a jury. He faced twenty-one charges of conspiracy, fraud and fraudulent conversion involving in all nearly £1 million.

There was a twenty-seven-day trial, with witnesses running into hundreds and documents into thousands.

He conducted his own defence. He declined the opportunity of giving evidence himself on oath from the witness-box (as any Accused is, of course, fully entitled to do) and chose to make an unsworn statement from the dock (as again is the right of any Accused). His statement lasted for three full days.

In the end the jury were only out for one hour forty minutes (from 8.20 p.m. until 10.00 p.m.). They found Singer Guilty on nineteen of the charges, involving over £¾ million. The Judge postponed sentence for a week, indicating plainly that this was an opportunity for Singer to give information about the missing money and to help to clear the whole matter up as far as possible.

After the week Singer merely confirmed his innocence and his ignorance. There was nothing for him to tell.

Mr Justice Haugh in passing sentence lashed Singer as a man who had deceived and defrauded on a wide and heartless scale and gave him a total of fourteen years' imprisonment – to date from that day. In other words not taking into account the period already spent in custody. a very long one here.

As is customary in Ireland – but not in England – a convicted person if he wants to appeal has first to apply to the trial judge for a certificate for leave to appeal, stating the grounds. If refused, he can still apply for leave to the Court of Criminal Appeal. The same effect is achieved in England by applying for leave to a single judge of the Court of Appeal (Criminal Division) and if refused to the full Court.

Dr Paul Singer promptly presented seventeen grounds of appeal to Mr Justice Haugh. One was broad-based, that he could not have received a fair trial in view of the publicity engendered and the extraordinary events which had taken place. One was personal, that Mr Justice Haugh was himself an interested party as being the judge in charge of the Shanahan liquidation. Many were technical, directed to particular charges. There were also strong objections to the confusing and allegedly prejudicial overlapping of charges. And there was one which came as a surprise and shock to everyone, namely that the foreman of the jury was (a) a partner of the person in the Chartered Accountant firm who was Liquidator of Shanahans and (b) himself an investor in Shanahans' Stamps and a claimant for £375 in the liquidation. When and how the ingenious doctor came to know the position about the foreman of the jury will remain a mystery.

The trial judge expectedly refused his certificate for leave to appeal and equally predictably Paul Singer went to the Court of Criminal Appeal. This was on 11 April 1961. The Court consisted of Mr Justice Walsh, Mr Justice O Dalaigh and Mr Justice Murnaghan. Singer continued to represent himself.

There were many exchanges between applicant and judges. They showed that they had the measure of him but were appreciative of many of his points and of the way he presented his case. One point which they early showed did not appeal to them at all was his constantly asserted theme that he could not get a fair trial. They were emphatic in the view that an Irish jury, properly directed, would certainly be prepared to try him on his merits. Another point they brushed aside was the ingenious but offensive suggestion that Mr Justice Haugh was, or might have been thought to be, prejudiced in the trial, and in the sentence, because of his being the judge in charge of the liquidation.

Other points troubled them, particularly the matter of the foreman of the jury and the question of overlapping of charges.

It was not perhaps altogether surprising to find some overlapping of charges, because of the nature of the case and because in the curious course of the case to trial three batches of charges were brought against Singer.

Complicated criminal cases seem to attract – in Ireland and in England too – a multiplicity of charges, many of them alternatives. There seems to be a feeling that to catch a big fish one must have a very big net.

Juries cope surprisingly well with complicated cases and a large number of counts, but complication in the charges as well as in the facts can tax them unduly. The ideal would be only four or five charges at most, but that, of course, just may not be possible.

The Court of Criminal Appeal reserved judgment. Then on 13 June 1961 they allowed Dr Singer's appeal, quashed his convictions, ordered a re-trial and confined it to nine charges, involving only a few thousand pounds. To his pleasure he got a sweeping order for costs, covering the trial, the appeal and the re-trial. Getting costs against the Attorney-General always gave the bearded doctor particular pleasure.

The Court based their decision on two grounds: the unsatisfactory situation created by the jury foreman's peculiar position, and the serious overlapping in the nineteen charges upon which Singer had been convicted. His personal and independent surety bail were reduced and became practical. A publican friend went surety, and after over two years in jail Dr Singer was free.

Before the re-trial there was yet another, different scene in the Singer saga, bringing everyone up to the Supreme Court once again.

Mr Justice Budd ordered in the liquidation proceedings that Dr Singer's examination on oath in those proceedings should be taken without regard to the outstanding re-trial. Objection was taken that such a course might prejudice the re-trial, but the Judge rejected this submission. Sean MacBride SC, in the case again, went on appeal to the Supreme Court for Dr Singer, and won. The examination would have to follow the re-trial.

The re-trial began on 7 November 1961, again at Green Street, before Mr Justice Walsh and a jury. Mr Justice Walsh was one of the three judges who had sat in the Court of Criminal Appeal, which, far from being a disqualification, was an advantage from everybody's point of view.

Despite the reduced number of charges the case lasted forty-seven days. At the end of the prosecution case there was a submission that there was no case to answer. That such a submission could even be attempted in this case surprised many until – in upholding it – the Judge explained his reasons to the jury in directing them to acquit Paul Singer of all charges. He pointed out that when the fraudulent transactions were alleged to have occurred there was nothing to show that the company's single bank account used clients' money. The evidence did not show that at the relevant times clients' money must have been used to carry out the fraudulent transactions. This was a revolving bank account.

The jury accordingly found Dr Paul Singer Not Guilty and he left Court a free man after two and a half years under charge and after something like 275 days actually in Court.

At his inevitable press conference afterwards the acquitted Doctor stated that he had always been confident of success. That is absolutely true, but he can never have predicted as to how it would eventually come about. He also expressed his love for Ireland and his desire to settle there – after a short visit to see his ill mother in Canada. He would, he said, gladly assist in the liquidation. Indeed he gave the impression that he could solve it satisfactorily.

Next morning it was found that he and his wife had left Ireland. He has never returned. There have been the usual "sightings" associated with every notable disappearance, but Dr Paul Singer has never surfaced in prominence again.

What of Diana Shanahan and Irma Singer?

In April 1961 the District Justice declined to commit Diana Shanahan for trial. In the Irish legal phrase he refused informations. The prosecution presented a Voluntary Bill of Indictment. Mr Justice Davitt upheld the District Justice's findings and rejected the prosecution case. However, in February 1962, after Singer had gone, the Supreme Court supported the State's right to proceed.

In early 1963 suddenly, without any warning and without any instant publicity, the prosecution dropped the case against both Diana Shanahan and Irma. A *nolle prosequi* was entered and the whole case was over. Irma's father got back his deposit of bail, with interest.

The prosecution, particularly in the person of the Attorney-General, Mr Andreas O'Keefe SC (later Chief Justice and then a member of the EEC Court) came in for a lot of criticism for the handling of the case. Much of the criticism was from political opponents seeking to make capital out of alleged ineptitude. Some of the criticism was more widely based.

It is easy to criticise, especially with hindsight. The prosecution obviously tried throughout to do what they thought was right. They certainly did not relent. It is, I think, possible to argue about certain aspects of the prosecution on the basis of an individual opinion, but I do not think it is fair to pass a judgment of criticism on them in respect of the case as a whole or any part of it.

When people say, even still, that the Singer case was a grave reflection on Irish law, its legal system and its courts, I most profoundly disagree. Indeed, I regard it as a striking example of Irish law and Irish Courts at their best. Every court involved, every time, was patient, painstaking and scrupulous to interpret the law correctly and fairly. The same court found sometimes for the defence, sometimes for the prosecution. The Court of Criminal Appeal analysed Singer's first trial to the very last detail. It plainly did not regard Dr Singer as having overpowering merit or being deserving of every sympathy and help. It fulfilled its duty in the highest traditions of the law. And, finally, the Judge who took the re-trial, Mr Justice Walsh – one of the three judges who formed the Court of Criminal Appeal – dealt with the case in a most careful, clear and logical way. His summary of reasons for upholding the submission of no case to answer was, respectfully, a model.

No sympathy need be felt for Dr Paul Singer at his long period in prison before trial. High bail requirements were inevitable until the extent of the charges was so drastically reduced by the decision of the Court of Criminal Appeal. It is quite true that when then able to fulfil the reduced bail requirements he made no attempt to abscond, but when he was acquitted at the re-trial he left the country quickly, secretly and permanently. He did not wait for his compulsory examination in the Liquidation. Furthermore, a fairly substantial part of the time he spent in prison was due to his own excursions in the law. As it was, bearing in mind the number of Court hearings and the mountain of evidence, one can only admire the promptness with which the Courts dealt with the various matters which arose.

The Singer case seems to me to focus attention on a question now being increasingly canvassed in both Ireland and England, namely the hitherto sacred principle of the criminal law of both countries – the Right of Silence. We differ from many other countries in giving an Accused person an absolute right of Trappist silence at every stage. Our Courts are at pains to point out that no inference of guilt is to be drawn from silence, that the Accused is not obliged to say anything, that suspicion is not enough to find a verdict of guilty.

Are we right about this? Should we not instead require an Accused to answer proper police questions? Should we not require him to give evidence on oath at trial? These are very debatable – but very important – questions. And without seeking myself to answer them it seems to me that the Singer case is one of the best instances one can find for focusing attention on these fundamental questions. He never gave evidence; he could not be compelled to in the criminal proceedings. But in the liquidation proceedings he was compellable. He successfully challenged Mr Justice Budd's decision that he should do so before the criminal proceedings ended. After they ended he disappeared and there was no opportunity to have him compulsorily examined on oath in the Liquidation.

In bankruptcy and liquidation, in other company enquiries as well, there is power to compel evidence. Does the Singer case, a classic example of company matters and criminal proceedings being closely connected, help the argument for abolishing or modifying the Right of Silence?

The Singer case was tragic for many people – the hundreds in Ireland, Britain and elsewhere who lost their investments, the many among them who had invested more than they could afford to lose, and the again many who lost virtually all they had. In a different way and in a different sense it was a tragedy for the Shanahan family.

It is a case which raises many important questions and provides much material for thought.

Judicial Reflection

It was not, I think, said in an Irish Court or by an Irishman, but it could have been:

"The matter does not appear to me now as it appears to have appeared to me then."

Noel and Marie Murray
 1976

WHENEVER THE QUESTION of the death penalty is discussed there is bound to be raised the point of retaining it for murder of a police officer or prison officer in the course of his duty.

When abolishing the death penalty for murder in 1964, the Irish statute retained it for those two offences and for murder of heads of state and diplomats and for treason.

Twelve years later the Courts had to decide what murder of a police officer in the course of his duty actually meant. In particular, if he were in plain clothes, not on actual duty but in pursuit of criminals who had just robbed a bank, was killing him capital murder or just ordinary murder? Did the killer have to know he was a policeman? Was reason to believe he was a policeman sufficient – or recklessness?

Noel and Marie Murray were two of an armed gang of four who robbed a branch of the Bank of Ireland at Killester, a suburb of Dublin, at about 4 o'clock in the afternoon of 11 September 1975. They drew up in a car near the bank. Mr and Mrs Murray, both then armed, went into the bank with one other man, also armed. The remaining man waited in the car. The gang held up the staff and threatened them not to move. Noel Murray held up the manager and a customer. Having got what they could, which was only about £7,000, the three ran out to the car which was ready to go.

As the car moved off it nearly crashed into a car which belonged to and was being driven by Guard Michael Reynolds, a police officer who had the afternoon off and was out with his wife and two-year-old child.

Having seen what happened, certainly having deduced it.

Guard Reynolds gave chase, blowing his horn continuously. The gang stopped the car at the entrance to a park and the four occupants tumbled out and began to run away. Guard Reynolds jumped out of his car and ran after them. He quickly caught or half-caught Noel Murray, by then unarmed. Marie Murray, by then armed with her husband's gun as well as her own (both loaded) shouted, "Let go my man," and almost simultaneously shot Michael Reynolds in the forehead at about two-and-a-half feet range, killing him.

The Murrays and one of the other two were caught and duly charged with the capital murder of Guard Michael Reynolds and with a number of connected offences as well. They were put on trial before the Special Criminal Court in Dublin, a tribunal consisting of three judges without a jury, brought in to deal with serious offences where for one reason or another (fear, intimidation or political sympathy) jury trial is considered inappropriate. It is a creature of crisis and had a predecessor forty years before, but few Irish judges or barristers would wish to see it a permanent feature of Irish legal life, exemplary though its record is.

The case against the third accused was adjourned and the trial proceeded against the two Murrays. They caused frequent disturbances and were extremely abusive to the Court so that for long periods they were removed from Court and put in cells where facilities existed for relaying the proceedings to them.

There was little defence possible in respect of ordinary murder. Noel Murray was not armed at the time of the killing and of course did not do the killing. But the Court held, with respect, rightly, that he and his wife were engaged in a common enterprise which contemplated the use of firearms to effect a crime and to escape, so that he was as responsible as she. The case of common enterprise is often put forward by the prosecution in murder and other gang crimes. It is sometimes not at all easy to apply, for example where only one accused uses a weapon or acts violently. Judge and jury have to look to see whether what was done was within or outside the common enterprise. Here there could be little reason for doubt.

Guard Reynolds was having the afternoon off at the time. Was he, therefore, acting "in the course of his duty" for the purpose of the capital charge? None of the judges who dealt with the case at any stage had any doubt about that; he was acting in the course of his duty. It may seem odd that when he was officially "off duty" he should be regarded as being "on duty", but the logic is clear and compelling. A police officer is always on duty and under a duty to prevent crime and apprehend criminals. Guard Reynolds was giving hot pursuit to criminals and was doing so in his capacity of a police officer. That is not to say of course that a police officer is always on duty for the purpose of the Act; when he is engaged in a purely personal capacity he is clearly not in the course of his duty. In practice the distinction should be easy enough to draw. The question of a prison officer might well occasion difficulty.

The crucial point which arose was whether it was necessary to prove knowledge in the murderers of the victim's identity as a police officer (or something akin to knowledge) in order to constitute the capital offence. Guard Reynolds was in his ordinary clothes, not in uniform. He was, in effect, a plain-clothes officer. He did not have the opportunity of calling out that he was a policeman.

I have used the phrase "or something akin to knowledge" because questions were canvassed as to whether recklessness of mind could be equated to knowledge, or whether, for example, "a reason to believe or to suspect" sufficed.

The defence claimed that actual knowledge was essential and that it had not been proved that either of the Murrays knew that Guard Reynolds was a police officer. They argued that the offence was a new one, and that where there was no specific state of mind mentioned in the Act the ordinary common law rule applied and guilty knowledge had to be proved to satisfy the test.

The prosecution contested that this was a new offence; it was the old offence of murder retaining the old penalty of death if certain conditions were fulfilled. Here, in the clear literal sense, the Murrays had killed a police officer. Knowledge was irrelevant. In effect, if you killed somebody you did so at your peril as to whether he was a police officer or not.

Each argument had a good deal to be said for it and the issue raised difficult questions of law, sociology and philosophy.

The Special Criminal Court rejected the defence argument, found both Guilty of capital murder and sentenced them to death. The verdict was on 9 June 1976 and the date of execution was fixed for 9 July.

An appeal to the Court of Criminal Appeal vacated that date. The appeal was heard at the end of July. The Court was an impressive one, consisting of Chief Justice O'Higgins, Mr Justice Doyle and Mr Justice McMahon. Grounds of appeal other than the crucial question of knowledge were soon rejected. The Court considered the question of knowledge with great care and anxiety. There were a great number of considerations to be taken into account.

The Court of Criminal Appeal, as is customary in Ireland and England, give a single judgment of the Court. This Chief Justice O'Higgins gave on 30 July 1976 and it dismissed the appeal.

There was in fact very great public interest in the case, universally and strongly adverse to the Murrays. Many who were in general opposed to the death penalty felt it was deserved here and no feminist sympathy was felt for the woman. A reprieve would not have been welcomed. The public naturally felt that the brutal murder of a young policeman in the presence of his wife and tiny child was unforgivable.

A new date for execution was fixed: 17 August 1976. But, reflecting public opinion, the Court of Criminal Appeal readily accepted that there was a point of law of exceptional public importance involved and accordingly certified for a final appeal to the five-judge Supreme Court. There the case was argued in November 1976 and judgment was given on 8 December 1976.

The Supreme Court consisted of Mr Justice Walsh, presiding, Mr Justice Henchy, Mr Justice Griffin, Mr Justice Kenny and Mr Justice Parke. The Irish Supreme Court enjoys a high reputation not only nationally but internationally. It is a Court of liberal and advanced thinking, markedly independent of any political or bureaucratic influence. This was a strong Court.

The scope of the problem was illustrated by Mr Justice Walsh pointing out that a uniformed, unarmed, police officer was only one side of the force; many police now were – and had to be – in plain clothes, and, moreover, when so acting had to be careful to pretend that they were indeed civilians. What of them?

In the Irish Supreme Court, as in the House of Lords in England, individual judgments are given.

All the judges agreed that the offence of capital murder was a new one and that therefore some mental element came into the question. Mr Justice Walsh decisively pronounced that knowledge, and nothing short of knowledge, of the fact that the victim was a police officer would suffice, so that in his view the verdicts of capital murder should be quashed and verdicts of non-capital murder substituted. This is an easily understandable, clean-cut point of view.

Recklessness as to state of mind is never an easy concept and it has additional difficulties when applied to knowledge. It suggests, as it were, a type of constructive or implied knowledge.

The other judges in one form or another held that recklessness or reason to believe was a necessary element. Although the concept is not an easy one and – as became clear – its application proved difficult, it seemed to many to accord with justice. Actual knowledge was too much to expect; complete unawareness of the identity of the victim might be unfair to the accused; but a state of mind between the two would do justice.

The four judges who found in favour of a state of mind less than actual knowledge differed as to what the result should be: should both appellants have their sentences reduced to non-capital murder? should both be re-tried? or should Mrs Murray alone be re-tried?

Mr Justice Griffin proposed a re-trial for both, but the prevailing view was in favour of re-trial of Mrs Murray alone and the conversion of Mr Murray's penalty into life imprisonment for non-capital murder.

In the result, therefore, Mrs Murray was ordered to be re-tried in the light of the majority view of the Supreme Court on the question of knowledge.

She was duly re-tried and on this occasion found guilty of non-capital murder and sentenced to life imprisonment.

The carrying of firearms is the curse of our time. Even those opposed to capital punishment have their confidence shaken by episodes such as the murder of Guard Reynolds. The taking of a loaded gun on an expedition of crime is as premeditated as anything can be and protestations that it was only brought to frighten not to kill are specious. There are many people who consider that a murderer should be held to kill at his own peril irrespective of any form of knowledge, but it would need a new Irish Act of Parliament to achieve this.

I told elsewhere the story of the Accused of over seventy who was making a plea on his own behalf at Cork Assizes and made the point that he was an orphan. Momentarily impressed, the Judge recovered himself and said, "But Good Heavens, man, I'm an orphan myself." Whereupon the Accused replied, "And when you're in trouble it will be taken into account in your favour." This prompted a well known North of Ireland lawyer to tell me of a much more recent occurrence, at the Belfast City Commission, when an elderly and rather deaf judge had a bad criminal case before him. Defending counsel began his mitigation by saying that his client knew it was a rather awful case. "What?" asked the Judge. "Your client is an orphan?" Counsel, rather nonplussed, said, "My Lord, I said it was an awful case." "I see," said the Judge, "from the Orkneys. An orphan from the Orkneys. I've never heard anything like that before." Counsel shook his head. "No," he said. "And I'm not surprised you haven't, either," commented the Judge. "I will show him all the sympathy I can, poor fellow. He never had a chance, I suppose."

That delightful Irishman the late Mr Justice Cusack, who is such a loss to the English legal scene, had – for all his apparent shyness – a store of Irish and English legal stories. On the Circuit which he led, the Oxford, there was one barrister who specialised in muddling things up. The climax came when he startled one judge who was trying undefended divorces by saying, "May it please your wife, this is a Lordship's petition."